COMFORT FOOD

Comfort Food

MEANINGS AND MEMORIES

Edited by Michael Owen Jones and Lucy M. Long

University Press of Mississippi / Jackson

www.upress.state.ms.us

The University Press of Mississippi is a member
of the Association of American University Presses.

First printing 2017
∞

Library of Congress Cataloging-in-Publication Data

Names: Jones, Michael Owen, editor. | Long, Lucy M., 1956– editor.
Title: Comfort food : meanings and memories / edited by Michael Owen Jones
and Lucy M. Long.
Description: Jackson : University Press of Mississippi, [2017] | Includes
bibliographical references and index.
Identifiers: LCCN 2016046900 (print) | LCCN 2016047575 (ebook) | ISBN
9781496810847 (hardcover : alk. paper) | ISBN 9781496810854 (pbk. : alk.
paper) | ISBN 9781496810861 (epub single) | ISBN 9781496810878 (epub
institutional) | ISBN 9781496810885 (pdf single) | ISBN 9781496810892
(pdf institutional)
Subjects: LCSH: Comfort food. | Food—Social aspects.
Classification: LCC TX714 .C6267 2017 (print) | LCC TX714 (ebook) | DDC
641.3—dc23
LC record available at https://lccn.loc.gov/2016046900

British Library Cataloging-in-Publication Data available

CONTENTS

COMFORT FOOD

COMFORT FOOD

Introduction

Michael Owen Jones and Lucy M. Long

According to the *Oxford English Dictionary*, "comfort food" is "food that comforts or affords solace; hence, any food (freq. with a high sugar or carbohydrate content) that is associated with childhood or with home cooking. orig. N. Amer." Merriam-Webster's 10th edition *Collegiate Dictionary* defines comfort food as fare "prepared in a traditional style having a usually nostalgic or sentimental appeal," while in the *Encyclopedia of Food and Culture* (2002), Julie Locher notes that it is "any food consumed by individuals, often during periods of stress, that evokes positive emotions and is associated with significant social relationships."

Typically linked with home, tradition, nostalgia, and positive feelings, the phrase "comfort food" appears to be an American invention that has begun to reach beyond US borders. Its first appearance in print may have been on Sunday, November 6, 1966, in a column by psychologist Dr. Joyce Brothers titled "Psychological Problems Play a Part in Obesity." Published in the *Des Moines Register* and many other newspapers, the essay states: "Studies indicate that most adults, when under severe emotional stress, turn to what could be called 'comfort food'—food associated with the security of childhood, like mother's poached egg or famous chicken soup." The *OED*, however, dates the expression's earliest use to an article in the *Washington Post* on December 25, 1977, in which restaurant critic Phyllis Richman describes a Southern dish. In 2013, Richman revisited the term, observing that she doubted that she created it, contending that the phenomenon likely exists worldwide and implying that although the specific foods might differ for us individually, we seem to understand the phrase.

The term has become widely adopted into everyday speech, restaurant menus, cooking shows, recipe books, magazines, and advertising. Recent years have seen a rapid increase in popular interest in comfort food. Numerous cooking magazines have devoted major sections and even entire issues to the subject. A number of recipe books have been published, some of which provide lower calorie and more healthful versions of comfort foods, from snacks to entrees and desserts. Restaurants attach the phrase to their menus, and the food industry exploits it in marketing. Meanwhile, individuals seem to use the notion as a way to both celebrate and justify eating certain foods that do not fit current concepts of healthful or nutritious eating.

Surprisingly little research has been done on comfort food from a cultural perspective. Medical sociologist Julie L. Locher may have first introduced it into food studies scholarship in 2002 through her essay, "Comfort Food," in the *Encyclopedia of Food and Culture*, edited by Solomon Katz. She went on to publish a foundational article in 2005 in the journal *Food & Foodways*, in which she and co-researchers drew from a survey among students to identify four categories of comfort foods based on the needs they fulfill: nostalgia, indulgence, convenience, and physical satisfaction. Other scholarship has come primarily from the fields of psychology, public health, and nutrition, focusing on the motivations for partaking of comfort foods as well as the impact of that consumption on the bodies of the consumers. As early as 1998, Paulette Wood and Barbra D. Vogen published "Feeding the Anorectic Client: Comfort Foods and Happy Hour" in *Geriatric Nursing*. Brian Wansink, Matthew Cheney, and Nina Chan later wrote about comfort food preferences across age and gender in *Physiology & Behavior*, concluding that "comfort foods are foods whose consumption evokes a psychologically comfortable and pleasurable state for a person" (2003). Carl T. Hall demonstrated that comfort food helped to relieve stress, at least in rats that were given high-fat foods (2003). Mary Dallman, Norman Pecoraro, and Susanne la Fleur, as well as other scholars, have examined the relationship between chronic stress, comfort food, and obesity, which, not surprisingly is a circular one, since most comfort foods tend to be high in fat, carbohydrates, and sugar (2003, 2005). Obesity resulting from consuming comfort food has continued to be a major concern among researchers. Robert D. Levitan and Caroline Davis, for example, examine the issue in their article on "Emotions and Eating Behavior" (2010).

The emphasis on gender differences has been a major thread in much of this research. Dubé Jordan, L. LeBel, and Ji Lu found that negative emotions tended to trigger comfort food consumption for women, but positive ones triggered it for men (2005). Other researchers also focused on the motivations for consuming comfort foods. For example, nutritionists Jayanthi Kandiah, Melissa Yake, James Jones, and Michaela Meyer stated the conclusion of their research in the title of their article: "Stress Influences Appetite and

Comfort Food Preferences in College Women" (2006). Similarly, Janet A. Tomiyama, Mary F. Dallman, and Elissa S. Epel claimed in the journal *Psychoneuroendocrinology* that "Comfort Food Is Comforting to Those Most Stressed: Evidence of the Chronic Stress Response Network in High Stress Women" (2011). Other researchers have expanded the scholarship to examine additional functions of comfort food. For instance, in an essay concerning the consumption of chicken soup in *Psychological Science* (2011), Jordan Troisi and Shira Gabriel observed that comfort food serves as a social surrogate, fulfilling a need to belong.

Speculations about comfort food have also been aired in news media and in professional arenas related to the food industry. As early as 2001, food writer Bret Thorn published "Seeking Comfort, Diners Indulge in Feel-Good Fare" in *Nation's Restaurant News*. A 2009 essay in a marketing internet forum summarizes findings from the Center for Culinary Development on differences in comfort food preferences by age (Lukovitz 2009). In the May 25, 2012, edition of the *New York Times*, journalist Daniel E. Slotkin asked "What's Your Comfort Food?" pointing out that personal preferences and definitions vary. Other popular writers and journalists have embraced the idea of comfort foods as individualistic and culture-specific, seeing the psychological value of them but also challenging the use of the concept as an excuse to indulge in foods deemed "guilty pleasures." For example, an essay in *Health Psychology* concerning "the myth of comfort food" (December 2014) elicited much discussion and debate. Nora Gomez Torres wrote of "Cubans Finding Comfort, Nostalgia in Russian Products" in the November 14, 2014, *Miami Herald*, and in *The Atlantic* (April 3, 2015), Cari Romm summarizes research on the efficacy of comfort food with "Why Comfort Food Comforts: A New Study Looks at the Intersection of Taste, Nostalgia, and Loneliness."

While this research offers a foundation for studying comfort food, it does not fully explore the implications of this category of food experience. The idea initially appears to be straightforward and self-explanatory—it is food that comforts. A closer examination, however, raises numerous questions about the concept, the specific foods belonging to this category, and the nature of food itself. After all, should not all food comfort in some way? As is commonly recognized by scholars and the general public, food fulfills multiple needs and functions beyond its most basic one of sustaining life. Not all of those functions are identified as their own category of food, so why does a genre such as comfort food exist? Does it reflect concerns related to contemporary life in the Western world, characterized by its industrial food system, an ethos that attaches specific moralities to eating, and a tendency towards nostalgia and romanticization of family, childhood, and the past? What foods fit into the category and why, and what is the role of commercialization and marketing in the rising popularity of the genre?

It is unclear whether comfort food is a universal concept or is particular to modern, Western societies. Food in general seems to act as a symbolic system in every cultural group,[1] but we do not have the data to know whether the idea of a separate category of foods that specifically and primarily offer comfort exists throughout the world. The very idea of food comforting may reflect the distance modernity has created between us and our food as well as between individuals. The modern world in general is one in which industrialization and capitalist economic philosophy have created a very real physical as well as emotional distance between our work and the things we use.[2] We rarely see an entire process of creating something from start to finish, causing, according to some scholars, a feeling of alienation. Similarly, modernity means that our lives are frequently fragmented into disparate social spheres, while the mobility associated with the freedom to explore new paths and new selves oftentimes cuts us off from our roots and dilutes a sense of continuity with places or people.[3] Modernity in this critique creates a need for comfort, and food because of its close association with personal relationships and identity, easily fulfills that function; hence, a category of foods that comfort. Modernity, however, can also erase those associations or enable them to be invented and manipulated for commercial or political gain.

Furthermore, the contemporary industrial food system contains numerous links in the chain between producers and consumers. Food in this system becomes a product that is initially grown or raised, but then processed, packaged, marketed, distributed, and sold. The producer rarely knows the consumer and vice versa, and food is transported from place to place without recognition of its origins or the people who have handled it along the way.[4] That many individuals find this system discomforting is evident in the diversity of current social movements surrounding the reconnection of consumer and producer and the reinvestment of meaning to activities around food as well as to food itself. Cultivating and cooking one's own food are presented now as means to emotional and psychological wholeness, for society as well as for individuals.[5] Food that comforts in this way can be seen as crucial to survival. Globalization, in spreading Western products and perspectives throughout the world, may also have spread these conditions for needing comfort.[6]

The industrial food system also turns food into a commodity rather than a cultural item recognized as having meaning and value outside its monetary worth. As such, it then becomes an item to be manipulated for optimal sales. Identities and meanings may be attached to it that are thought to appeal to customers, but are adapted to the whims of the marketplace.[7] Comfort food as a category seems to be undergoing such commodification, and specific dishes are being highlighted and turned into icons of the genre. Macaroni and cheese, for example, is now presented by restaurants, cookbooks, and cooking shows as the quintessential American comfort food. While it does historically have a significant place in the memories of many American childhoods, it is not universal among Americans. Its reputation for giving comfort, however, has become a large part of the marketing surrounding it, so that even those who do not have personal associations with it now also identify it as a comfort food. The processes of commodification and iconification manipulate the meanings of food, but also raise issues about who gets to select what foods mean and what they represent. Such cultural politics can frequently be seen in the foods that have been promoted as symbols of regions or ethnicities, such as lobster for Maine, crawfish for Cajuns, grits and barbecue for the South, and so on.[8]

Another aspect of modernity is nostalgia, a looking back on the past with wistfulness and affection. It is a longing for happier times, which might not actually have been as happy as remembered.[9] Food oftentimes plays a role in nostalgia, carrying or evoking specific memories, not only of the food itself but also of the relationships and contexts associated with it. French novelist Marcel Proust wrote eloquently of how the taste of a madeleine cookie evoked vivid memories of his childhood.[10] Grandmothers' and mothers' cooking is not so much about the taste of the food as the feelings of security and safety represented by it. Family tends to be idealized and romanticized through nostalgia, rendering pleasant and warm memories. The reality, of course, can be very different, and the idea of comfort food may demonstrate that.[11] Individuals differ in the dishes they consider comforting, and those differences reflect, in part, different family experiences as well as different personalities.

Comfort food also seems to be complicated by morality. Saying that an item is comfort food relieves the eater of being concerned with its nutritional or caloric qualities, suggesting that those foods in other contexts should not be eaten. This implies a moral system of "good" and "bad" foods or food experiences. How does morality get attached to certain foods? Sidney Mintz points out that morality is sometimes tied to the self, to one's relationship to a religious system (purity) or ethical system or even sense of self,[12] but at other times to the impact of one's actions on the larger society (1996). These moralities are culturally specific, not universal. In his groundbreaking study of the place of sugar in Western Europe at the end of the 1600s, he traced the movement of sugar from an exotic luxury to being considered a necessary part of everyone's diet. He demonstrated that sugar was invested with both types of morality by Europeans. It was tied directly to slavery by abolitionists who recognized the connection of slavery to sugar production in the Caribbean and called for boycotting sugar, saying that consuming it was essentially murder. Sugar itself also had morality attached to it. It was considered unhealthful for the body in large quantities and "corrosive of the will" (1996: 71). However, it was also used as a medicine; it was allowed by the church during fasting if it was taken to aid digestion rather than for nourishment.

Mintz brings up another perspective on comfort food when he refers to the asceticism and puritanism foundational to American culture that has long viewed pleasure, especially physical and sensual pleasures, as immoral. Comfort food is frequently perceived as dishes that give us pleasure. They tend to satisfy our appetites and our taste buds, both of which are suspect in the Western moral universe. Comfort food, however, is understood to satisfy deeper psychological and emotional needs, therefore relieving consumers of the moral judgment assigned to eating purely for the pleasure of it.

The anthology *Comfort Food: Meanings and Memories* explores the concept of "comfort food" primarily within a Western context. Examples are taken from Atlantic Canadians, Indonesians, the English in Britain, and various ethnic, regional, and religious populations, as well as rural and urban residents in the US. It includes studies of particular foods, ways in which they comfort or in some instances cause discomfort, and how these foods produce such an effect. The foods they focus on range widely from bologna to chocolate, sweet and savory puddings, fried bread with an egg in the center, dairy products, fried rice, cafeteria fare, sugary fried dough, soul food, and others. Some essays analyze the phenomenon in daily life; others consider comfort food in the context of cookbooks, films, internet blogs, literature, marketing, and tourism. Recognizing that what heartens one person might discomfort another, the collection includes essays on comfort foods that are problematic in some way and is organized accordingly, from pleasant to unpleasant or discomforting food experiences. These foods are then related to concepts and issues such as identity, family, community, nationality, ethnicity, class, sense of place, tradition, stress, health, discomfort, guilt, betrayal, and loss, contributing to a deeper understanding of comfort food as a significant social category of human behavior around food.

Contributors to the anthology come primarily from the field of folklore studies and apply this perspective to their essays. They attend to food as an aesthetic experience through which individuals and groups construct and perform their identities, relationships, values, and understandings of the universe.[13] This approach emphasizes personal agency in creating meaning, but also recognizes the role of power structures and systems in shaping the possibilities for each individual. It also tends to highlight the overlooked and mundane, the foods or individuals not usually thought of as significant. Comfort food, for example, is often associated with home and family—the feminine, domestic sphere—and with unrefined cooking that warrants little attention from those trained in the culinary arts or of more gourmand tastes. At the same time, a folkloristic approach sees all cultural products as potential sources for the expression of creativity and the construction of meaning, so that mass-produced commercial foods can become integral traditions just as much as those foods that have been handed down over generations within a family by imitation or word-of-mouth. From this perspective, comfort food is an ideal subject for examining the interplay of marketing, commodification, iconization, and other such processes in which individuals find and attach personal meaningfulness to their food.

The authors draw upon a diversity of ethnographic and archival sources for data to analyze, ranging from personal interviews and observations to auto-ethnography. The last refers to "ethnography of one's self or one's group,"[14] and lends itself also to reflexive analysis of the impact of the ethnographer on the people being studied and the information gleaned from them. Comfort food is a rather "elastic" category, representing different foods to different people; therefore, it is highly subjective. It also seems to be particularly subject to current trends in the marketplace and in attitudes towards food and health. Discussing it tends to open the proverbial "can of worms," so that individuals being interviewed or observed begin questioning it and their own responses to it.

Scholarship in the ethnography of the senses is also relevant to comfort food and is implicit in much of the research in this volume. As Paul Stoller points out in his groundbreaking book, *The Taste of Ethnographic Things: The Senses in Anthropology* (Philadelphia: University of Pennsylvania Press, 1989), academia in the West has privileged sight over other senses, leading to an emphasis in scholarship on intellectual and cognitive understanding over more sensory ways of experiencing the world. Food offers full use of all the senses, and some aspects of it can be perceived only at a sensual level rather than a verbal (oral or written) one. The researcher therefore should attend to a range of possible ways in which individuals may perceive the world. Also, memory is literally embodied in the senses. The taste of food conjures images of the past or particular people; its aromas remind one of places; its texture can take one back to a previous experience, sometimes literally.[15] Comfort food seems to function as a category partly because of its appeal to the senses. It frequently gives literal comfort by warming the body or filling the stomach, but it also evokes memories of pleasant sensory experiences. Recognition of the significance of the senses in people's relationships to comfort food runs throughout the essays in this volume.

Chapter 1 concentrates on the emotional and physiological satisfaction afforded by comfort food that is usually emphasized in conceptualizations, along with the relationship between stress and consumption. Among the hypotheses for craving and partaking of comfort food that Michael Jones explores are the role of emotional relief, physical sensations and satiety, pharmacological components of the item, and associations with people, places, and events. In particular, he considers chocolate, "the food of the gods," which for many American women is the quintessential comfort food, a conception reinforced by folklore, the mass media, and popular culture objects.

Rachelle Saltzman, in the second chapter, examines pudding as an integral part of English national identity. Through historical research supplemented with observations and interviews, she explores the development of whim whams, spotted dick, jam roly-poly, and other savory and sweet puddings and the processes by which they became so associated with the English that they were referred to in the nineteenth century as the "Pudding Eaters." More recently, the National Trust's "pudding campaign" encouraged pudding consumption, and the environment secretary urged citizens to eat more sweet puddings made with local ingredients rather than unpatriotically consuming foreign products. Although many immigrants reside in the country, and their non-pudding fare is impacting the culinary culture, a taxi driver told Saltzman, "They may be British but they'll never be English." Pudding as comfort food, then, is intimately tied to national identity.

In Chapter 3, Susan Eleuterio, with the assistance of three longtime Chicago residents, focuses on the ways in which a sense of community and feelings of belonging are generated in commercial contexts, such as in local cafeterias. Focusing on Valois, a favorite breakfast spot of former Senator and then President Barack Obama, in Chicago, Eleuterio explores how a place of business can not only offer comfort food, but also become a place of comfort. Although it is also a tourist destination, Valois is known among certain community members as a place where you can "see your food," interact easily with others over a leisurely meal, feel at home, enjoy familiar fare, and experience a haven of comfort and normality; in sum, an opportunity for commensality. Sharing the political values associated with its most famous fan contributes to the sense of community.

Authored by Alicia Kristen, the fourth chapter concerns the summer custom of going for doughboys (sugary fried dough) at clam shacks in seaside Rhode Island. A tradition among the working class from mill cities nearby, both the practice and the food itself are markers of class distinctions, insider identity, and cultural pride. Crafted on the coast, doughboys acquire the scent of Oakland Beach and, cooked in the same oil as the clam cakes, they have a hint of the flavor of locally harvested clams; as such, they exhibit terroir, "a sense of place," which comforts many of the diners.

Chapter 5, by Jillian Gould, examines the intergenerational connections of a single, simply prepared item. Called "egg-in-the-hole," "man on the raft," "Popeyes," "one-eyed Jacks," and other names, the food consists of a piece of bread in which the center is torn out and an egg is fried in the hole. Utilizing auto-ethnography and historical analysis of the tradition, the author reveals how this source of comfort and memories, through its preparation rather than taste, unites three generations of women, two of whom are now deceased, connecting the survivor with the past and, in the present, with her daughter. The dish, then, exemplifies comfort food grounded in home and the family.

In the sixth chapter, Yvonne and William Lockwood consider the concepts of heritage and nostalgia as significant, perhaps even primary, motivations for some Finnish Americans in the upper Midwest to perpetuate or revitalize the tradition of preparing and eating Finnish fare, including "poverty food." A favorite item is *viili*, a fermented milk product, despite the fact that those of Finnish descent have an astonishingly high rate of lactose intolerance. Lovers of viili enjoy the stringy, slippery texture that frequently repulses most non-Finnish Americans to the extent that children compare it with snot. For many Finnish Americans, the nostalgia satisfied through this dish is for a childhood, family, or experiences not from the home country but from the strong ethnic community as it existed through the 1940s; thus, the comfort offered by this food represents an idealized past.

In Chapter 7, Lucy Long investigates the emergence of culinary tourism featuring comfort food. The opposite of the more usual exotic, fine dining, and unique foods found in such tourism, comfort food would not seem to be of interest to tourists; however, it appears to be growing in popularity. Based on her own experiences and observations, as well as an examination of advertisements for tours in the Midwest and other locations throughout the world, she identifies the qualities of comfort food that are highlighted in culinary tourism and examines the ways in which comfort food might function for tourists. A major theme in both categories of experience is home, either as a physical space or a metaphor for security and familiarity; its role in tourism suggests that home itself may now be considered exotic.

The chapters to this point consider the positive associations of comfort food, such as combatting stress and feelings of loneliness, identification with home, intergenerational connections and other social linkages, commensality and community, memories of joyful events and cordial relations, and nostalgia about the past. These characteristics are implied or stated in dictionary definitions and they are apparent from survey research conducted by Locher et al., Wansink et al., and Troisi and Gabriel; they are developed and discussed more fully in *Comfort Food: Meanings and Memories*. Subsequent chapters in this anthology, however, address negative aspects of comfort food by exploring health concerns, feelings of discomfort, and the subversion of taken-for-granted assumptions about family, tradition, and history.

In her essay on bologna in Chapter 8, Diane Tye raises the specter of unhealthful qualities in what has become a pervasive comfort food in the Canadian Atlantic region. Although it is loaded with high amounts of sodium, saturated and trans fat, and cholesterol (along with sodium nitrate, which has been linked to the formation of carcinogenic nitrosamines), people nevertheless persist in avidly consuming bologna. In a diet historically low in protein, fruits, and vegetables, this processed meat product remains relatively inexpensive, requires little preparation, is convenient, and lends itself to creative dishes. Turning a blind eye to nutritional deficiencies and high rates of chronic disease, residents tout "Newfoundland steak" as "traditional," a regional food commemorating earlier times and common in the ritual of homecoming and family visits.

Chapter 9, by Sheila Bock, focuses on soul food, which has become a contested cuisine providing, on the one hand, comfort through racial pride and cultural achievement, and on the other, discomfort owing to the health crisis that has arisen among African Americans because of the high fat and sodium content of some dishes and their preparations. Through an examination of recent cookbooks, the author delineates ways in which some African Americans are re-conceptualizing and re-presenting "tradition" as a tool of intervention.

In Chapter 10, LuAnne Roth turns her attention to concepts of memory and discomfort as she explores food-centric films, both ethnographic and fictional. While in daily life memories are recalled through smell, taste, and mouthfeel, in film they are generated and conveyed through sound and visuals. Her explorations reveal how key cinematic scenes regarding food depict otherwise unexpressed emotions, conflict, chronic binging, efforts at controlling others, trauma, and the combatting of loneliness stemming from childhood neglect.

Annie Tucker, in the last chapter, examines three short stories by Puthut EA, a young writer from Yogyakarta, Central Java, whose works have frequently appeared in major national publications and numerous anthologies. He establishes familiar associations of comfort food, such as family, identity,

belonging, and pleasure, but then subverts them to address instances of overbearing parental authority, ruthless exploitation of the environment, and brutal political violence. He imbues foods with a "culinary conscience," asking
readers to ponder what happens when comforting foods of identity become
haunted by aching memories.

The essays in *Comfort Food: Meanings and Memories* offer a foundation
for further exploration of comfort food. As a subject of study, the category
is relevant to a number of scholarly disciplines, most obviously food studies, folkloristics, and anthropology, but also American culture studies, cultural studies, global and international studies, tourism, marketing, and public
health. It also represents a category of eating experiences that resonates with
most of us and that can be easily understood in one's own life, enabling us as
scholars to better understand the significance of emotions and memories in
human behavior. It therefore offers a window for exploring the relationships
among our foodways patterns, our own past experiences, and larger forces
in society that shape those relationships. Whether such foods generate feelings of comfort or cause distress, unite families or produce conflict, celebrate
tradition or challenge it, remind individuals of pleasant experiences or force
them to confront painful memories, they warrant close examination for what
they reveal about the human condition and people's relationship to the fare
that they consume.

Notes

1. The recognition that food carries meaning is standard in scholarship today. Anthropologist Sidney Mintz explains: "For us humans . . . eating is never a 'purely biological' activity
. . . The foods eaten have histories associated with the pasts of those who eat them; the techniques employed to find, process, prepare, serve, and consume the foods are all culturally
variable, with histories of their own. Nor is the food ever simply eaten; its consumption is
always conditioned by meaning. These meanings are symbolic, and communicated symbolically; they also have histories" (1996: 7).

2. The idea of modernity creating a sense of distance comes originally from critiques
of industrialization that tended to somewhat romanticize the pastoral and the past. For an
overview of Romantic Nationalism's influence on the discipline of folkloristics, see William
A. Wilson, "Herder, Folklore and Romantic Nationalism," in *Folk Groups and Folklore Genres:
A Reader*, ed. Elliot Oring (Logan: Utah State University Press, 1989), 21–37. Marxist critiques
tie modernity to capitalism and probably are most famous for promoting the idea of distance as a result of the two forces.

3. One of the most influential writings on the isolation created by modern life is sociologist Robert D. Putnam's *Bowling Alone: The Collapse and Revival of American Community*

(New York: Simon & Schuster, 2000). His powerful application of the French culture theorist Pierre Bourdieu's notion of social capital ("The Forms of Capital," in *Handbook of Theory and Research for the Sociology of Education*, ed. J. Richardson [New York: Greenwood, 1986], 241–58) introduced the concept to the larger public.

4. There are numerous excellent critiques of the industrial food system. One that combines ethnography with insightful explorations into the mindset and ethos behind Western agriculture is Deborah Barndt's *Tangled Routes: Women, Work, and Globalization on the Tomato Trail* (Lanham, MD: Rowman & Littlefield, 2008), in which she clearly articulates the foundation laid by Rene Descartes's dualism between man and nature. Other scholarly critiques include Deborah Kay Fitzgerald, *Every Farm a Factory: The Industrial Ideal in American Agriculture* (New Haven: Yale University Press, 2003); Julie Guthman, *Agrarian Dreams: The Paradox of Organic Farming in California* (Berkeley: University of California, 2004); Damian Maye, Lewis Holloway, and Moya Kneafsey, eds., *Alternative Food Geographies: Representation and Practice* (Amsterdam: Elsevier, 2007); and Moya Kneafsey, Rosie Cox, Lewis Holloway, Elizabeth Dowler, Laura Venn, and Helena Tuomainen, *Consumers, Producers and Food: Exploring Alternatives* (New York: Berg, 2008). Journalist Michael Pollan brought these issues to the attention of the general public in his book, *The Omnivore's Dilemma: A Natural History of Four Meals* (New York: Penguin, 2006).

5. For example, the concept of "mindfulness" is currently being applied to eating, with classes, online instructions, and the media popularizing the notion of finding "wholeness" in this way. Numerous "how-to" books are available on the subject.

6. For insightful treatments of the issues surrounding food and globalization, see Alexander Nützenadel and Frank Trentmann, eds., *Food and Globalization* (Oxford: Berg, 2008); James L. Watson and Melissa L. Caldwell, eds., *The Cultural Politics of Food and Eating* (Malden, MA: Blackwell, 2005); and Richard R. Wilk, *Home Cooking in the Global Village* (Oxford: Berg, 2006).

7. Food as an expression of identity, as well as a medium through which identity can be constructed, performed, and negotiated, was a major theme in foundational folkloristic studies of food in the 1970s and '80s. See, for example, Michael Owen Jones, Bruce B. Giuliano, and Roberta Krell, eds., *Foodways and Eating Habits: Directions for Research* (Los Angeles: California Folklore Society, 1983); Linda Keller Brown and Kay Mussell, eds., *Ethnic and Regional Foodways in the United States: The Performance of Group Identity* (Knoxville: University of Tennessee Press, 1984); Theodore C. Humphrey and Lin T. Humphrey, *We Gather Together: Food and Festival in American Life* (Ann Arbor, MI: UMI Research, 1988); Charles Camp, *American Foodways: What, When, Why, and How We Eat in America* (Little Rock: August House, 1989); and Kathy Neustadt, *Clambake: A History and Celebration of an American Tradition* (Amherst: University of Massachusetts, 1992). For more recent summaries of folkloristic approaches to food and identity, see Lucy M. Long, "Learning to Listen to the Food Voice: Recipes as Expressions of Identity and Carriers of Memory," *Food, Culture and Society: An International Journal of Multidisciplinary Research* 71 (2004): 118–22; Lucy M. Long, "Food and Identity in the Americas: Introduction," *Journal of American Folklore* 122, no. 483 (2009): 3–10; and Lucy M. Long, ed., *The Food and Folklore Reader* (New York: Bloomsbury, 2015). Anthropologists have also been concerned with food and identity; an

excellent introduction is Carole Counihan and Penny Van Esterik, eds., *Food and Culture: A Reader* (New York: Routledge, 2013). Also see references in endnote 11. The implications of food as commodity are explored in Warren James Belasco and Philip Scranton, eds., *Food Nations: Selling Taste in Consumer Societies* (New York: Routledge, 2002).

8. George H. Lewis, "The Maine Lobster as Regional Icon: Competing Images over Time and Social Class," in *A Taste of American Place: A Reader on Regional and Ethnic Foods*, eds. Barbara G. Shortridge and James R. Shortridge (Lanham, MD: Rowman & Little-field, 1998), 65–83; C. Paige Guttierrez, "The Social and Symbolic Uses of Ethnic/Regional Foodways: Cajuns and Crawfish in South Louisiana," in *Ethnic and Regional Foodways in the United States: The Performance of Group Identity*, eds. Linda Keller Brown and Kay Mussell (Knoxville: University of Tennessee Press, 1984), 169–92; Marcie Cohen Ferris, *The Edible South: The Power of Food and the Making of an American Region* (Chapel Hill: University of North Carolina Press, 2015). For overviews of ethnic and regional foods as symbols from a folkloristic perspective, see Susan Kalck, "Ethnic Foodways in America: Symbol and the Performance of Identity," in Brown and Mussel (1984), 37–65; and Lucy M. Long, *Regional American Food Culture* (Santa Barbara, CA: Greenwood Press, 2009).

9. Nostalgia in relation to food has been studied by a number of scholars, particularly from a cultural perspective, and is oftentimes tied to notions of nationalism, modernity, and globalization. See, for example, Anita Mannur, "Culinary Nostalgia, Authenticity, Nationalism and Diaspora," in *Culinary Fictions: Food in South Asian Diasporic Culture* (Philadelphia: Temple University Press, 2010), 27–78; Susan L. Stowers, "Gastronomic Nostalgia: Salvadoran Immigrants Craving for Their Ideal Meal," *Ecology of Food and Nutrition* 51, no. 5: 374–93; Mark Swislocki, *Culinary Nostalgia: Regional Food Culture and Urban Experience in Shanghai* (Palo Alto: Stanford University Press, 2008); Maria Amelia Viteri, "Nostalgia Food and Belonging: Ecuadorans in New York City," in *Ethnicity, Citizenship, and Belonging: Practice, Theory, and Spatial Dimensions*, eds. Sarah Albiez, Nelly Castro, Lara Jüssen, and Eva Youkhana (Vervuert: Iberoamericana, 2011), 221–36; and Allen S. Weiss, ed., *Taste Nostalgia* (New York: Lusitania Press, 1997). An article specifically on comfort foods, loneliness, and nostalgia is Karen Stein, "Comfort Foods: Bringing Back Old Favorites," *Journal of the American Dietetic Association*, 108, no. 3 (March 2008): 412, 414. Scholarship on food and memory is also relevant here: David E. Sutton, *Remembrance of Repasts: An Anthropology of Food and Memory* (New York: Berg, 2001).

10. Proust is commonly cited in reference to the power of food to bring about what he called "involuntary memory." His musings about eating a madeleine were published originally (in French) in seven parts between 1913 and 1927 as *À la recherche du temps perdu*. The novel was translated into English with two titles, *Remembrance of Things Past*, trans., C. K. Scott-Moncrieff, Joseph Wood Krutch, and F. A. Blossom (New York: Random House, 1934), and *In Search of Lost Time*, trans., C. K. Scott-Moncrieff, Terence Kilmartin, and D. J. Enright (London: Vintage, 1996).

11. Diane Tye's auto-ethnography of her mother's baking is an excellent example of the complexity of family food traditions. Her mother baked out of duty and did not enjoy it, but it was a central part of the family routine and figures significantly in Tye's memories of her childhood and of her mother. See *Baking as Biography: A Life Story in Recipes* (Ithaca:

McGill-Queen's University Press, 2010). Also, while sharing meals is frequently thought of as a positive and bonding experience, many individuals have negative memories of eating together, as suggested poignantly by Alice P. Julier in the title of her book, *Eating Together: Food, Friendship, and Inequality* (Urbana: University of Illinois Press, 2013). For more critical analysis of the social act of eating together, see *Commensality: from Everyday Food to Feast*, eds. Susanne Kerner, Cynthia Chou, and Morten Warmind (New York: Bloomsbury, 2015).

12. That food is tied to our sense of self—our identity and our worth—is not surprising considering that it bridges so many aspects of our lives. Isabelle de Solier explores this role of food in *Food and the Self: Consumption, Production and Material Culture* (New York: Bloomsbury, 2013). Also see Leon R. Kass, *The Hungry Soul: Eating and Perfecting of Our Nature* (Chicago: University of Chicago Press, 1994) and Fabio Parasecoli, *Bite Me: Food in Popular Culture* (New York: Berg, 2008).

13. For discussion of folkloristic perspectives on food, see Lucy M. Long, ed., *The Food and Folklore Reader* (New York: Bloomsbury, 2015).

14. Kirin Narayan, *Alive in the Writing: Crafting Ethnography in the Company of Chekhov* (Chicago: University of Chicago Press, 2012), 95.

15. Along with Stoller, other foundational works on these concepts include Constance Classen, *Worlds of Sense: Exploring the Senses in History and Across Cultures* (London: Routledge, 1993); Yi-Fu Tuan, *Passing Strange and Wonderful: Aesthetics, Nature, and Culture* (Washington, DC: Island Shearwater, 1993); C. Nadia Seremetakis, *The Senses Still: Perception and Memory as Material Culture in Modernity* (Boulder: Westview, 1994); and Carolyn Korsmeyer, *Making Sense of Taste: Food & Philosophy* (Ithaca, NY: Cornell University Press, 1999). An excellent introduction to the concepts and issues surrounding an anthropology of the senses is given by David Howes in his edited volume, *Empire of the Senses: The Sensual Culture Reader* (Oxford: Berg, 2005). See, in particular, his "Introduction: Empire of the Senses" (1–17) and Alain Corbin's essay, "Charting the Cultural History of the Senses" (128–39), for the larger cultural contexts for this scholarship. Issues of how to document and interpret sensory experiences are discussed in Sarah Pink's *Doing Sensory Ethnography* (Los Angeles: Sage, 2009) and in Mark Dingemanse, Clair Hill, Asifa Majid, and Stephen C. Levinson, "Ethnography of the Senses," *Field Manual* 11, ed. Asifa Majid (Nijmegen: Max Planck Institute for Psycholinguistics, 2008), 18–28.

"Stressed" Spelled Backwards Is "Desserts": Self-Medicating Moods with Foods

Michael Owen Jones

A survey of grocery store food sales across the country following the September 11, 2001, terrorist attack in New York City showed a spike of more than 12 percent over the previous year in the purchase of snack food items and an almost 13 percent rise in the sale of instant mashed potatoes.[1] Restaurateurs reported increased sales of soup, macaroni and cheese, puddings, and similar fare.[2] Conventional wisdom has it that we crave and often eat comfort foods—high in fat, starch, and sugar—because we feel "depressed" or "stressed out" about events, which calls to mind the dictum, "Life's uncertain; eat dessert first." Numerous greeting cards, bumper stickers, rubber stamps, beverage mugs, and T-shirts refer to chocolate in particular: "Next to you, the best thing in life is chocolate!"; "Chocolate is proof that God loves us"; "Chocolate: It's not just for breakfast anymore." A popular saying claims that "chocolate is cheaper than therapy and you don't need an appointment."[3]

Widely spread, the post-burial practice of providing a funerary meal at a reception, usually in the home of the deceased's survivors, focuses on the needs of the living: "Take time to stuff, O mourner. Full stomachs cannot cry."[4] In *Up a Country Lane Cookbook*, Evelyn Birkby includes a recipe for Mabel Lewis's Jell-O dish composed of pineapple and grapes in red gelatin with whipped topping: "This was truly a comfort salad, for Mabel always took this to a family at the time of serious problems." Birkby also comments that "we learned, during those long, painful days that the quiet offer of food provided sustenance for our bodies and comfort for our aching hearts, as our family weathered the terrible storm of our daughter's death."[5]

Rubber stamp: "Life's Uncertain, Eat Dessert First."
Author's collection. Photo by Laura Layera.

In their studies of foodways, folklorists have overlooked comfort food or relegated it to the back burner.[6] In this chapter, therefore, I explore some of the manifestations of comfort food consumption in folklore and popular culture, consider variations in patterns of food choice, and examine several hypotheses about causes, effects, and correlations regarding the consumption of comfort foods by a large percentage of the population. The purpose is to address a range of questions that will help delimit this important area of inquiry that has long been neglected in folkloristics. The focus is on the US inasmuch as cross-national comparisons are few; these concern chocolate cravings, which appear to be dominant among women rather than men in the US,[7] in contrast to more equal desire in Spain[8] and the virtual absence of chocolate cravings in Egypt.[9] Hence, some of the chapter will concentrate on chocolate—the "food of the gods" with a history spanning thirty centuries—which has its self-proclaimed "chocoholics," sayings, rituals, celebrations, jokes, folk knowledge, and stories about hoarding and clandestine consumption. The chapter begins with surveys reporting the association of comfort food choice with gender, age, and locale; it then considers definitions of comfort food, some of the biological, hedonic, emotional, and social bases for cravings and consumption, as well as instances of discomfort and illness resulting from indulgence. Next is a section on chocolate that includes explanations for why this substance seems to be the quintessential comfort food for many American women. The final topics are the impact of folklore and popular culture in establishing eating patterns, the process of conceptualizing an item as comfort food, and future research needs.

Comfort Food: Patterns, Definition, and Explanations for Ingestion

Although comfort food choice is idiosyncratic, patterns are evident—for example, the preference for such side dishes in the US as mashed potatoes and macaroni and cheese. Questionnaire studies indicate that men are more likely to choose hot foods and main meal items such as steak, casseroles, and soup while women have a propensity for sweets or snack foods including chocolate, ice cream, and potato chips. Generally speaking, the male choices possess a nostalgic quality associated with meals prepared by others in their youth. Female selections more often exhibit convenience, indulgence, and perhaps in some instances an implicit rejection of the traditional role of homemaker.[10]

Younger people gravitate toward flavor-saturated options of saltiness and intense sweetness.[11] In one survey of 3,700 respondents, 46 percent said they preferred sweets. Fifty-one percent of women versus 36 percent of men opted for ice cream, chocolate, and brownies. In terms of age categories, Baby Boomers favored braised meats, casseroles, and ice cream; Gen X'ers tended to desire fast food such as burgers and burritos, as well as particular brands of packaged cookies, candies, and snacks; and Generation Y respondents fancied burritos, ramen noodles, and global comfort food in the form of Indian and Thai curries and Vietnamese noodle soup.[12]

In another survey, mashed potatoes headed the list of favorites; 27 percent of respondents said they were reminiscent of Mom, 18 percent found them soothing when stressed, and others remarked on associations with childhood, security, and warmth. Thirty-six percent of women versus 19 percent of men ate comfort food under stress while 36 percent of men versus 27 percent of women chose feel-good food to put them in a positive mood. With respect to seasons, 51 percent of respondents consumed more comfort foods during the winter; 29 percent mentioned holidays. Those self-medicating with food when stressed differed regionally: 57 percent in the Northeast and 48 percent in the West, in contrast to 24 percent in the South and 23 percent in North Central US. In regard to the rate of craving mood foods, 51 percent desired them one to three times per week and 58 percent ate comfort foods as often as thrice weekly. Thirteen percent longed for them daily while 11 percent enjoyed a dose of this kitchen therapy every day of the week.[13]

According to the *Oxford English Dictionary*, "comfort food" is "food that comforts or affords solace; hence, any food (freq. with a high sugar or carbohydrate content) that is associated with childhood or with home cooking. orig. N. Amer." The *OED* dates the term's use in print to a statement in the magazine section of the *Washington Post* on December 25, 1977: "Along with grits, one of the comfort foods of the South is black-eyed peas." Merriam-Webster's

Wooden wall plaque: "Keep Calm and Eat a Cupcake."
Author's collection. Photo by Laura Layera.

10th edition *Collegiate Dictionary* defines comfort food as fare "prepared in a traditional style having a usually nostalgic or sentimental appeal." One researcher writes that it is "any food consumed by individuals, often during periods of stress, that evokes positive emotions and is associated with significant social relationships."[14] Other investigators contend that "comfort foods are foods whose consumption evokes a psychologically comfortable and pleasurable state for a person."[15] The co-owner of a restaurant in Los Angeles specializing in Japanese comfort food (learned from his mother and grandmother and popular along the streets of Tokyo) summed it up: Comfort food is "familiar, flavorful, and filling." The restaurant's reviewer adds, "No matter the ethnic origin, it invariably involves a degree of nostalgia; a familiar component that resonates with your past."[16]

Definitions and conventional wisdom frequently relate comfort food consumption to stress. Several experiments and observations offer a degree of confirmation. Male rats and mice subjected to extreme levels of stress, including frequent exposure to social subordination by an older aggressor, engaged in frantic wheel running and compulsive feeding of high-energy foods such as pure lard and a 30 percent sucrose solution. Female rhesus monkeys harassed by higher ranking females showed an increased intake of a high sugar diet of banana flavored pellets.[17] Stress creates a state of hyper-vigilance, the fight or flight response. Normally, fat deposits in the body generate a signal that reduces the amount of a stress-related chemical. In chronic stress, however—when there is a torrent of anxieties, threats, and burdens over days or weeks—the hormone cortisol in the adrenal gland remains elevated, which often appears to be correlated with compulsive, pleasure-seeking behavior and a marked preference for high-energy foods.[18] Although the mechanisms are not fully known, this research on the consumption of high-energy fare in relation to stress suggests the presence of a system of signals bi-directionally between the body and the brain.[19]

Recent experimental research also suggests that some people might be more sensitive to the presence of fat in foods owing to their bodies' production of a greater amount of a protein referred to as CD36.[20] In addition, there appears to be a fat receptor in the tongue along with the sweet, salty, sour, and bitter tastes and that of umami (savory).[21] Rats and mice in controlled taste tests show a decided preference for foods with fat. Eating fat might reduce vulnerability to sadness in people. After experimentally inducing feelings of sadness in human subjects, clinical investigators found that a gastric infusion of a fatty acid solution apparently lowered the intensity of the sad emotions by nearly half, which is comparable to the pharmacological effects of antidepressants.[22]

In addition to biological explanations, several of which are at present speculative, experiential evidence points to a number of reasons for craving or consuming comfort food. One is the hedonic response: the sensory pleasures derived from the taste, texture, aroma, and mouthfeel of certain foods. Each month in Florida, prison inmates purchase 270,000 honey buns, the dense, glazed snacks that weigh in at six ounces and boast 680 calories, 30 grams of fat, and 51 grams of sugar. Craved and consumed avidly, they sometimes are fashioned into cakes for cellmates' birthdays or to celebrate release from prison, bet on sports events, and barter in the underground economy. According to one inmate, a honey bun "sticks to the gut and fills the gap left from the state food that's badly prepped . . . and at times spoiled to a point that it's uneatable."[23]

Comfort foods vary across societies, from the warm, soft-textured, soupy rice congee in China to the stir-fried rice noodle dish Pad Thai served as street food and in casual eateries in Indonesia to vegemite, the dark brown, salty paste rich in umami favored by Australians. Dining on death row, many prisoners about to be executed request a calorie-loaded last meal of savory fried chicken, juicy burgers, and sugar-laden pies, cakes, and sodas that they have been deprived of for years and that often encode emotional meanings.[24] The reviewer of a book about what top chefs would choose as their last meal writes that "when it comes to our deepest desires, it turns out that food isn't just about taste. It's tied right into memory and the longing for the sensations of when we felt happiest or most loved." The reviewer quotes a restaurant owner: "If someone can hand us those memories . . . it's the culinary equivalent of a big hug."[25]

Besides possible physiological factors and the yearning for particular sensory experiences, the desire for comfort food is often social, emotional, or associational. One account about food brought to a prison conveys the sense of comfort and past memories that food may conjure up. At Christmas, a woman took her husband some homemade biscuits, "not because I can bake good biscuits but because he asked me to try. They turned out . . . different." He shared his Christmas food with others who had received none, including an elderly man with no teeth who consumed nothing but the biscuits. No one else liked them. Asked if he thought they were good, the man replied, "Every morning when I was a little boy, my mama baked biscuits for breakfast. When I came to prison, she still baked biscuits for me every Christmas. My mama died a few years ago, and I ain't had any homemade biscuits since then. Your wife's biscuits taste just like my mama's—God rest her soul, that woman never could bake a decent biscuit! They taste awful, but they remind me of my mama."[26]

Some prisoners and many in the free world endeavor to combat feelings of boredom, unhappiness, frustration, anxiety, loneliness, resentment, enmity, and grief by seeking comfort in food. A woman in a British prison said, "You've got to get solace somehow . . . so I eat. I eat the sweets because the dinner's disgusting, but also because it makes me feel better, cheers me up."[27] As a female college student put it: "Food is a friend, a consolation, a hobby, a companion."[28]

In a survey of comfort food, researchers who queried 264 undergraduate students found that the choices and reasons for them fell into four categories.[29] One is nostalgia: the identification with a particular time and place in one's past evoking feelings of peace and happiness. A male student said that SpaghettiOs symbolized being taken care of by his mother when ill. Indulgence food, a second category, was exemplified by a desire for something expensive and calorically rich, often chocolate but also in one instance a student recalled her impoverished childhood in which her mother sometimes had enough money to prepare breaded pork chops. A third is convenience food. One woman explained: "When I am feeling depressed . . . I want something that is convenient. It is more convenient for me to go to the store and buy some cheese curls than it is for me to go in the kitchen and cook."[30] The fourth category consists of physical comfort food: the sensory aspects of a food that is warm, soft, smooth, easily eaten and digested, and provides a sense of fullness.

A theme running through many accounts is that individuals consume comfort food when alone—and perhaps when feeling lonely.[31] As numerous definitions indicate, comfort food tends to be identified with family tradition, holidays, and special events in which an individual participated. The physiological experience of ingesting a palatable food activates emotional associations with other people that become encoded with the food.[32] After losing her olfactory sense owing to head injuries suffered in an auto accident, my mother sometimes prepared chicken and dumplings like the dish made by her grandmother who had reared her and about whom she reminisced fondly. Mother could not smell the aroma of the food, which is much of its sensory satisfaction, but she recalled her grandmother whose dish was "soooooo good!"[33] Comfort food, then, may serve as a social surrogate.[34] For my mother, chicken and dumplings held "autobiographical meanings."[35]

Their sensory qualities lauded and symbolic connections recalled, comfort foods are often considered to be junk food or harmful to health.[37] Mashed potatoes, macaroni and cheese, pasta dishes, ice cream, and even chocolate are not inherently unhealthful, however. Nevertheless, fifty-two out of ninety-four teenage respondents to a student opinion poll on the *New York Times* learning blog indicated that their choices, and comfort foods generally, are bad for one's health.[38] But several added comments such as: "I don't care if it's healthy or not"; "I don't think it matters"; and "People just want to feel good, and if their comfort food makes them feel that way for a moment then that's all that matters."

Nearly a dozen of the ninety-four teenagers who contributed comments on the blog referred to emotional motivations for and consequences of consuming comfort foods. Among the remarks were: "it does make me feel better when I'm eating them"; "they [mashed potatoes and French fries] just hit the spot and make my life feel like I have been lifted up"; and "When I am upset or if I had a stressful day I go to the store and buy a Reese's candy or something. Another comfort food that I have is ice cream. It's not very healthy for you, but I swear it takes your problems away the second you put a spoonful in your mouth."

Emotional reasons for partaking of comfort foods differ with age. Older individuals tend to consume them when feeling positive while younger people are somewhat more inclined to turn to them when in a dysphoric state.[39] Gender is also a factor. In one survey, more than one third of the women, compared to one fifth of the men, found solace in comfort foods when feeling "stressed"; and more than one third of the men ate them to maintain or enhance positive emotions in contrast to one fourth of the women who did so.[40] Hunger triggers food cravings in many men regardless of the substance;

post-consumption feelings are apt to be positive. Women often attribute their cravings to television commercials, boredom, and stress;[41] after succumbing to their craving, many feel anxious and guilty, particularly if they have been on a restricted diet.[42]

Of the five male and six female teens writing on the *New York Times* blog who commented on the relationship between emotions and comfort food, the females most often focused on counteracting negative mood states rather than sustaining positive ones. "My comfort food is ice-cream," said one. "I seem to always go for this when I'm sad. . . . I feel that this is the only food that really will make me feel better." Another stated, "Whenever I need a break or want to wallow in my sadness, I grab those [chocolate, ice cream, or chips]." A third explained, "I eat snacks as comfort food, but it all depends on my mood. When I am stressed, I will eat anything quick and simple. Something I can just grab and not have to make. I will keep eating and eating and just nonstop eating. . . . When I am sad or depressed, I will eat simple flavors of ice cream, not the exotic. I don't think that the health[fulness] of the comfort food matters because it's for your own personal comfort."

In the late 1990s, two practitioners utilized their understanding of comfort food to help elderly anorexic clients in a nursing home who frequently refused to eat and whose quality of life had diminished greatly. Dieticians design and serve meals representing a "balanced diet" to all patients even though the food remains uneaten meal after meal. "Comfort foods may be a viable alternative," suggest the creators of an alternative approach that proved successful. Comfort foods, they write, are "associated with bygone years, intended to trigger recollections of pleasant childhood experiences and feelings of caring and healing."[43] The authors surveyed 115 individuals in an Iowa care facility, asking them "to identify special foods fed to them by their mothers when they were sick or having an especially difficult time."[44] At 44 percent, chicken soup ranked highest on a list of forty-eight items, followed by toast (33 percent), milk toast (29 percent), ice cream (19 percent), and other items. Offers of comfort food to the patients were accompanied by solicitous comments from the staff to help them recall early experiences in which caring individuals gave them the food. The goal was "to use family traditions, ethnicity, and religious or traditional beliefs to stimulate digestion and trigger hunger," write the authors. "Many residents are comforted by nostalgia. They enjoy thinking of times past and people they loved."[45]

Thoughts of loved ones, past times, and attachments to family, community, and birthplace abound as a result of transnationalism—the migration of people from one country to another—and are manifested in culinary longings. Every few weeks and at holidays, couriers transport coveted comestibles to the Oaxaqueña/os in California from their relatives in Mexico. Items consist of peppers, cheese, seeds, and particularly homemade foods such as *mole* (a cooking sauce consisting of twenty to thirty ingredients, including chili peppers, seeds, nuts, and often chocolate), *tlayudas* (a tortilla unique to Oaxaca), and *chapulines* (fried grasshoppers, which are considered a delicacy). "If my mom sends me things, it's such a treasure," said one woman. "When I receive these things, I'm receiving something from my family. It makes us feel connected to our people."[46] The *envios* (shipments) are prepared by the senders, paid for by the recipients, and carried by representatives of community-based businesses. Beneficiaries "commonly talk about the 'authenticity' of the food, both in regards to the taste and the fact that it came from their homes and was made by their mother." Although the "'home' may be the anchor, the food, be it tlayudas or grasshoppers, is the chain connected to the anchor."[47] A cultural nutrient thus provides emotional comfort, for "food represents 'home,' the family, the household, and the local community. . . . It signifies a person's identity."[48]

While a food might be or might once have been comforting, ingesting it can also produce negative feelings, discomfort, and even anxiety. Those who are dieting to lose weight sometimes feel remorse after having succumbed to their gustatory and emotional cravings for calorie-laden comfort foods, especially sweets. Some Latinas with diabetes bemoan having to adhere to a restricted diet or chastise themselves for not abiding by it. Remarked one woman: "Desserts: those are my comfort foods." Another admitted, "The day of Thanksgiving . . . that one pie made of pumpkin: I know that I shouldn't eat it, but I get tempted and I take nibbles . . . nibbles." A third woman told me, "There are times I see ice cream [sold by vendors] in the streets and my mouth waters, and I say, 'Oh, my God!' I tell my daughters that one day, when I know I am really sick, I am going to eat a really big one, even if I die—but I will die happy. The day will arrive, but not yet. . . . One makes a huge sacrifice. A lot of sacrifice." Another woman who has struggled along with her husband, often unsuccessfully, to control diabetes through diet, commented: "I mean, it's just . . . we're bad . . . we are. We're just bad, period."[49] While Spam is a highly desirable food for many Hawaiians and Southerners, partaking of it may evoke issues of class. "Being an African-American, looking good was always important, showing some kind of status," said one man who quit eating it after eight years. "Being associated with Spam would take that away from that good image."[50] Eating foods rich in positive associations with home, family, and identity can also trigger alarm. The American-born children of Oaxacan immigrants in Monterey County, California, exhibit exceptionally high levels of lead poisoning caused by ingesting lead through fried grasshoppers and other homemade foods sent to them as envios.[51] "My first thought was, 'What's going to happen to us, to our unique way of getting what makes us who we are, our traditional foods,'" said a community worker at a binational organization.[52]

Consuming the Food of the Gods

One oft-mentioned comfort food tied to memorable occasions in childhood, emotional eating, thoughts of others, sensory experiences, and perhaps physiological processes is chocolate, which is the most commonly craved food in North America.[53] Several questions arise: Which gender is more susceptible to chocolate's allure? Is chocolate craving culture-specific or is it cross-national? Are some people addicted to chocolate as they claim?

American folklore and popular culture have a field day with this food item. T-shirts read: "If the answer is chocolate, who cares what the question is." "Save Planet Earth. It's the only one with chocolate." "A balanced diet is chocolate in both hands." In 1990, the Complete Chocoholic First Aid Kit became available; it consisted of bite-sized chocolate bandages, "quick fix" chocolate tablets, chocolate "aspirins," and a chocolate "diet pill." Sayings on shirts, mugs, and rubber stamps refer to chocolate as therapy: "When no one understands you, chocolate is there." "Here, have some chocolate. Feel better now?" There

Rubber stamp: "Chocolate is proof that God loves us."
Author's collection. Photo by Laura Layera.

are also emailed jokes concerning why chocolate is better than sex: "You can *get* chocolate. You can have chocolate in public. No need to fake your enjoyment of chocolate. Size doesn't matter—though more is still better."

Consumption of cacao or chocolate—the "food of the gods"—originated in the New World with the Olmec, Maya, and Aztec at least 3,000 years ago and diffused to Europe in the mid-1500s. From the sixteenth century to the present, more than 100 medicinal uses have been proposed.[54] Frequently mentioned today is chocolate as a stimulant, relaxant, antidepressant, and aphrodisiac.[55] People describe chocolate as heavenly, irresistible, decadent, naughty, dangerous, erotic, immoral, sinful, unhealthful, and addictive—but also therapeutic.[56]

Surveys indicate that substantially more American women than men crave chocolate; e.g., in one study the ratio was 40 percent female to 15 percent male.[57] According to a T-shirt: "Chocolate is a girl's best friend." Remarked actress Sandra Bullock: "Chocolate is the greatest gift to women ever created, next to the likes of Paul Newman and Gene Kelly. It's something that should be had on a daily basis." Then there's the joke about the man who finds a bottle on the beach containing a genie that grants him three wishes. The first is for one million dollars. The second is for a convertible. For his third wish, the man asks to become irresistible to women. The genie turns him into a box of chocolates.

For years, researchers and the public have puzzled over chocolate's appeal and effects. Four explanations are common. One is that the craved food, in this instance chocolate, serves homeostatic needs; i.e., ingesting the substance will redress a nutritional deficiency. Sometimes women cite this belief in "the wisdom of the body" to account for chocolate craving in relation to their menstrual cycle, contending that chocolate restores depleted magnesium or aids in the release of serotonin to improve mood.

Arguing against magnesium deficiency, however, is the fact that other foods—including rice bran, flax seeds, cornmeal, and seaweed—are high in magnesium but not craved.[58] Moreover, individuals could simply take a magnesium pill but don't.[59] Dark chocolate contains cacao mass, coco butter, and some sugar, but milk chocolate, the form that most people prefer the taste of with its added milk solids and sugar, contains lower amounts of cacao and hence less magnesium; in addition, white chocolate does not include cocoa solids. Many women contend that they crave chocolate perimenstrually, but few eat more chocolate during the two to three days before and after the onset of menses, and non-PMS sufferers do not show signs of cyclic changes in eating.[60] In one of the rare cross-national studies, a survey indicates that while 40 percent of American female respondents associated chocolate craving with their menstrual cycle, only 4 percent of Spanish females did.[61] In addition, among people craving sweets, the difference between men and women in Spain who desired chocolate was small—22.2 percent and 28.6 percent, respectively—compared to 17.4 percent men and 44.6 percent women in the US.[62] In a questionnaire study undertaken in Egypt, researchers found that the craved food first mentioned by both men and women was savories, not sweets. Only 6 percent of women and 1 percent of men named chocolate.[63] The white chocolate preferred by women in Spain has no cacao base; and although Egypt has a sizeable candy and confectionary industry, sweets including chocolate are not the most craved items. This casts doubt on a homeostatic cause, suggesting instead a cultural origin for chocolate cravings.

A second popular claim is that chocolate improves mood and counters depression. Among the 380 chemical elements in chocolate are tyramine and phenylethylamine, which are arousing and might stimulate the release of dopamine, but these compounds are higher in some sausages, cheddar cheese, and pickled herring, which are not often craved; in addition, too much dopamine may produce negative emotions.[64] Chocolate contains caffeine but the amount is insignificant compared to coffee and tea. A common belief is that chocolate or carbohydrate craving addresses serotonin deficiency, especially in depressed individuals who then self-medicate. Carbohydrates stimulate insulin production that increases the proportion of tryptophan, which is converted into serotonin. The fat content in chocolate slows the absorption of carbohydrate, however, and 5 percent of chocolate's calorie content is protein, negating the serotonin effect.[65] In sum, a "depressed mood cannot be the sole trigger of chocolate cravings," write a set of researchers. "Many women report ingesting chocolate to improve mood, but these individuals exhibit no more depression-like symptomatology than women who do not use chocolate for these purposes."[66] Alleviating a negative mood more likely occurs through the hedonic effects of eating, not a nutritional or physiological mechanism. Conclude a pair of investigators: "This proposed link between serotonin, mood and 'craving' for carbohydrates . . . has become part of the folklore of the psychology of eating" with little evidence to support it."[67]

A third assertion is even more doubtful. Self-identified "chocoholics" often insist that psychoactive constituents in chocolate cause addiction to it, which explains their intense desire for and over-consumption of this food. "I'm sure it's addictive, I do think that," remarked one woman. It has a "drug-like effect," said another; "some of the ingredients in chocolate, it works on your brain and then you feel happy."[68] But theobromine is a weak stimulant, caffeine concentrations are low, and other compounds exist in greater amounts in foods that are not craved or said to be addictive.[69] A T-shirt proclaims, "When it

Refrigerator magnet: "Chocolate, the fifth basic food group."
Author's collection. Photo by Laura Layera.

comes to chocolate, resistance is futile." Indulgence, however, is stigmatized in our current climate of "healthism," in which chocolate is considered "bad" and the 2.8 billion pounds consumed annually in the US (11.7 pounds per capita) is said to contribute to the "obesity epidemic" (the Swiss eat twice as much chocolate, however, and the Austrians are not far behind them). Employing a medical model to justify overindulgence in eating chocolate, to explain why one succumbs to its "moreish" quality (wanting to consume more, like the ad for Lay's potato chips: "Bet you can't eat just one!"), and to account for failing to exercise restraint relieves individuals of personal responsibility; they are victims of forces beyond their control.[70] A T-shirt advises that there are "3 steps for chocoholics. Admit you have a problem. Admit there is no cure. Don't worry about it anymore."

Not a staple but rather a highly palatable treat, chocolate possesses orosensory properties providing immense gratification. It dissolves at a slightly lower temperature than a person's body warmth; one observation is that "if you've got melted chocolate all over your hands, you're eating it too slowly." Because it is calorically dense as well as exhibits a unique combination of

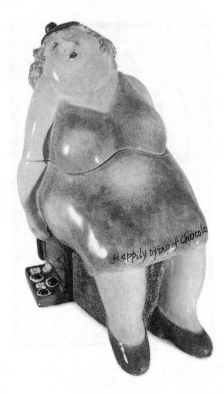

Cookie jar: "Happily dying of chocolate." Author's collection. Photo by Laura Layera.

sweetness, creamy texture, characteristic taste, and tantalizing aroma, chocolate "seduces the palate."[71] As the cartoon character Dennis the Menace
remarks to his friend while eating a chocolate ice cream cone, "Joey, the only
thing better than chocolate is ... well ... nothing!"[72] This is the fourth hypothesis concerning chocolate's allure.

Chocolate, which is "a real pleasure thing," commented one woman,[73] may
be eaten either as a reward for an achievement or as therapy for a difficult,
trying day. In other words, to celebrate or to medicate.[74] Its excessive consumption is viewed as evidence of lack of self-control; hence, one lay construction views it as unhealthful, harmful, or simply "bad." Little wonder that
there are stories about people hoarding, hiding, and clandestinely consuming
chocolate. "The taste of chocolate is a sensual pleasure in itself, existing in the
same world as sex," observed the therapist and media personality Dr. Ruth
Westheimer. "For myself, I can enjoy the wicked pleasure of chocolate . . .
entirely by myself. Furtiveness makes it better." Viewed as sinful because it
provides sensual pleasure, chocolate often evokes a sexual analogy: ". . . eating

chocolate is a bit like having sex . . . it just feels so good," said one woman in a study of alleged chocoholics.[75] Remarked the actress Alicia Silverstone: "My favorite thing in the world is a box of fine European chocolates which is, for sure, better than sex."

Encounters with chocolate are unavoidable. Thoughtful hotel staff leave a piece on your pillow at night; chocolate bars and bags of Hershey's Kisses sit temptingly near the cash register in pharmacies and grocery stores; greeting cards incorporate references to it; and it appears in various forms at major holidays, including chocolate eggs and bunnies at Easter, chocolate coins on Hanukkah, chocolate snowmen and Santa Claus at Christmas, chocolate skulls, cats, bats, witches, and jack-o'-lanterns at Halloween, and red, heart-shaped boxes of gold or silver foil-wrapped chocolate cherries, caramels, truffles, nougats, fudge, and bonbons on Valentine's Day. Gift boxes of choco-lates emphasize femininity, luxury, and allure:[76] They are glossy white, gold, silver, or chocolate brown, a colorful ribbon adorns one corner, and images on the cover depict some of the delicious confectionaries inside. A symbol of romance and sexuality, chocolate figures in the ritual of seduction. Often men give women gifts of chocolate to "sweeten them up"—"sweets for the sweet" as the saying goes—as a step in breaking down sexual resistance.

The Process of Conceptualizing a Food as Comfort-Giving

To recapitulate hypotheses about the appeal of comfort food, recent animal studies point to a possible correlation between intense stress and the con-sumption of high-energy foods to alleviate the negative state. Perhaps we eat what we do sometimes because of "what's eating us," but alternative or additional influences have been proposed. For instance, other experimen-tal research suggests the possibility of a fat receptor on the tongue provid-ing a way for gustatory sensations to reach the brain. Yet other investigators claim to have identified a protein that may cause people to react differently to the presence of fat: When some individuals consume more fat, they might become less sensitive to it and therefore require a greater amount to be satis-fied (leading to obesity), or those who make more CD36 protein could have increased sensitivity and therefore need less fat, or perhaps diet itself influ-ences the amount of the fat protein that is produced.[77] Besides a possible bio-logical basis for comfort food craving, the orosensory characteristics of food, particularly chocolate, have long been recognized: the warm, soft, soothing, and filling nature of some foods, or the crunchy and salty features, or the sweetness or savory quality that provide hedonic rewards. Carbohydrates are known to promote insulin production resulting in increased tryptophan that is converted to serotonin, which has a positive influence on mood. Whether in biology, psychology, or sociology, researchers seem to be seeking a "unifying explanation of food cravings,"[78] but none of the hypotheses conclusively identifies the origin of comfort food eating.[79]

Several articles implicate yet another set of influential factors that have not been investigated thoroughly. For example, the researchers who mentioned that carbohydrate "addiction" has "become part of the folklore of the psychology of eating"[80] also note that a "widely believed motive to eat chocolate is to improve mood" and refer to "belief," "a popular idea," and "everyday discourse." Others comment on "terms in common use," "popular claims," and "a popular hypothesis";[81] "lay definition," "common view," and "conventional explanation";[82] and "the popular media and personal anecdotes."[83] There are references as well to "socially constructed" notions, "folk wisdom," and the "vernacular of everyday life," along with "family traditions," "cultural traditions," and "traditional beliefs." In other words, folklore, popular culture, and symbolic behavior play a significant role in establishing patterns of comfort food choice, perpetuating ideas about certain food items, influencing expectations, and affecting cognitive processes.

The process of conceptualizing items as comfort foods seems to follow a particular set of occurrences. It entails having a pleasurable gustatory experience, repeated exposure to the item, emotional meanings attributed to the food, learned expectations of the alleviation of an aversive mood or maintenance of a positive frame of mind, and social reinforcement. To elaborate: Certain foods are highly palatable owing to their sweet, salty, savory, aromatic, or other properties. Combined with the hedonic satisfaction they offer as well as the simple pleasure of eating and feelings of satiety, carbohydrate-rich fare and the fatty acids in some of the items may have physiological consequences affecting moods.[84] Foods providing such desirable outcomes will be sought again as a conditioned response; some items are given in childhood as treats and rewards, the indulgence leading to learned behavior patterns and anticipation.[85] Often an item is associated with one or more individuals, and these emotionally charged connections become part and parcel of the food. For example, one of the teens who mentioned a comfort food on the *New York Times* blog noted, "It is a special recipe that only my aunt knows." Another wrote, "My mom made them for me when I was little." A third stated, "My family has pizza night every Friday and I look forward to it every week." Yet another commented, "My comfort food is my mom's fried chicken, mashed potatoes and gravy, hot biscuits and gravy (or Honey) and corn or green beans. Nobody can cook it like my mom. . . . It's just a wonderful meal and makes for a great family time together." A dish, then, becomes cognitively linked to family or other relational partners,[86] to be served on such special occasions as holidays. A repast might carry markers of ethnicity because of the "flavor principle," a distinctive taste owing to herbs, spices, and manner of preparation.[87] As either family fare or cultural cuisine, the food often becomes conceived of as "traditional," that is, exhibiting continuities through time and consistencies in space,[88] and therefore imbued with value.[89]

Scholarly studies and the media contribute to promoting the concept of comfort food and to shaping conceptions and expectations. Authors who address what they refer to as conventional or popular ideas about comfort food are clearly aware of some of the lore surrounding the topic. Yet other investigators seem implicitly motivated to test common beliefs to determine possible physiological mechanisms accounting for alleged effects. Journalists report on novel and potentially important findings,[90] typically interviewing an author to obtain explanations in lay language. Whether degree-holders or self-styled health and fitness gurus, bloggers simplify research further, sometimes misrepresenting or overstating a study's initial findings and its implications. Terms and hypotheses derived from these sources become part of vernacular speech and hence elements of "folk knowledge" as "the everyday, taken-for-granted understandings that shape people's perceptions, thinking, actions, and reactions to events and situations."[91] The popular lexicon now includes "comfort food," "stress," "chocoholic," "sugar addict," "wisdom of the body," "tryptophan," and "serotonin."

An example of folk knowledge is the oft-heard remark at a Thanksgiving feast that tryptophan in the turkey has caused a person's fatigue. Amino acid is a natural sedative metabolized into the neurotransmitters serotonin and melatonin, but the food needs to be eaten on an empty stomach and turkey contains no more tryptophan than does pork, beef, chicken, or beans, the devouring of which is not alleged to put people to sleep. The drowsiness owes much to the carbohydrate-rich side dishes and sugar-laden desserts that lead to increased serotonin levels, not to mention the depressant effect of the accompanying alcohol or the fact that the body redirects blood from elsewhere to the digestive system, a process that is pronounced after overeating.[92] "Another popular myth that is widespread on the Internet is that bananas improve mood because of their serotonin content. Although it is true that bananas contain serotonin, it does not cross the blood–brain barrier."[93] It is not necessarily a matter of lay constructions being incorrect; rather, members of the public may have incomplete information in their efforts to understand their behavior and that of others.

Future Research

More research needs to be done, especially ethnographic. Few ethnic, multi-ethnic, and cross-national studies of comfort food cravings and consumption exist. The emphasis has been on food; beverages are rarely considered. Also not investigated is the topic of unusual food mixtures, often eaten clandestinely. The one study of "secretive food concocting" concerns binge eating, attributing the behavior to cravings.[94] Most of the examples described by the college students in this survey involve the incorporation of chocolate, sugar, and peanut butter—e.g., sugar on scrambled eggs, peanut butter and chocolate chip sandwiches, oatmeal with Oreo cookies, bananas with peanut butter wrapped in cheddar cheese, tortilla chips and peanut butter, French fries in ice cream, ham and cheese with syrup, and so on. The researchers report that a majority of respondents indicated that having a craving rather than being hungry or even bored predominated among motives. Judging from my own occasional queries to others, it seems that sometimes the consumption of unusual combinations provides or is motivated by a desire for not only gustatory but also emotional satisfaction, and hence what is prepared might well be considered "comfort food."

Surveys involving questionnaires, chiefly among college students, have identified some comfort foods and, through respondents' attempts at recall, when or under what conditions cravings were triggered, but direct observation and interviews or having people keep diaries for a period of time usually produces more accurate records of behavior and cognitive processes. Daily journals that document what was eaten, when, and in what circumstances (including a notation about others present, mood, and post-ingestion feelings) can be discussed with the diary keepers in regard to items they identify as comfort food, thus providing insight into eating patterns during normal and stressful circumstances, the variety of beverages as well as foods (and their manner of preparation) that were consumed, items claimed to alleviate or maintain particular moods, and other data revealing what is conceived of as comfort fare and why it was consumed, when, where, and by whom.

Since the term "comfort food" entered print three-and-a-half decades ago, it has become a household word. Many restaurants, blogs, and cookbooks now promote comfort food or propose ways of preparing less fattening versions of it, cutting one third to one half or more of the calories in chicken pot pie, Philly cheesesteaks, and tuna melts. Research on comfort food cravings and consumption is important for several reasons. A large percentage of the American population partakes of comfort food, often wittingly and willingly as either celebration or medication. One application of research, described earlier, is encouraging elderly anorexic patients to eat by offering them comfort food given to them in years past by caring individuals. Laboratory studies of stress among animals and their increased intake of fat and sucrose usually justify research by suggesting that there are implications for human beings, principally in regard to eating disorders, depression, corpulence, and cardiovascular disease. Some note the rising incidence of stress in our lives, along with the growing obesity "epidemic," wondering if there is a correlation.[95] An oft-circulated email presents its own view of fat and disease: "The Japanese eat very little fat and suffer fewer heart attacks than the British or Americans. On the other hand, the French eat a lot of fat and also suffer fewer heart attacks than the British or Americans. Conclusion: Eat what you like. It's speaking English that kills you."

Although the logic is twisted, the joke nevertheless points to the fact that people construct systems of health and healing beliefs. Further research on comfort food can reveal more fully the process by which individuals attach meanings to food, how and why they self-diagnose and self-medicate with food, the ways in which they draw upon multiple "sources of authority" (tradition, personal experience, the media, formal medicine, academic research), and "*how* these health belief systems of authority interact—sometimes competing, sometimes conflicting, sometimes remarkably congruent."[96] Longstanding questions in folkloristics can also be addressed, shedding new light on comfort food, foodways, and our own field of study. These issues include how and why traditions come into being, why they are perpetuated, and how and why they remain stable as well as change.[97] In sum, research in folklore studies can contribute to understanding how and why food is as much a symbolic object as it is a substance to nourish the body. Perhaps, as the saying goes, "chocolate solves everything." Although folklore studies might not be able to make a similar claim, it can nevertheless add much to the growing body of literature about comfort food cravings and consumption.

Notes

1. "A Nation Turns to Comfort Food," *ABC News*, November 7, 2006, accessed February 20, 2013, http://abcnews.go.com/US/story?id=92217&page=1.

2. Bret Thorn, "Seeking Comfort, Diners Indulge in Feel-Good Fare," *Nation's Restaurant News* 35 (2001): 32.

3. For these and similar examples in this chapter, see such websites as Cafepress.com, Zazzle.com, Facts-about-chocolate.com, and Jokes.com.

4. From a poem by Jeanne Nail Adams quoted in Lonnie Yoder, "The Funeral Meal: A Significant Funerary Ritual," *Journal of Religion and Health* 25 (1986): 149–60.

5. Michelle Huneven, "Meanwhile, Back on the Farm," review of *Up a Country Lane Cookbook* by Evelyn Birkby, *Los Angeles Times*, September 1, 1994, H11.

6. Exceptions to varying degrees include Michael Owen Jones, "Food Choice, Symbolism, and Identity: Bread-and-Butter Issues for Folkloristics and Nutrition Studies (American Folklore Society Presidential Address, October 2005)," *Journal of American Folklore* 120 (2007): 129–77; Sojin Kim and R. Mark Livengood, "Ramen Noodles & Spam: Popular Foods, Significant Tastes," *The Digest* 15 (1995): 2–11; Sarah E. Newton, "The Jell-O Syndrome: Investigating Popular Culture/Foodways," *Western Folklore* 51 (1992): 249–67; and LuAnne Roth, *"Last Supper"* [review], *Journal of American Folklore* 124 (2011): 105–108. In addition, some of the recipes labeled "traditional" in Humphrey's article, associated with the contributor's mother or grandmother, might well be thought of as comfort foods by that individual; see Lin T. Humphrey, "Traditional Foods? Traditional Values," *Western Folklore* 48 (1989): 169–77.

7. H. P. Weingarten and D. Elston, "The Phenomenology of Food Cravings," *Appetite* 15 (1990): 231–46.

8. Jamie L. Osman and Jeffery Sobal, "Chocolate Cravings in American and Spanish Individuals: Biological and Cultural Influences," *Appetite* 47 (2006): 290–301.

9. Gordon Parker, Isabella Parker, and Heather Brotchie, "Mood State Effects of Chocolate," *Journal of Affective Disorders* 92 (2006): 149–59.

10. Julie L. Locher, William C. Yoels, Donna Maurer, and Jillian Van Ells, "Comfort Foods: An Exploratory Journey into the Social and Emotional Significance of Food," *Food & Foodways* 13 (2005): 273–97; and Brian Wansink, Matthew M. Cheney, and Nina Chan, "Exploring Comfort Food Preferences Across Age and Gender," *Physiology & Behavior* 79 (2003): 739–47.

11. Locker et al., "Comfort Foods"; Wansink et al., "Exploring Comfort Food Preferences."

12. Karlene Lukovitz, "Does Meaning of 'Comfort Foods' Vary by Age?" July 31, 2009, accessed February 22, 2013, http://www.mediapost.com/publications/article/110781/does-meaning-of-comfort-foods-vary-by-age.html#axzz2Leodj8ws.

13. unileverusa.com/mediacenter/pressreleases/2004/countrycrockcomfortfoodpr.aspx, accessed February 18, 2013.

14. Julie L. Locher, "Comfort Food," in *Encyclopedia of Food and Culture*, ed. S. Katz (New York: Charles Scribner's Sons, 2002), accessed February 9, 2013, http://www.encyclopedia.com/doc/1G2-3403400153.html.

15. Wansink et al., "Exploring Comfort Food Preferences," 739.

16. Brad Japhe, "Japanese Comfort Food at Del Rey Kitchen from Satoru Yokomori and Michael Yee," *LA Weekly*, November 10, 2014, accessed November 11, 2014, http://m.laweekly.com/squidink/2014/11/10/japanese-comfort-food-at-del-rey-kitchen-from-satoru-yokomori-and-michael-yee. Among the dishes served are *nankotsu* (bite-sized pieces of deep-fried chicken cartilage) and *itameshi* pasta (a spaghetti hybrid infused with umami-rich flavors of such items as shaved *bonito*, *nori*, and *ponzu* butter).

17. For studies of rat behavior, see Mary F. Dallman, Susan F. Akana, Susanne E. la Fleur, Francisca Gomez, Hani Houshyar, M. E. Bell, Seema Bhatnagar, Kevin D. Laugero, and Sotara Manalo, "Chronic Stress and Obesity: A New View of 'Comfort Food,'" *Publications*

of the National Academy of Sciences 100 (2003): 11696–701; and Jen-Chieh Chuang, Mario Perello, Ichiro Sakata, Sherri Osborne-Lawrence, Joseph M. Savitt, Michael Lutter, and Jeffrey M. Zigman, "Ghrelin Mediates Stress-Induced Food-Reward Behavior in Mice," *Journal of Clinical Investigation* 121 (2011): 2684–92. For observations of primates, see Marilyn Arce, Vasiliki Michopoulos, Kathryn N. Shepard, Quynh-Chau Ha, and Mark E. Wilson, "Diet Choice, Cortisol Reactivity, and Emotional Feeding in Socially Housed Rhesus Monkeys," *Physiology & Behavior* 101 (2010): 446–55; John Tierney, "Comfort Food, for Monkeys," *New York Times*, May 20, 2008, accessed February 9, 2013, http://www.nytimes.com/2008/05/20/science/20tier.html; and M. E. Wilson, J. Fisher, A. Fischer, V. Lee, R. B. Harris, and T. J. Bartness, "Quantifying Food Intake in Socially Housed Monkeys: Social Status Effects on Caloric Consumption," *Physiology & Behavior* 94 (2008): 586–94.

18. Carl T. Hall, "'Comfort Food' Research Finds Medicinal Effect / High-Fat Fare Helps Rats in Dealing with High Stress Levels," *San Francisco Gate*, accessed February 19, 2013, http://www.sfgate.com/health/article/Comfort-food-research-finds-medicinal-effect-2573565.php; and A. Tomiyama, Mary F. Dallman, and Elissa S. Epel, "Comfort Food Is Comforting to Those Most Stressed: Evidence of the Chronic Stress Response Network in High Stress Women," *Psychoneuroendocrinology* 36 (2011): 1513–19.

19. Further complicating matters is that, according to one study, it might not be negative emotions in response to stress that prompts ingesting comfort foods as much as it is the "regulation strategies" people utilize to deal with their emotions. That is, experimental participants who suppressed the expression of negative emotions ate more comfort foods than those who reappraised their emotions in order to change the emotional impact once the situation occurred: "Rather than focusing on emotional experience as being responsible for increased food intake, we assumed that different strategies that individuals employ to regulate these emotions are responsible for the changes in eating behavior." See Catharine Evers, F. Marijn Stok, and Denise T. D. deRidder, "Feeding Your Feelings: Emotion Regulation Strategies and Emotional Eating," *Personality and Social Psychology Bulletin* 36 (2010): 800.

20. Julie Wan, "Fat Might Be the Sixth Basic Taste," *Washington Post*, June 4, 2012, accessed February 17, 2013, http://articles.washingtonpost.com/2012-06-04/national/35462005_1_fat-taste-nada-abumrad-meatiness. See also Gary Wenk, "Why Does Fat Taste So Good? The Importance of Fat-Tasting Proteins on the Tongue," *Psychology Today*, January 2012, accessed February 17, 2013, http://www.psychologytoday.com/blog/your-brain-food/201201/why-does-fat-taste-so-good. Both authors report on recent research concerning CD36, which was discovered by Nada Abumrad. See Marta Yanina Pepino, Latisha Love-Gregory, Samuel Klein, and Nada A. Abumrad, "The Fatty Acid Translocase Gene CD36 and Lingual Lipase Influence Oral Sensitivity to Fat in Obese Subjects," *Journal of Lipid Research* 53 (2012): 561–66.

21. Kikunae Ikeda, a chemistry professor at Tokyo's Imperial University, discovered umami in the early twentieth century. The name of the taste is derived from the Japanese word *umai* (delicious). See Bernd Lindemann, Yoko Ogiwara, and Yuzo Ninomiya, "The Discovery of Umami," *Chemical Senses* 27 (2002): 843–44.

22. Lucas Van Oudenhove, Shane McKie, Daniel Lassman, Bilal Uddin, Peter Paine, Steven Coen, Lloyd Gregory, Jan Tack, and Qasim Aziz, "Fatty Acid–Induced Gut-Brain

Signaling Attenuates Neural and Behavioral Effects of Sad Emotion in Humans," *Journal of Clinical Investigation* 121 (2011): 3094–99.

23. Drew Harwell, "Honey Buns Sweeten Life for Florida Prisoners," *Tampa Bay Times*, January 2, 2011, accessed August 13, 2012, http://www.tampabay.com/features/humaninterest/honey-buns-sweeten-life-for-florida-prisoners/1142687.

24. Michael Owen Jones, "Dining on Death Row: Last Meals and the Crutch of Ritual," *Journal of American Folklore* 127 (2014): 3–26.

25. Joel Stein, "You Eat What You Are," *Time*, October 18, 2007, accessed August 5, 2010, http://www.time.com/time/magazine/article/0,9171,1673252,00.html.

26. Bookgirl, 2002, accessed August 12, 2010, http://www.prisontalk.com/forums/archive/index.php/t-150289.html.

27. Catrin Smith, "Punishment and Pleasure: Women, Food and the Imprisoned Body," *The Sociological Review* 50 (2002): 204.

28. Carole M. Counihan, *The Anthropology of Food and Body: Gender, Meaning, and Power* (New York: Routledge, 1999), 120.

29. Locher et al., "Comfort Foods."

30. Ibid., 287.

31. Locher et al., "Comfort Foods."

32. Jordan D. Troisi and Shira Gabriel, "Chicken Soup Really Is Good for the Soul: 'Comfort Food' Fulfills the Need to Belong," *Psychological Science*, May 2, 2011, accessed October 19, 2011, http://pss.sagepub.com/content/early/2011/05/02/0956797611407931.

33. Michael Owen Jones, *Exploring Folk Art: Twenty Years of Thought on Craft, Work, and Aesthetics* (Ann Arbor, MI: UMI Research Press, 1987), 99.

34. Troisi and Gabriel, "Chicken Soup Really Is Good for the Soul."

35. Gill Valentine and Beth Longstaff, "Doing Porridge: Food and Social Relations in a Male Prison," *Journal of Material Culture* 3 (1998): 139.

36. John Lancaster, "Incredible Edibles," *The New Yorker*, March 21, 2011, 68.

37. Wansink et al., "Exploring Comfort Food."

38. Daniel E Slotkin, "What's Your Comfort Food?" May 25, 2012, accessed August 11, 2013, http://learning.blogs.nytimes.com/2012/05/25/whats-your-comfort-food/?_r=1&apage=2#comments.

39. Laurette Dubé, Jordan L. LeBel, and Ji Lu, "Affect Asymmetry and Comfort Food Consumption," *Physiology & Behavior* 86 (2005): 559–67.

40. Unilever. See also Levitan and Davis, "Emotions"; Weingarten and Elston (1991), "Food Cravings"; and Wansink et al., "Exploring Comfort Food."

41. Weingarten and Elston (1991), "Food Cravings."

42. Benford and Gough, "'Unhealthy' Practices"; Parker et al. (2006), "Mood State"; and Rogers and Smit, "Food Craving."

43. Paulette Wood and Barbra D. Vogen, "Feeding the Anorectic Client: Comfort Foods and Happy Hour," *Geriatric Nursing* 19 (1998): 192.

44. Wood and Vogen, "Feeding the Anorectic Client," 193.

45. Ibid., 194.

46. Sandip Roy, "There's Lead in My Grasshopper Snack: Environmental Problems Cross Borders," *New America Media*, April 3, 2007, accessed October 21, 2014, http://news

.newamericamedia.org/news/view_article.html?article_id=93856b1c427e995ccdb2aca6cdd5 b303.

47. James I. Grieshop, "The *Envios* of San Pablo Huixtepec, Oaxaca: Food, Homes, and Transnationalism," *Human Organization* 65 (2006): 404.

48. Grieshop, "The *Envios*," 405.

49. Michael Owen Jones, "Latina/o Local Knowledge about Diabetes: Emotional Triggers, Plant Treatments, and Food Symbolism," in *Diagnosing Folklore: Perspectives on Health, Trauma, and Disability*, eds. Trevor J. Blank and Andrea Kitta (Jackson: University Press of Mississippi, 2015), 97–103.

50. Jones (2007), "Food Choice," 146.

51. Margaret A. Handley, Kaitie Drace, Robert Wilson, Mary Croughan, Celeste Hall, Evie Diaz, Eric Sanford, Enrique Gonzalez-Mendez, and Mario Villalobos, "Globalization, Binational Communities, and Imported Food Risks: Results of an Outbreak Investigation of Lead Poisoning in Monterey County, California," *American Journal of Public Health* 97 (2007): 900–906.

52. Roy, "There's Lead in My Grasshopper Snack."

53. Willa Michener and Paul Rozin, "Pharmacological Versus Sensory Factors in the Satiation of Chocolate Craving," *Physiology & Behavior* 56 (1994): 419–22.

54. Teresa L. Dillinger, Patricia Barriga, Sylvia Escarcega, Martha Jimenez,Diana Salazar Lowe, and Louis E. Grivetti, "Food of the Gods: Cure for Humanity? A Cultural History of the Medicinal and Ritual Use of Chocolate," *Journal of Nutrition* 130 (2000): 2057S–72S.

55. Dillinger et al., "Food of the Gods." See also Parker et al. (2006), "Mood State Effects."

56. D. Barthel, "Modernism and Marketing: The Chocolate Box Revisited," *Theory of Culture and Society* 6 (1989): 429–38; Rebecca Benford and Brendan Gough, "Defining and Defending 'Unhealthy' Practices: A Discourse Analysis of Chocolate 'Addicts'' Accounts," *Journal of Health Psychology* 11 (2006): 427–40; Peter J. Rogers and Hendrick J. Smit, "Food Craving and Food 'Addiction': A Critical Review of the Evidence from a Biopsychosocial Perspective," *Pharmacology, Biochemistry & Behavior* 66 (2000): 3–14; and H. E. Yuker, "Perceived Attributes of Chocolate," in *Chocolate: Food of the Gods*, ed. Alex Szogyi (Westport, CT: Greenwood Press, 1997), 35–43.

57. Michener and Rozin, "Pharmacological"; see also Debra A. Zellner, Ana Garriga-Trillo, Soraya Centeno, and Elizabeth Wadsworth, "Chocolate Craving and the Menstrual Cycle," *Appetite* 42 (2004): 119–21.

58. Michener and Rozin, "Pharmacological"; Parker et al. (2006), "Mood State"; and P. Rozin, E. Levine, and C. Stoess, "Chocolate Craving and Liking," *Appetite* 17 (1991): 199–212.

59. H. P. Weingarten and D. Elston, "Food Cravings in a College Population," *Appetite* 17 (1991): 167–75.

60. Rogers and Smit, "Food Craving."

61. Zellner et al. (2004), "Chocolate Craving."

62. D. A. Zellner, A. Garriga-Trillo, E. Rohm, S. Centeno, and S. Parker, "Food Liking and Craving: A Cross-Cultural Approach," *Appetite* 33 (1999): 61–70.

63. Scott Parker, Niveen Kamel, and Debra Zellner, "Food Craving Patterns in Egypt: Comparisons with North America and Spain," *Appetite* 40 (2003): 193–95.

64. Michener and Rozin, "Pharmacological"; Rozin et al., "Chocolate Craving"; and D. Benton and R. T. Donohoe, "The Effects of Nutrients on Mood," *Public Health Nutrition* 2 (1999): 403–409.

65. Parker et al. (2006), "Mood State."

66. Weingarten and Elston (1990), "Phenomenology," 239.

67. Rogers and Smit, "Food Craving," 6.

68. Benford and Gough, "'Unhealthy' Practices," 436.

69. Rogers and Smit, "Food Craving."

70. Ibid.

71. Weingarten and Elston (1990), "Phenomenology."

72. Hank Ketcham, "Dennis the Menace [cartoon]," *Los Angeles Times*, June 18, 2013, D6.

73. Benford and Gough, "'Unhealthy' Practices," 433.

74. Indeed, the survey reported in "Exploring Comfort Food," by Wansink et al. found that, contrary to popular belief, 86 percent of respondents consumed comfort food as reward in contrast to 36 percent who used it as therapy when depressed.

75. Benford and Gough, "'Unhealthy' Practices," 434.

76. Barthel, "Modernism and Marketing."

77. Jim Dryden, "Tongue Sensors Seem to Taste Fat," 2005, accessed February 17, 2013, http://news.wustl.edu/news/Pages/6285.aspx.

78. Weingarten and Elston (1990), "Phenomenology," 241.

79. Weingarten and Elston (1991), "Food Cravings."

80. Rogers and Smit, "Food Craving," 6.

81. Parker et al. (2006), "Mood State."

82. Weingarten and Elston (1990), "Phenomenology."

83. Chuang et al., "Ghrelin Mediates."

84. Edward Leigh Gibson, "Emotional Influences on Food Choice: Sensory, Physiological and Psychological Pathways," *Physiology & Behavior* 89 (2006): 53–61.

85. Jayanthi Kandiah, Melissa Yake, James Jones, and Michaela Meyer, "Stress Influences Appetite and Comfort Food Preferences in College Women," *Nutrition Research* 26 (2006): 118–23; see also Wansink et al., "Exploring Comfort Food."

86. Troisi and Gabriel, "Chicken Soup Really Is Good for the Soul."

87. Elisabeth Rozin, *Ethnic Cuisine: The Flavor Principle Cookbook* (Brattleboro, VT: Stephen Greene, 1983).

88. Robert A. Georges and Michael Owen Jones, *Folkloristics: An Introduction* (Bloomington: Indiana University Press, 1995).

89. Humphrey, "Traditional Foods?"

90. Elliott Oring, "Legend, Truth, and News," *Southern Folklore* 47 (1990): 163–77.

91. Benjamin D. Steiner, William J. Bowers, and Austin Sarat, "Folk Knowledge as Legal Action: Death Penalty Judgments and the Tenet of Early Release in a Culture of Mistrust and Punitiveness," *Law & Society Review* 33 (1999): 461–506.

92. Anne Marie Helmenstine, "Does Eating Turkey Make You Sleepy? Tryptophan & Carbohydrate Chemistry," accessed August 14, 2013, http://chemistry.about.com/od/holidaysseasons/a/tiredturkey.htm.

93. Simon N. Young, "How to Increase Serotonin in the Human Brain without Drugs," *Journal of Psychiatry and Neuroscience* 32 (2007): 394–99.

94. Mary M. Boggiano, Bulent Turan, Christine R. Maldonado, Kimberly D. Oswald, and Ellen S. Shuman, "Secretive Food Concocting in Binge Eating: Test of a Famine Hypotheses," *International Journal of Eating Disorders* 46 (2012): 212–25.

95. Giovanni Cizza and Kristina I. Rother, "Was Feuerbach Right: Are We What We Eat?" *Journal of Clinical Investigation* 121 (2011): 2969–71.

96. Erika Brady, "Preface," in *Healing Logics: Culture and Medicine in Modern Health Belief Systems*, ed. Erika Brady (Logan: Utah State University Press, 2001), vii.

97. Georges and Jones, *Folkloristics*, 317–19.

From Whim Whams to Spotted Dick: "Pudding, [England's] Universal Dish"

Rachelle H. Saltzman

... Pudding, that universal Dish,
The Swain's Delight, the Plowman's Wish,
The Housewife's Pride, the Husband's Choice,
The darling Food of Girls and Boys,
....
Pudding! the Idol of the Priest,
The Farmer's constant *Sunday*'s Feast,
The Ornament of each Man's Table,
Down from the Noble to the Rabble,
The sole Characteristick Food
Of true-born *Englishmen* abroad:
From whence, to good Old-*England*'s Fame,
Jack-Pudding takes his ancient Name. ... [1]

—verses from Edward Ward, *British Wonders: Or, A Poetical Description of the Several Prodigies and Most Remarkable Accidents That Have Happen'd in Britain Since the Death of Queen Anne* (London: John Morphew, 1717)

"What's for pudding?" is possibly the most asked question in the United Kingdom. Since at least the beginning of the twentieth century, pudding, in British English, has come to mean dessert, since most (though not all) are, in fact, sweet. Puddings encompass a broad category of foods, including both savory and sweet dishes, cooked and uncooked, as well as sausages of various types. But it is all a matter of context. What Americans think of as pudding is really boiled custard, usually thickened with cornstarch and/or eggs. Jell-O and Royal instant and cooked pudding mixes fit into this category. English puddings are considerably more complex and varied, as this essay details.

As the quintessential comfort food of the English at home and abroad, puddings are often equated or used synonymously with the larger vernacular category of "nursery food," simply prepared custards and puddings as well as plain fish and chicken dishes. This category also includes the foods of a typical working-class tea (supper): eggs, beans, chips,[2] buttered toast, sausages, and puddings, especially of the sweet variety. Redraspberrygirl, a frequent poster to the British online discussion board "Cook's Corner" on the Taste of Home website, defined the nursery food on February 25, 2006, as "childhood favourites made by your nanny or your mum, depending on where you stood on the social scale." In the introduction to her online book *Nursery Puddings*, Jenny Robertson notes that "nursery puddings are those wonderfully comforting desserts." They constituted a reward for children who had cleaned their plates; what made school dinners bearable was "that fat slab of syrup sponge, Bread Pudding, Jam Roly Poly[3] . . . covered in lashings of lovely yellow vanilla custard."[4]

Nursery food has also come to refer to the large group of sweet puddings that adult baby boomers and their parents recall from childhoods in the 1950s and 1960s, and the 1930s and 1940s, respectively—from weekends with grandparents to the "puddings" served for dessert at school dinners (lunches), from the stodgy, familiar meals offered at gentlemen's clubs to the nostalgic puddings found on menus at fine restaurants. I suspect that there is scarcely a person alive in the UK today, regardless of ethnic background, who does not know exactly what is meant by this term. Frequently mentioned childhood favorites are spotted dick, jam roly-poly, and sticky toffee pudding.[5] Redraspberrygirl noted on February 25, 2006, that "'old-fashioned' (read, British nursery) foods such as macaroni and cheese, cod cakes, mashed potatoes, and rice pudding have become chic treats." For more than three decades, the (British) National Trust has promoted such foods as traditional, classic, and representative national and regional specialties.[6] In current parlance, these are place-based,[7] heritage foods that draw upon a centuries' old history of slow cooking, which involved boiling, steaming, and baking basic ingredients into memorable and uniquely named dishes.

What is it about puddings that makes them the logical choice for nursery foods? While the ingredients, for both savory and sweet pudding, are generally simple, few, and modest, the very name conjures up nostalgic memories and stories of childhood that appear to transcend age and class boundaries. In nineteenth-century America, egg and milk custards were promoted as health-ful foods, as they were in Great Britain. More recent, twenty-first-century Jell-O advertisements featuring Bill Cosby, everybody's one-time favorite dad, promote the benefits of pudding for children.[8] Rice, tapioca,[9] and other such bland foods appeared in early medical texts, recommended as nourish-ing the very young, old, and infirm long before they showed up in recipe books.[10] During the nineteenth century and into the twentieth, housekeep-ing books noted that such foods were particularly appropriate for children.[11] Yet although puddings represent the lion's share of those dishes described in recent years as nursery food, food scholarship, if not popular culture, has rather neglected nursery puddings.

As a general food group, however, puddings have been the recipient of much popular attention, from the earliest of cookbooks to television food shows. The numerous and diverse varieties, both savory and sweet, have enjoyed a long history in Britain and throughout the former empire.[12] They make their appearance in historical texts, novels, folk poetry and tales; wit-ness the plum pudding in Dickens's *A Christmas Carol*. Beatrix Potter's *The Tale of Samuel Whiskers or The Roly-Poly Pudding* describes Tom Kitten's near demise as a savory pudding filling. And Tom Thumb suffers a similar close call from a tumble into a bowl of pudding fat in a seventeenth-century folk tale.[13] Agatha Christie's Hercule Poirot solves a murder while eating a Christ-mas pudding, and novelist Nancy Mitford's social comedy, *Christmas Pudding* (1932), describes a holiday spent in the Cotswolds. Published pudding recipes show up with increasing frequency in cookbooks from the mid-eighteenth century onward, peaking in the late nineteenth and early twentieth centuries, as the British Empire reached its high point and then its nadir.

This food became so characteristic of national identity that the English acquired the sobriquet of "pudding-eaters" in the eighteenth century. They are, as praised in the verse above, the very essence of Englishness—and the term "Jack-Pudding" (also noted in that opening verse) was a common name for a "buffoon who performs pudding tricks, such as swallowing a certain number of yards of black-pudding."[14] The town of Manchester even hosts the World Black Pudding (sausages made of oatmeal or other grains, fat, blood, and spices) Throwing Championships, which involves tossing blood pud-dings at a huge stack of Yorkshire puddings (baked batter puffs made of eggs, flour, and milk)[15]—rather a pudding war! And the residents of Mytholmroyd in Calderdale, West Yorkshire, fearing the extinction of their own specialty, created a dock pudding (an oatmeal-based herb pudding) competition as part of their annual spring celebration.[16]

Puddings make their first known in-print appearance in Homer's *Odyssey* as a black or blood pudding made from pig's blood and other ingredients, which were roasted inside the pig's stomach. Conventional wisdom has it that the Romans introduced the idea of pudding (i.e., stuffed entrails or sausage) to Britain. According to the *Oxford English Dictionary*, and reported in several articles, websites, and books about pudding, the word comes from the Latin *botellus* (sausage or intestine); the Anglo-Norman *bodin* or *bodeyn* and the later French *boudin* and the English pudding come from this root. The *Oxford English Dictionary* also notes that the old English *pudec* (swelling) may be related, hence the words "podge," "pod," and "pudge," and the related "porridge."[17]

Those early stirred porridges became known as "hasty" puddings, mixtures of water or milk combined with a ground grain (rice or semolina) and heated until the grain released a gelatinous starch. Besides the pottage, oatmeal, brose, and pease porridge, several varieties developed over the centuries. As historian Will Ryan[18] reminded me in an email on February 25, 2015, pease porridge, a thick soup of dried split peas, is still quite popular today and served "with boiled bacon or ham dishes."[19] The seventeenth-century poet Robert Herrick wrote of "frumentie" (frumenty) in a verse that celebrated this wheat and milk porridge, flavored with cinnamon and honey. Eaten at court, to mark the Yule season, and at harvests, frumenty dates back at least to the reign of Henry IV.[20] In New England, hasty pudding became Indian pudding, so named for the Native American cornmeal substituted for European oats or wheat. It started out as a cornmeal porridge (cornmeal mush, aka polenta) mixed with "sweet" spices such as cinnamon and ginger, milk and eggs, molasses, raisins and nuts, and then steamed in an oven for several hours. A long, slow cooking process, which allows the cornmeal to absorb the liquid, results in a silky rather than a grainy texture. Like other steamed sweet puddings, the early American version was once served topped with pouring cream or custard—but whipped cream or ice cream eventually replaced traditional British toppings.

As noted, the Romans, followed by the British and others, made puddings by stuffing ingredients into a variety of containers, from the earliest animal casings (cleaned intestines or stomachs—naturally, hollow body parts), then paste (dough) wrapped in cloth, cloths themselves, and eventually "pudding" basins (a variety of differently sized, thick ceramic bowls). Once cooks prepared the ingredients, they boiled, baked, steamed, or grilled both sweet and savory puddings. Those early and even present-day savory puddings or sausages provide a way to use all parts of an animal, ensuring the availability of much-needed protein. In Britain, Continental Europe, and North America, farmers traditionally slaughtered cows and pigs in the late autumn, when the weather was cooler and other harvesting was done. Sausages and various kinds of headcheese (also known as scrapple and souse in parts of the United States) could be cooked and eaten immediately after slaughter and processing, or dried or smoked to make them last through the winter.[21]

Most early puddings were both sweet and savory at once, and included spices (cinnamon and nutmeg) and ingredients (dried fruits and nuts) that today we associate with desserts rather than with main courses, vegetables, or meats. Although sweet puddings as such start to appear in the sixteenth century, cooks continued to make both types. They boiled suet-based mixtures in well-cleaned cow, pig, or sheep intestines or stomachs along with beef, pork, or mutton, or cooked them underneath roasting meat to catch the flavorful drippings.

The pudding cloth, which emerged in the seventeenth century, apparently revolutionized pudding preparation, making it possible to dispense with intestines or stomachs as containers for all but actual meat and blood sausages. Some have speculated that this was a matter of hygiene, given the necessity of carefully washing intestines before use and the sheer amount of attention paid to this issue in early housekeeping books, such as Hannah Glasse's *Art of Cookery* (1747).[22] It is also likely that most found the cloth to be much more convenient[23]—and certainly less expensive and easier to obtain—than animal innards. With the pudding cloth as their new kitchen tool, cooks could prepare savory and sweet puddings throughout the year. The cloth, which seems to have been rapidly followed by the pudding basin, made it possible to create a pudding of filled, then boiled or steamed suet dough.

As nearly everyone writing about British puddings seems to note, George I (1714–27), the first of the German British monarchs and a non-English speaker, was said to be so fond of pudding that he became known as the Pudding King or Pudding George. Folklore has it that he is the "Georgie Porgy" referred to in the nursery rhyme. His sons, George II and George III, were also said to be inordinately fond of elaborate, sweet suet puddings, making them the dessert of choice for the court, nobility, the upper classes, and for those literate middle-class wives and housekeepers for whom cookbooks were written.

The eighteenth century, when householders started to build ovens into chimneys, at least in middle-class homes, brought the advent of the steamed pudding pye (custard-filled dough or crust) and eventually baked pudding. Working-class people, usually those in rural areas, with the wherewithal to have a stovetop or an open outdoor fire, continued to boil or steam their puddings; ovens were a luxury until well into the twentieth century. Before then, many urban poor and working-class folks instead brought their food for local bakers to cook.[24] According to Jeri Quinzio, until the time of World War I, some working-class families served boiled or steamed suet puddings (often just flour, suet, water or milk) as the only course or as a substantial first course, meant to fill one up prior to relatively smaller bits of boiled meat and vegetables.[25]

The Victorian era seems to have been the golden age of puddings, both savory and sweet, though the former began to differentiate as meat pies and sausages. Sweet puddings and their names proliferated and included such treats as the aforementioned spotted dick, jam roly-poly, bread and butter pudding, Christmas or plum pudding, treacle tart, and so on. Prince Albert, Queen Victoria's consort, not only shared his German countrymen's love of puddings, but he also brought Germanic Christmas customs to Great Britain, including the iconic tree. Sara Paston-Williams makes the claim that Albert's "German taste" for "rather heavy nursery-style puddings" shifted British preference away from the lighter, French-influenced puddings, those jam and fruit sponges (cakes) topped with meringue known as "Queen's Pudding, Her Majesty's Pudding, Empress Pudding and Albert Pudding."[26] Mid-nineteenth-century magazine covers show the royal family enjoying a large, fat, round plum pudding—what soon came to be known as Christmas pudding, a bagged and steamed suet dough sweetened with golden syrup (a liquid cane sugar) or treacle (molasses), and filled with nuts and dried fruit such as raisins, sultanas or dates, and dried citrus peel. With great ceremony, a servant would carry this glorious concoction to the table, the warmed pudding surrounded by blue-flamed brandy fumes.

To make a plum pudding, cooks poured a thick flour and suet batter into pudding molds (no longer just basins). They wrapped the entire thing in a pudding cloth, tied at the top, and then placed it in a larger water-filled basin to steam on the stovetop or the oven, for those who had them, for a couple of hours. Left to cool, the puddings were unmolded and served with a custard sauce (eggs beaten into hot milk or cream and stirred until thickened) or a hard sauce (brandy and butter).

Sponges are a more recent variety of pudding, usually involving a cake layer (flour, baking soda, eggs, sugar) that is either baked first and then layered with other ingredients or iced. Sponge puddings have a fluffy egg-yolk batter with various spices and flavoring ingredients and folded-in egg whites beaten to soft or stiff peaks. Baking in a dish placed in a *bain marie* (water bath), the sponge (cake) would separate out from what became a "puddle" or sauce. More modern versions use baking soda to help to leaven or lighten the sponge, and what Americans know as lemon or chocolate pudding cake is the same as the English lemon or chocolate sponge. Other forms of sponge cake include a layer of prebaked sponge cake topped with jam or other filling and often finished with a browned meringue. There are also summer puddings, for which one layers dry slices of bread in a pudding basin or bowl with sugared fresh berries, a dish put on top, and a weight placed on the dish to compress the ingredients. The entire mass is turned out several hours later and topped with cream or custard.

A related pudding is the trifle, for which one places dry pieces of sponge cake or lady fingers in an ornamental glass bowl; wets them with sherry or brandy; layers some jam or fruit; pours cooled, boiled custard over the lot; and tops the whole thing with whipped cream. Eighteenth-century trifles included various combinations of broken sponges, macaroons, or other dry biscuits (cookies) soaked in sherry and topped with a boiled custard, then a syllabub (a mixture of cream, sugar, and wine), and finally garnished with jelly and flowers. During the next century, among the various names for this pudding were King's Pudding, Easter Pudding, Victoria Pudding, and Colchester Pudding. The last often had a pink-colored meringue or whipped cream topping. Tipsy cake was another name for this sort of trifle, and the famed cookbook author Mrs. Beeton prepared it in one of the many fashionable decorative molds popular in the nineteenth century. The whim wham featured in the title of this essay is also a trifle but one that could be prepared quickly and with a mixture of whipped cream and wine instead of boiled custard.[27]

Despite their seeming ubiquity in different forms and with different kinds of ingredients from the nineteenth century on, the historical record makes clear that not everyone ate puddings at every meal year in and year out, though certainly bread and pottage were common.[28] The working classes had neither the time and equipment nor the money to be making spotted dicks, plum duffs, or even rice pudding except on special occasions. Mince pies and plum puddings were a Christmas treat and more likely a gift from the better-off than made at home.[29] The middle classes were much more inclined to serve them but, again, not more than a few times a week at most. And even the well-to-do were not likely to consume such heavy fare in its entirety.[30]

Nursery food, as distinct from holiday or special occasion dessert puddings, emerges in the mid-nineteenth century as the food for the young of the upper and upper-middle classes. It referred then to bland, "wholesome," and often milk-based foods such as custards, simple grain-based porridges of rice, oats, or wheat (semolina), plainly prepared fish and chicken, batter puddings such as pancakes or toad in the hole (Yorkshire pudding with sausages baked in),[31] and a variety of steamed or baked suet and flour-based sweet puddings (desserts) usually served with a poured custard or cream topping. Puddings were also the stuff of the countryside and rural villages, where cookbook author Mary Norwalk contends that many of the cooks, nurses, and nannies who worked at great houses were reared, especially from the middle of the nineteenth century through the first few decades of the twentieth century.[32] Thus, the advent of the nurses who cared for the babies of the well-heeled and nannies for somewhat older children still not of school age ensured that this particular class of foods became codified and transmitted as appropriate for children. Most of these dishes came from relatively inexpensive, easily obtained, and very filling ingredients, which made for familiar foods that cooks at private and state schools prepared for their charges as well. With several generations raised on such food, especially those who suffered the deprivations of rationing during and after World War II, nursery food assumed the patina of nostalgia for simpler times. In this spirit, I suspect, the immensely popular *Downton Abbey* included in the third show of the fifth season a mention of spotted dick. Interestingly, Mrs. Patmore, the cook, reminds the footman not to forget the spotted dick for the servants' pudding—not for the gentlefolk upstairs—perhaps indicating that such a simple, straightforward sweet was more appropriate for those below stairs in the early twentieth century.[33]

Comfort foods, including puddings and especially nursery puddings, are indeed foods of indulgence. Unlike the puddings of earlier times, they are not meant for everyday consumption but special occasions or for treats. During the close of the twentieth century and the beginning of the twenty-first century, people have tended to reserve the more elaborate, time-consuming puddings for the seasonal round, with Christmas cakes (an iced fruitcake) or plum pudding bought or made for Christmas (a few who responded to my email queries mentioned Stir-up Sunday, the Sunday before Advent, when all members of the family take a hand in stirring the batter for the pudding),[34] mince pies for Christmas or first-footing (New Year's), haggis for Burns Night around January 25, pancakes for Shrove Tuesday (Mardi Gras) to use up fat and rich ingredients before the Lenten fast, hot cross buns for Easter, parkin (gingerbread) for Guy Fawkes Night in November, and a rich, heavily decorated fruitcake for weddings.[35] Such foods have their place in the national consciousness and in individual recollections because they were the dishes that stood out, that were consumed (mostly) in comfortable, safe places, for special occasions, and among blood kin or the tight-knit "familial" groups of schoolmates.

Between the wars, making many of the old-style puddings themselves went out of fashion as the employment of servants declined, more women worked outside the home, and packaged commercial products such as powdered custards, cornstarch puddings, and flavored jelly (gelatin) became increasingly available.[36] From the 1960s through the 1970s or so, a number of trends, including French *nouvelle cuisine*, forced sweet puddings and nursery foods into further decline; the savory variety, including such childhood favorites as toad in the hole, bangers and mash (sausages and mashed potatoes), or bubble and squeak (cabbage and potatoes), managed to survive.[37] Along with ready-to-eat commercial products, concern with health and reducing fat and sugar consumption increased, and the stereotype of English food as bland, stodgy, overcooked, and tasteless seemed to overtake popular culture.[38] In the 1980s, however, a revival and a taste for "old-fashioned" foods began at the same time that Prince Charles helped to popularize vegetarian and homegrown foods, the health food movement really started, and boomers came of age.

According to R. W. Apple, Francis Coulson and the Cotswold's Pudding Club fueled that revival, which began in the Lake District.[39] Apple and others credit Francis Coulson (Coulson and partner Brian Sack opened the Sharrow Bay Country House) with the invention of sticky toffee pudding, which most agree occurred in the early 1970s. Blogger Felicity Cloake did some further digging and found that Coulson acquired the recipe from Mrs. Martin of Lancashire, who had gotten it from a Canadian friend.[40] Despite its mention in every pudding or traditional English/British cookbook since (and usually described as "good old-fashioned"), sticky toffee pudding, while amazing, is neither old-fashioned nor even English (though British origins could be argued, given the Canadian connection).

For Americans, STP, as Cloake styles it, tastes like a moist gingerbread cake, though moister and stickier from chopped dates, covered in a thick toffee (caramel) sauce and finished with a rich, warm custard sauce. Cloake writes that a "good sticky toffee pudding should be more than a simple sugar hit—add nuts, for texture, and cloves, for a hint of spice." My own experience with sticky toffee pudding occurred in a cozy place, enjoyed with a friend in London, England, in 1985. Loaded with thick, warm custard sauce and fragrant with spices, chewy, hot, and creamy all at once, STP fulfilled the very definition of comfort food.

Another recent and popular addition to the list of favorite English puddings is Sussex pond pudding, which consists of butter, sugar, and a whole lemon encased in a suet crust, steamed for hours, and then turned out into a serving dish. Cutting into the pudding releases a fragrant pond of hot lemon sauce. Although several food history books, including Quinzio's, Norwalk's, and Paston-Williams's, as well as Eleanor Morgan's blog, indicate or imply that this is one of the oldest and most traditional puddings, it may not have been quite so ancient. While Hannah Wooley did include a similar recipe in *The Queen Like Closet* (1672),[41] it was for a dough filled with either butter or an apple—rather like an apple dumpling. Food historian and writer Sharon Hudgins explained in an email on February 25, 2015, that she had come across the same recipe with the name Edge Lemon Pudding in a 1930s cookbook; Hudgins pointed out that, like many recipes, it was likely made in home kitchens before it was published. Either way, these more recently created puddings completely fulfilled the structural requirements of comfort food, which is why it has inserted itself so easily into the pantheon of nursery puddings and acquired the aura of tradition.

Food historian Jane Garmey, writing first in 1981, noted that chefs were rediscovering recipes and "restaurants [were] beginning to sneak onto their menus such dishes as Sussex Pond Pudding, Hindle Wakes, Cockie Leekie [*sic*], and Syllabub. British cooking may even be in danger of becoming fashionable."[42] In the ensuing years, the slow food movement and the heritage cooking trend have led to an increasing recognition on the part of the upper-middle and middle classes that regional British cuisines not only existed and were not just something to joke about but quite tasty, redolent as they are of animal fat, sweetener, cream, and starch. Despite this trend, Eleanor Morgan asserts that only certain types of traditional puddings appear in restaurants, and the more homely spotted dick is not to be found,[43] possibly because of its name, which, far from being suggestive, is a shortening of the old "puddick."[44] Will Ryan, contradicting Morgan, explained to me that spotted dick "is often found in pubs which offer cooked food, as most do nowadays, sometimes advertising themselves as 'gastro-pubs.' Sometimes I think it is there mostly to amuse American tourists."[45] Likely because of its "funny" name, spotted dick has been and continues to be one of the most cited of the old puddings (first noted in the mid-nineteenth century).[46] Cookbooks seem to always provide at least one recipe and usually a variation or two, along with the alternative, spotted dog.

Alongside the growing vernacular appreciation for a national cuisine has been the increasingly voracious appetite of tourists, particularly American visitors, for "authentic" English food. I emphasize English, because despite the larger category of British foods and the clear influence that the heritage of various groups (Irish, Scottish, and Welsh, not to mention the range of foods that different immigrant groups brought to the UK, e.g., Jewish, Italian, Caribbean, Chinese, Thai, Asian Indian, and various African cultures) have had on local foods, the marketing, perception, and consumption has been specifically about heritage foods of *England*. First put forward were the traditional and well-known dishes: roast beef and Yorkshire pudding, lamb with mint sauce, afternoon cream teas, elaborate trifles, and plum or Christmas pudding. The popularity of London's Carvery restaurants and hotel teas at Browns, the Ritz, and elsewhere cemented eating those foods and doing so in particular contexts—white tablecloth restaurants or cozy tea rooms with plush, comfy chairs around intimate tables.

In 1978, I had my own first encounter with a "traditional English trifle" at a restaurant in London. Served after what was also described as a traditional meal of joints (roast beef or roast lamb) with a wondrous side of (suet) roasted potatoes, the trifle was full of creamy custard, cake, some kind of fruit, and flavored with sherry.[47] The Brits had clearly mastered this amazing dish, and I searched it out whenever I could during and after that first trip to the UK.[48]

As other tourists (and upper-middle-class British urbanites)[49] visited the countryside in search of what historian Patrick Wright refers to as "Deep England" during the 1970s and '80s,[50] they went beyond those stereotypical and solidly middle-class dishes and hunted down more working-class meals and pub food, including steak and kidney pie (or pudding); ploughman's lunches of cheese, bread, and pickle; and cottage pie, fish pie, or shepherd's pie, as well as more recognizably regional fare such as Cornish pasties. Eventually chip shops and cafés became part of the mix, and travelers on a budget searched out local and very affordable fish and chips (not so much eel pie), beans on toast, bacon butties (sandwiches), sausage rolls (sausage encased in pastry), and the like. For tourists and UK residents, London's excellent (and not-so-excellent) Asian Indian, Italian, Thai, Chinese, and other ethnic restaurants also became part of the British experience, especially the Indian white tablecloth establishments in the theatre district as well as the inexpensive takeaways.

While the meat and fish pies, the sausages, and bubble and squeak certainly fit into the definition of nursery food, the other foods did not. They may have been part and parcel of the food offerings of the United Kingdom, but they were not of ethnic English heritage. And nursery food is, first and foremost, an in-group term that encodes class, ethnicity, a particular time period, and a very specifically English category of food. Jane Garmey writes that "the native cuisine" found in the home kitchen is "practiced and passed on to successive generations with little or no fanfare."[51] This is not to say the term does not describe a specific set of traditional foodways, but it is critical to recognize that it has its own roots and implicit meanings for a certain cultural group.

As part of the dominant culture, nursery food, especially in its current incarnation, represents a worldview that promotes English customs, traditions, and foodways as those of all classes and all times in the United Kingdom.[52] Julian Barnes's *England, England*, a not-so tongue-in-cheek novel about the "Disneyfication" of England, puts this kind of food right in the middle of a satirical tale about the commodification of culture and its reduction to a series of stereotypical tourist sites and experiences. Not only was the

> roast beef of Old England approved on the nod by the Gastronomic Sub-Committee [charged with deciding what to include on the "programme"], as were Yorkshire pudding, Lancashire hotpot, Sussex pond pudding, . . . and Kentish chicken pudding. A swift tick was given to fish and chips, bacon and eggs, mint sauce, steak and kidney pudding, . . . cottage pie, plum duff, . . . bread and butter pudding. . . . Approved for their picturesque nomenclature . . . were . . . Queen of puddings, Poor Knights of Windsor, Hindle Wakes, stargazey pie, wow-wow sauce, maids-of-honour, . . . and parkin.[53]

During the same period as this revival of English food heritage, there has been much scholarly, popular, and contentious debate about the vagaries of national identity in the United Kingdom, particularly with regard to the meanings underlying Britishness, which refers to a civic identity, and Englishness, which has to do with ethnicity. In fact, the impulse to define a national identity has been part and parcel of English and British culture since the Battle of Hasting, the Magna Carta, and so on. Not surprisingly, the foodways promulgated as British or English have become a rather determined part of this cultural debate, most recently during the late twentieth and the early years of the twenty-first century.[54]

The traditional cooking revival was partly a result of the larger identity issue but also emerged as a way to differentiate and defend British foodways against a negative stereotype of unhealthful, fried, vegetable-free, stodgy, and overcooked food. Of course, many stereotypes do have their basis in fact, and it is not difficult to find this kind of "greasy spoon" sort of food in the UK, then and now. It is cheap, easy, and filling. But what many today forget or never knew was that English food as a national cuisine did not always have such a reputation, which seems to have been started with the strict rationing during World War II through the 1950s and has continued largely unabated, despite evidence to the contrary.[55] Food historians Laura Mason, Jeri Quinzio, Sara Paston-Williams, Jane Garmey, and numerous others have dealt in depth with the reasons for this unfair image and the history of British food. Suffice it to say that the image arose largely due to postwar shortages, an abundance of cafés offering cheap fried food for workers and students, the rise and ubiquity of "foreign" food restaurants, and the custom of overcooking fresh vegetables (also common in the United States during the middle years of the twentieth century), along with the fact that most tourists had little to no access to traditional home cooking in England during this time. But it is important to acknowledge this stereotype as the context for the vociferous defense of traditional English food and the recent spate of popular blogs and publications about what is probably the UK's most iconic food group—pudding, which resonates with all sorts of nostalgic memories about childhood and the ideal world of "Deep England."

Regardless of all the rhetoric, for a simple everyday pudding (dessert), many people serve baked apples, biscuits, plain fruit, or something store-bought. Homemade puddings tend to be for special occasions, with cookbooks and websites providing ready sources of instruction. One starts with a batter of eggs, suet or butter, milk, flour, and various spices and fruit, dried and fresh. The cook pours the batter into a pudding basin, covers and seals the container with paper, foil, or cloth (tied to prevent leakage), and then steams it over a rack in a pot of boiling water on the stovetop, cooks it in a *bain marie* (water bath) in the oven or bakes it for some hours. The final sponge (cake) or pudding is cooled, unmolded, and served with thick cream or cooked, hot custard, and often with reconstituted Bird's custard powder. Variations include pies or tarts, which are made of a pastry crust (flour, suet, salt, and very cold liquid) filled with some sort of fruit and/or plain or flavored custard, which is baked, then served as above.

Encouraging people to make their own puddings seems to be the goal of all the bloggers and cookbook authors. But one can find puddings just about anywhere in the UK, from the most modest (working man's) café to London's clubland to the finest of dining establishments (e.g., 2015 menus for Simpson's-in-the-Strand, Hoi Polloi, and Hawksmore), which feature Yorkshire parkin (a gingerbread cake made with oatmeal and treacle) and Cambridge burnt cream (crème brûlée), Eton mess (a tumble of sugared raspberries, broken pieces of meringue, and whipped cream) and fruit crumble, or sticky toffee pudding and Christmas pudding and custard (for Christmas menus). While not everyone is a fan, the connection between the familiar food of childhood and comfort food for adult men is clear. Writing in the *Telegraph*, the conservative British newspaper, Rowan Pelling noted, somewhat tongue in cheek, in an essay about the infiltration of women into London men's clubs, that the latter would hardly be attracted by the "ghastly nursery food" for which such institutions are known; not so men. "My uncle took the line that adult men need schoolboy space, with rules, regulations and jam roly-poly."[56]

In keeping with the nursery theme, Sara Paston-Williams, author of the National Trust's *Good Old-Fashioned Puddings*, tempts her readers while acknowledging that "despite our obsession with calories, 'pudding-time' still brings murmurs of delight from guests as they tuck into a syrup sponge or plum crumble. Our traditional puddings are glorious—rich and indulgent and comforting. Naughty? Yes, but oh so nice!"

Further indication of the nostalgic allure and touristic lure of puddings is the aforementioned Pudding Club (http://www.puddingclub.com), which Keith and Jean Turner started in the Cotswolds in 1985 "to revive the traditional British pudding."[57] Christine Knight, Wellcome Trust Senior Research Fellow at the University of Edinburgh, responding on December 11, 2014, to a query I posted on the Food and Culture listserv, alerted me to this rather amazing place, as did folklorist Michael Owen Jones. As Knight says, the website alone is "a great source of material on the more stereotypical/oddly named British puddings. Clearly the existence of Pudding Club only raises again the question of the relationship between nostalgia, memory, culinary history, 'comfort foods', and indeed tourism!"

The Pudding Club, based at the Three Ways House Hotel, which has rooms named for various puddings (and decorated accordingly), offers a light Friday evening dinner that concludes with seven (!) puddings served on a rotating basis, and a vote for the favorite pudding. The hotel also hosts pudding-making workshops and other events. In a 2010 review of the Pudding Club for Britain's left-leaning newspaper, the *Guardian*, Laura Barton wrote: "The club's enduring appeal is perhaps down to its British eccentricity as much as its excellent puddings; there is something both wonderful and faintly peculiar about sitting in a room with 60 strangers to worship at the altar of the jam roly-poly."[58]

Knight told me that the establishment also "produces a range of pre-made puddings sold in Waitrose (the high-end British supermarket chain) and presumably other outlets." Thus, the comfort food experience can be exported or carried away as a souvenir of this most English of all English foods.[59] Further witness to this phenomenon are several websites that also enable expatriates to enjoy the foods of home; one that Jones pointed out to me includes six items, five of which could be easily classified as puddings (three pies, one sausage, and a Cornish pasty—a pie itself and likely a descendent of the early crusted puddings).[60]

British puddings evoke not just memories of comfort but also of discomfort. Several years ago, at the American Folklore Society (1990) in St. Johns, Newfoundland, I had my first (and last) taste of black pudding.[61] It was aromatic, chewy, a bit gritty, and the cause of considerable mental discomfort when I found out what kind of pudding it was, not to mention its primary ingredient (blood). Others have had similar experiences. Robert Graves's short story "Treacle Tart" describes how a young scion of the peerage at a private school refuses to eat his treacle tart and ends up leaving after a few days rather than give in to the headmaster's demands that he will be given no other food until he consumes "the oblong of tough burned pastry."[62] As cookbook author Jane Garmey warns: "Scratch the surface, and you may be given gory descriptions of such school horrors as Boiled Baby, Wet Nelly, Dead Man's Leg and Washerwoman's Arm (all nicknames for poorly made steamed puddings [and part of the folklore of puddings])."[63]

Several correspondents who responded to a query about nursery puddings I posted on the Talking Folklore listserv expressed similar sentiments: not everyone reveled in the stodgy, steamed suet puddings or the texture of the tapioca, sago, or other more "porridgey" desserts of post-World War II English childhood. In response to comments about texture, Caroline Oates wrote on December 8, 2014, that "even more revolting was the slimy 'frog spawn with tadpoles' ([typical school slang for] tapioca with sultanas) served at primary school. The semolina pudding was marginally less disgusting, redeemed slightly by a spoonful of rosehip syrup." Texture is clearly part of what makes something comforting or not, as with my own reaction to the grittiness of that blood sausage.

My experience with haggis was entirely different from that with the black pudding. A 1986 fieldwork trip to Peterhead, Scotland, resulted in a chance encounter with the dish that Scottish poet Robert Burns immortalized as the "great chieftain o the puddin'-race!" Although I did not know it at the time, haggis is made with minced sheep heart, lungs, and liver combined with chopped onion, suet, and spices, which are stuffed into a cleaned sheep's stomach and boiled in broth. According to the *Oxford English Dictionary*, this description constitutes the original definition of pudding in the thirteenth century.[64] My first taste reminded me of the bread-based savory "stuffing" (dressing) my mother made with roast chicken, my favorite meal as a child (and, as I've discovered, an early sort of pudding itself—leftover bread and aromatics cooked inside an animal and served alongside). I asked for seconds of the haggis, something few Americans apparently do, which amazed the local fishermen's wives and had the result of endearing me to them. More haggis, as well as talk about knitting patterns and childcare, was immediately forthcoming. My love affair with all things pudding continues to this day, except for that aforementioned blood sausage.

For the most part, British puddings are celebrated and remembered fondly, particularly those involving suet, the fat of choice in Great Britain. Available since the late nineteenth century, when a Frenchman in Manchester developed prepackaged suet, Atora, an early convenience food, is shredded and floured to prevent lumps and sticking. It has a higher melting point than butter, which means that suet dough is less likely to become sodden or stodgy.

Will Ryan, responding on December 10, 2014, to my follow-up question about suet on the Talking Folklore listserv, explained its allure:

> suet [a pure, white fat from around the kidneys] is a hard natural fat that could and still can be bought cheaply and unprocessed from the butcher. Suet dough has a distinctive flavour and consistency … Its popularity may have fallen off a bit in the last few decades as we have become more weight conscious—but plenty of people, and pubs and restaurants, in Britain still cook and eat the various fruit, jam, syrup, and raisin puddings already mentioned … and savoury suet dumplings, and suet pie crusts. … Suet dishes are the great comfort food, cheap and satisfying and classless, and their greatest manifestation is the Steak and Kidney Pudding—it sustains the British and makes the French turn pale. Its only disadvantage is that in its more exquisite forms (Steak and Kidney pudding [steamed instead of baked] and Christmas pudding) it takes several hours of cooking to reach perfection.

Online blogger Eleanor Morgan commented: "The British pudding is so special because it cannot be separated from love and affection. Yes, there is a utility to baking frugally, but you'd never give a piece of sponge [cake] to someone you didn't want to make feel good."[65] Thus, for puddings to work as comfort food, they have to be first lodged in one's memory as the food of affection and childhood or to remind one of that time of life or an idealized version of someone's lovely past.

Once you start considering pudding as a food category, it becomes readily apparent that most if not all cultures have some version of both sweet and savory varieties. With roots in Southeast Asia, especially Vietnam and Laos, my Tai Dam American friends in Des Moines, Iowa, make a savory pudding, i.e., sausage: ground chicken and pork, spiced, wrapped in banana leaves, tied tightly, boiled, and then sliced and served cold with a variety of other foods on holidays and special occasions. Tamales, a Latino favorite, also constitute a pudding: ground masa de maiz (dried field corn),[66] wet and formed around ground pork or chicken for the savory version, or ground sweet corn mixed with sugar and butter and occasionally raisins or nuts for the sweet—both kinds are wrapped in soaked corn husks (Mexican or banana leaves for Colombian), tied, steamed or sometimes boiled, and served hot. Again, "everyone" traditionally made them for Christmas, and now people serve them year-round.

My own relationship with puddings has its roots in several cultures. Those I grew up with as an American Jew of Eastern European heritage were, at first glance, very different from those British examples. They included potato *kugel* (literally, potato pudding in Yiddish)—a soft-centered, crispy-on-the-outside scoop of total comfort—fragrant with onions and potatoes, held together with matzo meal and eggs, and made by my grandmother but only for holiday meals. And then there were the cornstarch chocolate and lemon puddings, sometimes made from Jell-O or Royal boxed mixes, sometimes homemade. There was also my father's favorite: the local, Pennsylvania Dutch (German) scrapple, consisting of cornmeal filler, pork scraps, and sage—ground, boiled, sliced, fried, and served hot and crisp with fried eggs, this was a pudding by any other name. Savory or sweet, these were certainly the comfort foods of my childhood, and that is one of the keys to the more generic popularity of puddings—their ability to evoke those long-gone days when life and its needs were simple and easily fulfilled.

Yet despite the ubiquity of pudding-like foods in general, the British versions, with their whimsical names and endless varieties, seem somehow more magical than those of other cultures. As with all folklore, the various names for pudding have somewhat obscure origins. Some reference famous individuals or places, others for the way the thing looks, and still others acquired nicknames from schoolboys or common usage, with words changing, eroding, or new words being substituted for others.

Not surprisingly, pudding history ignores the others whose cultures and foodways have made a huge impact on British culinary culture. The rhetoric surrounding English puddings tends to reify and essentialize a history that includes only certain kinds of people and certain kinds of food: the ethnic food of the English mainstream. Perhaps it goes without saying to note, as one taxi driver did to me in 1986, "They may be British but they'll never be English."[67] And neither will their desserts.

Nonetheless, and as evidenced by the very real and even overwhelming marketing of nursery puddings on internet blogs, websites, and television cooking shows, as well as in women's magazines, published cookbooks, and both the mainstream and the popular press, traditional puddings do remain a very real and relevant cultural category for the English. They reference warm memories of granny, or less comforting thoughts of ghastly school dinners. Puddings are the stuff of English heritage, of both country villages and great houses. But while traditional puddings may help the British food economy and reinforce national identity, they are also not the most healthful choice; some books and websites note that yogurt or crème fraîche could provide a less indulgent option than full cream,[68] though the "grown-up" version may not be quite as "nice."[69] Even the National Trust, while encouraging and incentivizing the consumption of traditional puddings, took the opportunity to promote its properties and ameliorate the damage, noting "there's also the chance to walk off those autumn puddings on a Great British Walk with the National Trust."[70]

That recommended walk was part of the trust's autumn 2012 "pudding campaign," which offered free pudding with lunch during October at all trust cafés and restaurants. To encourage consumption of local British foods with homegrown ingredients, "Environment Secretary Owen Paterson urged people to be patriotic with their puddings, choosing traditional British recipes over foreign imports . . . and encouraged diners to [choose] . . . traditional favourites like apple crumble, treacle tart and spotted dick."[71] Unawares, the consumption of pudding had become a declaration of one's loyalty to the British polity or, more precisely and implicitly, the English.

Notes

Thanks are due to Lucy Long for enticing me to think about comfort food, to Michael Owen Jones and Lucy for inviting me to be part of this lovely collection, to Michael for fine editing, and to those generous people who responded to my email queries and allowed me to pick their brains and quote their words. Of particular assistance were Sharon Hudgins and Will Ryan, who were especially diligent and saved me from some egregious errors. Simon Talbot added a note of levity to the proceedings at his distant and near pudding-less post in Madrid. I also owe a huge debt of gratitude to Nick Rieser and Eva Saltzman for enabling me to disappear for hours and days without seeming end to research and write this piece. Now that we own so many pudding cookbooks, I have promised to treat them to at least a few of the comforting and indulgent puddings—with more than a few lashings of warm custard sauce.

1. Thanks to Erica J. Peters (email to author, December 11, 2014, response to my query on the Food and Culture Listserv) for this reference from Edward Ward, *British Wonders: Or, A Poetical Description of the Several Prodigies and Most Ridiculous Accidents That Have Happen'd in Britain Since the Death of Queen Anne* (London: John Morphew, 1717), accessed January 4, 2015, http://en.wikisource.org/wiki/British_Wonders. And see (accessed February 24, 2015) https://books.google.co.uk/books?id=OCZWAAAAYAAJ&printsec=frontcover&d q=inauthor:%22Anne+%28Queen+of+Great+Britain%29%22&hl=en&sa=X&ei=6LzsVMaE N5XhoAT25ILwDg&ved=0CCgQ6AEwAQ#v=onepage&q&f=false.

2. As Will Ryan reminded me in an email, February 27, 2015, chips are "a good half inch or more thick, and less crisp than [American] 'French fries.'"

3. Jam roly-poly is a typical schoolboy's pudding, consisting of a suet dough spread with jam, rolled up like a jelly roll, traditionally steamed and now sometimes baked and served with custard or poured cream.

4. Jenny Robertson, *Nursery Puddings: Comforting Desserts from Child-hood, Introduction* (2012), Kindle edition, http://www.amazon.com/ Nursery-Puddings-Comforting-Desserts-Childhood-ebook/dp/B007BN0POK.

5. Spotted dick is a steamed, boiled, or baked roll of sweetened suet-dough dotted with raisins or currants, and served with custard sauce; "it can be either round, bowl-shaped, or long and about four inches thick," as Will Ryan noted in an email, February 27, 2015. Sticky toffee pudding is a rich cake of butter, eggs, sugar, chopped dates, flour, and walnuts, flavored with cloves; once baked, the cake is drenched in toffee (caramel) sauce, and then served with a warm egg custard, "pouring" cream (heavy cream), or ice cream.

6. Sara Paston-Williams, *Good Old-Fashioned Puddings*; NTSteve, "Save the Great British Pud with the National Trust," National Trust Press Office Blog, September 18, 2012, accessed February 20, 2015, https://ntpressoffice.wordpress.com/tag/british-puddings/.

7. See my study of Iowa place-based foods, http://www.iowaartscouncil.org/programs/folk-and-traditional-arts/place_based_foods.

8. While many of these ready-to-serve or packaged "instant" desserts include cornstarch as a thickener, the original pudding mixes instructed home cooks to add milk and beaten eggs for a true custard that mothers could take pride in serving as homemade, if not entirely from scratch.

9. Will Ryan clarified that "the base is the rice etc., and the milk is the liquid in which it is cooked. Rice boiled in water was/is sometimes served as a sweet pudding with Golden Syrup."

10. Lynne Olver, ed., "What is Pudding," The Food Timeline, accessed February 16, 2015, http://www.foodtimeline.org/foodpuddings.html#whatis.

11. Daniel Pool, *What Jane Austen Ate and Charles Dickens Knew* (New York: Simon & Schuster, 1993), 205; and Laura Mason, *Food Culture in Great Britain* (Westport, CT: Greenwood Press, 2004), 49, 53.

12. Helen Leach, "Translating the 18th Century Pudding," accessed January 25, 2015, http://press.anu.edu.au/wp-content/uploads/2011/03/ch24.pdf; Helen Leach, "The Pavlova Wars: How a Creationist Model of Recipe Origins Led to an International Dispute," *Gastronomica: The Journal of Food and Culture* 2 (2010): 24–30, accessed January 25, 2015, http://www.jstor.org/stable/10.1525/gfc.2010.10.2.24; Jeri Quinzio, *Pudding: A Global History* (London: Reaktion Books, 2012), Kindle edition, http://www.amazon.com/Pudding-Global-History-Jeri-Quinzio-ebook/dp/B00BLP4DRY/ref=tmm_kin_swatch_0?_encoding=UTF8&sr=&qid=; and Rafia Zafar, "The Proof of the Pudding: Of Haggis, Hasty Pudding, and Transatlantic Influence," *Early American Literature* 2 (1996): 133–49, accessed January 25, 2015, http://www.jstor.org/stable/25057047.

13. Erica Peters alerted me to the Tom Thumb connection and the various mentions of his connection with pudding.

14. *Brewer's Dictionary of Phrase and Fable: Bibliographic Record, New Edition, Revised, Corrected and Enlarged* (Philadelphia: Henry Altemus, 1898, New York: Bartleby.com, 2000), accessed January 25, 2015, http://www.bartleby.com/81/9061.html.

15. Jeri Quinzio, "Puddings in Black and White: Pudding Revels," *Pudding: A Global History* (London: Reaktion Books, 2012), Kindle edition, http://www.amazon.com/Pudding-Global-History-Jeri-Quinzio ebook/dp/B00BLP4DRY/ref=tmm_kin_swatch_0?_encoding=UTF8&sr=&qid=.

16. Jeri Quinzio, "Vegetable Pudding: Springtime Pudding," *Pudding: A Global History*.

17. "Pudding," The Virtual Linguist; Alan Davidson, *Oxford Companion to Food* (Oxford: Oxford University Press, 2006), 2nd edition, 638–39; Jeri Quinzio, *Pudding: A Global History*; and Lynne Olver, ed., "What is Pudding," The Food Timeline.

18. Ryan responded to a query I put out on the (British) Talking Folklore listserv. He has had a varied career, including working as the museum curator in the Oxford History of Science Museum, teacher of Russian in London University (language and medieval literature), and "for the last 27 years of my working life Academic Librarian and Professor of Russian Studies at the Warburg Institute, London," email, February 27, 2015.

19. And note the nursery rhyme, which I remember my mother reciting to me when I was a child:

Pease pudding hot
Pease pudding cold,
Pease pudding in the pot
Nine days old

20. Mary Norwalk, *English Puddings: Sweet & Savoury* (London: The Book People, 2010), 85; and Dorothy Hartley, *Lost Country Life: How English Country Folk Lived, Worked, Threshed, Thatched, Rolled Fleece, Milled Corn, Brewed Mead* (New York: Pantheon Books, 1979), 191, 274–76.

21. Disagreeing with this point, which several food historians, including Jeri Quinzio have made, Sharon Hudgins explained in an email, February 25, 2015, that in many places "intestines were available year-round, not just at slaughter time in autumn. They were cleaned and blown up with air, then tied at both ends (looking like long balloons) for preservation until needed.... I have certainly seen this myself in the Balkans and Hungary, where those intestines were sold in local open-air markets—and I know that intestines can be preserved this way (walrus, seal, whale) from my recent research into Native foods (and clothing made from these intestines) in Alaska and Russia. Certainly the meat sausages themselves were made during the slaughter season, but there's no reason that the preserved intestines couldn't be used at other times of the year as wrappings for other fillings that were to be cooked in them."

22. Quinzio, *Pudding: A Global History*.

23. "Sussex Pond and Kentish Well Pudding," *The Art and Mystery of Food*, January 28, 2007, accessed February 20, 2015, http://adambalic.typepad.com/the_art_and_mystery_of_fo/2007/01/post.html.

24. Daniel Pool, *What Jane Austen Ate and Charles Dickens Knew: From Fox Hunting to Whist—the Facts of Daily Life in Nineteenth-Century England* (New York: Simon & Schuster, 1993), 204.

25. Quinzio, "A Pudding Chronology," *Pudding: A Global History*; and Mason, *Food Culture in Great Britain*, 49.

26. Paston-Williams, *Good Old-Fashioned Puddings*, 7.

27. Norwalk, *English Puddings: Sweet & Savoury*, 44–50.

28. Mason, *Food Culture in Great Britain*, 45.

29. Frank Dawes, *Not in Front of the Servants* (New York: Taplinger Publishing Company, 1974), 72–73, 134–37.

30. Paul Thompson, *The Edwardians: The Remaking of British Society* (London: Weidenfeld and Nicolson, 1984).

31. Sue Style, "Toad in the Hole Is Uniquely British Comfort Food," *Zester Daily*, January 27, 2015, accessed February 6, 2015, http://zesterdaily.com/world/toad-hole-uniquely-british-comfort-food/.

32. Norwalk, *English Puddings: Sweet & Savory*, 11.

33. Thanks are due to Mike Jones for having brought this mention to my attention.

34. Maria Grace, "800 Years of Plum Pudding," *English Historical Fiction Authors*, December 11, 2012, accessed February 17, 2015, http://englishhistoryauthors.blogspot.com/2012/12/800-years-of-plum-pudding.html. "The last Sunday before Advent is considered the last day on which one can make Christmas puddings since they require aging before they are served. It is sometimes known as 'Stir-up Sunday.' This is because opening words of the main prayer in the Book of Common Prayer of 1549 for that day are: 'Stir-up, we beseech thee, O Lord, the wills of thy faithful people; that they, plenteously bringing forth the fruit of good works, may of thee be plenteously rewarded; through Jesus Christ our Lord. Amen.' Choir boys parodied the prayer: 'Stir up, we beseech thee, the pudding in the pot. And when we do get home tonight, we'll eat it up hot.'"

35. Mason, *Food Culture in Great Britain*, 176–94.

36. Ibid., 116–21.

37. R. W. Apple, Jr., "The Worldly Pleasures of Nursery Puddings: In England, There Will Always be Whim Wham and Apple Dappy," *New York Times*, March 22, 2000, accessed February 21, 2015, http://www.nytimes.com/2000/03/22/dining/worldly-pleasures-nursery-puddings-england-there-will-always-be-whim-wham-apple.html.

38. Eleanor Morgan, writing about puddings for *Munchies* on July 15, 2014, recalls that "the heavy, palate-sticking puddings of yore are, unless you eat at your nan's every weekend, almost a memory. If you ask any British person what their favourite childhood dishes were, though, they'll almost certainly come back with something hot, spongey, and sweet, invariably involving custard from a packet. It's the stuff we were fed at school in neatly compartmented plastic trays, the stuff our grandparents taunted us with to make us eat all the over-boiled carrots on our Sunday lunch plates, the stuff that stuck to our ribs when we went out to play on freezing cold 'summer' evenings."

39. Apple, "The Worldly Pleasures of Nursery Puddings."

40. Felicity Cloake, "How to Cook Perfect Sticky Toffee Pudding," Word of Mouth Blog, *Guardian*, April 14, 2011, accessed February 21, 2015, http://www.theguardian.com/lifeandstyle/wordofmouth/2011/apr/14/cook-perfect-sticky-toffee-pudding.

41. "Sussex Pond and Kentish Well Pudding," *The Art and Mystery of Food*, January 28, 2007, accessed February 20, 2015, http://adambalic.typepad.com/the_art_and_mystery_of_fo/2007/01/post.html.

42. Jane Garmey, *Great British Cooking: A Well-Kept Secret* (New York: Harper Collins, 1992), xv–xvi.

43. Eleanor Morgan, "British Puddings Are the Best in the World," Munchies, July 15, 2014, accessed January 15, 2015, http://munchies.vice.com/articles/british-puddings-are-the-best-in-the-world.

44. Ed Zotti, ed., "What's the Origin of 'Spotted Dick'?" The Straight Dope, August 27, 2002, accessed February 13, 2015, http://www.straightdope.com/columns/read/2031/whats-the-origin-of-spotted-dick.

45. Will Ryan, email, February 27, 2015.

46. Zotti, ed., "What's the Origin of 'Spotted Dick'?"

47. Ryan, email, February 27, 2015, noted that "the Italians call it zuppa inglese 'English soup.'"

48. I came up with my own version, modified over the years to include raspberry jam (instead of the flavored gelatin some British friends use), a melted dark chocolate layer, and pound cake soaked in orange liqueur (instead of sponge cake soaked in sherry). This was definitely a hit with American friends and family, and even my visiting British and Scottish friends seemed to enjoy it, though perhaps they were merely being polite and didn't really consider my concoction to be a proper trifle.

49. Ryan, email, February 27, 2015, suggested that this may have occurred earlier, and had "to do with the growing availability of the family car after WWII."

50. "Deep England" is a core concept for Wright's book and refers to an idealized, mostly rural, vision of a middle- to upper-middle-class normative lifestyle. Patrick Wright, On Living in an Old Country: The National Past in Contemporary Britain (London: Verso, 1985).

51. Garmey, Great British Cooking, v.

52. Paul Ward, Britishness since 1870 (London: Routledge, 2004), 8–9, 45, 94–95.

53. Julian Barnes, England, England (London: Picador, 1998), 90–91. Stargazey pie is a crusted pie with pilchards (small, herring-like fish) peeping out. Wow-wow sauce is a savory sauce made with meat stock, wine vinegar, Worcester sauce, mustard, and parsley, and is often served with bubble and squeak. Maids-of-honour are almond custard tarts made with puff pastry, and parkin is a kind of gingerbread cake.

54. Rachelle H. Saltzman, A Lark for the Sake of Their Country: The 1926 General Strike Volunteers in Folklore and Memory (Manchester: Manchester University Press, 2012), 21–22, 26. A host of British historians and sociologists, most notably Krishan Kumar, Robert Colls, Philip Dodd, Jeremy Paxman, Paul Ward, and Arthur Aughey, have comprehensively written about the distinction between a British civic identity (includes the non-English ethnic groups in the UK and national beliefs about civic virtues) and a more restrictive English ethnic identity (cultural heritage), which also gets at what Patrick Wright means by "Deep England."

55. Jeremy Paxman, The English: A Portrait of a People (London: Penguin Books, 1999), 256–59.

56. Rowan Pelling, "Hurrah for the R and A members who let women across the invisible line," Telegraph, September 19, 2014, accessed January 21, 2015, http://www.telegraph.co.uk/sport/golf/11109232/Hurrah-for-the-RandA-members-who-let-women-across-the-invisible-line.html.

57. Laura Barton, "Life Is Sweet at the Pudding Club," Guardian, January 9, 2010, accessed February 20, 2015, http://www.theguardian.com/travel/2010/jan/30/the-pudding-club-the-cotswolds.

58. Ibid.

59. After reading a draft of this chapter, Simon Talbot, in an email dated February 25, 2015, commented on the absence of puddings in Madrid, noting that in "the better Irish pubs, The James Joyce on Calle Alcala, for example, one can find a delightful Apple Crumble; so I think your point about pudding being an international symbol and export is well made." He also speculated that climate might have something to do with the British love of puddings, an observation that Redraspberrygirl made as well. "It's a truth universally acknowledged that when the temperature drops our craving for old-fashioned comfort puds goes into overdrive. Hot sponge puddings oozing with syrup or treacle, nursery food like bread-and-butter pudding made extra indulgent with lashings of double cream, even school-dinner jam roly-poly served with masses of reassuring proper custard—puddings like these make winter something actually worth looking forward to." "Cook's Corner," Taste of Home, February 5, 2006, accessed December 12, 2014, http://community.tasteofhome.com/community_forums/f/30/t/250311.aspx#ixzz3SgxgB177 .

60. Homesick Brit Sampler, accessed January 30, 2015, http://www.igourmet.com/shoppe/shoppe.aspx?cat=Dinners&subcat=Dinners.

61. Black pudding is not just British, of course, and can be found in Ireland as well as in Spain, Germany, Scandinavia, and France.

62. Robert Graves, "Treacle Tart," *Collected Short Stories* (Harmondsworth, Middlesex: Penguin Books, 1984), 43.

63. Garmey, *Great British Cooking*, 166.

64. "Pudding," The Virtual Linguist, June 30, 2014, accessed January 31, 2015, http://virtuallinguist.typepad.com/the_virtual_linguist/2014/06/pudding.html.

65. Morgan, "British Puddings are the Best in the World."

66. As Sharon Hudgins reminded me in an email, February 25, 2015, masa is "lime-slaked corn processed to make masa dough (the fresh, moist mass) or dried to make masa harina (flour, which is then moistened for making tortillas, tamales, etc.)."

67. Rachelle H. Saltzman, "Fieldwork in a Green and Pleasant Land," paper presented at the annual meeting of the American Anthropological Association, 1991.

68. Paston-Williams, *Good Old-Fashioned Puddings*, 7.

69. In her Hammersmith (London) gastropub review, Fay Maschler writes, "The English nursery and boarding school has influenced the list of puddings but poached prunes are rendered grown-up by their accompaniment of Greek yogurt, pistachio nuts and honey." Fay Maschler, "Nursery Food Grows Up," *London Evening Standard*, January 16, 2008, accessed February 24, 2015, http://www.standard.co.uk/goingout/restaurants/nursery-food-grows-up-7402848.html.

70. NTSteve, "Save the Great British Pud with the National Trust," National Trust Press Office Blog, September 18, 2012, accessed February 20, 2015, https://ntpressoffice.wordpress.com/tag/british-puddings/

71. Ibid.

Even Presidents Need Comfort Food: Tradition, Food, and Politics at the Valois Cafeteria

Susan Eleuterio with Barbara Banks,
Phillis Humphries, and Charlene Smith

Diners and cafeterias have long played an important role in America's food-ways—most often through popular culture, but also in fine art, notably in Edward Hopper's painting "Nighthawks," completed in 1942 and owned by the Art Institute of Chicago. A Chicagoan, John Kruger, is credited with the creation of the first named "cafeteria" (his word) at the 1893 Chicago's World's Columbian Exposition, eventually running a chain of them.[1] Valois (pronounced Vah loys[2]) Restaurant is a traditional cafeteria, complete with a "smorgasbord" line of offerings (which first interested Kruger on a trip to Sweden) served up by Greek and Hispanic short order cooks along with African American women who take drink orders and a no-nonsense cashier. While a plain exterior and menu of basic American foods may seem familiar to those who frequent cafeterias, the cafeteria's history as a favorite hang-out of President Barack Obama offers an opportunity to explore connections among comfort food, politics, community, and tradition.[3]

This essay is based to a great extent on a facilitated conversation with three longtime African American customers of the Valois: Phillis Humphries, Barbara Banks, and Charlene Smith. These three women have all written about various aspects of food traditions as part of their membership in a community writing group within the Neighborhood Writing Alliance, where I served as a volunteer coordinator for a number of years. The chapter also draws on personal and field observations by me, a white folklorist who has worked in Hyde Park over the years and now lives there part-time; a sociological study of some of the restaurant's regulars, staff, and owners conducted in 1992;[4]

news articles; and social media reviews. Our dialogue about the role of comfort food at Valois and similar cafeterias and diners in America took place over a leisurely breakfast. Barbara had her traditional steak and two eggs *over easy*, Phillis and I ate the "Obama Mediterranean omelet," and Charlene had grits, ham, and eggs. Three of us chose biscuits over toast. We met at 9:30 in the morning, a good time for sitting over coffee at the Valois, which opens for breakfast at 5:30 a.m. and has been known to have lines down the street, depending on the time of day and who is in town.[5]

Charlene, a retired public school teacher, has been eating at Valois for over fifteen years. She noted: "I like the atmosphere; that you can stay and sit and talk and feel at home there. They are always very cordial, and it's in the neighborhood." Phillis, a former loan officer who in retirement is studying spiritual writing, commented: "I ate at Valois all the time during my working years. It was convenient; open early, no waiting, in a reasonably safe area at the time. I used to live here near 52nd and Blackstone. Then I moved home when my dad died to take care of my mom. Now parking is a hassle and I'm not up as early." Barbara's tradition, while working as a medical technician, was to have Saturday breakfast with her mother. "It was a ritual, nice to come for the first meal of the day, a 'break of the fast,' have eggs and bacon. They used to have a big coffeepot like my grandmother had. There's the tradition of coffee, a 'cup of joe.' Now you have to pay if you want another cup."

Located in the Hyde Park neighborhood on Chicago's South Side, Valois was founded in 1921 and has become legendary in part because it was (and remains) a favorite of President Barack Obama when he taught at the nearby University of Chicago Law School, and before that, when he worked as a community organizer. "Before he become senator, he was always around the neighborhood, organizing and helping," said Spiros Argiris, the cafeteria's Greek owner. "He was here off and on. Sometimes he'd be by himself, sometimes with friends, sometimes with family." Obama leaned toward Argiris's massive bacon and cheese omelets but also bounced around the menu, from his fluffy pancakes to his $12.95 prime rib. Argiris often sent food to Obama's office when he was too busy to stop.[6]

Unpretentious and decorated with wall and ceiling murals reflecting both Chicago and University of Chicago scenes (the downtown skyline, "the Point" on Lake Michigan a few blocks away, the Fermi nuclear accelerator memorial at University of Chicago), Valois shares a mix of student, local, and tourist clientele with a number of other Hyde Park eateries, including the Medici and Mellow Yellow.

First opened by William Valois, a French Canadian, the restaurant has been run by Greek families (Spiro Argiris and Gus Sellis have co-owned it

Valois Restaurant

5:30am to 10:00pm Everyday

We Serve Lunch, Dinner And NOW...

BREAKFAST ALL DAY!

Breakfast All Day. Photo by Susan Eleuterio.

since 1973) since its sale by William Allman in 1969.[7] It had a previous period of fame, locally and nationally, when it was the subject of University of Chicago student Mitchell Duneier's thesis in Sociology, which was published as a book in 1992. *Slim's Table: Race, Respectability, and Masculinity* showcased the unpretentious and comforting atmosphere of Valois where a group of African American men gathered regularly to eat, talk, argue, and share their lives.

Duneier interviewed Allman's widow, who described the clientele in the '60s as "largely white," and in the afternoons, "mostly the women."[8] By 1992, Duneier wrote, "social life in the cafeteria is not typical of the wider society in that there is sometimes an almost total absence of women there." This is not true today. Perhaps one more example of changing gender roles is that women are now more comfortable eating alone in public. Phillis refers to Valois as "a neighborhood comfort joint." In a 2013 profile, *Chicago Tribune* writer Charles Johnson observed: "Church groups meet at the big center table, happy to share the Gospel or debate scripture with anyone who will listen."[9] Phillis noted that a group from the Illinois Humanities Council's Odyssey Project (a program designed to provide a college education to community members) meets here every Thursday night.

As Duneier wrote: "Old-fashioned food with natural ingredients, a meeting place that conjures up both an old barbershop and an old neighborhood, and frequent discussion of beliefs and opinions that originated in the old black community—all serve to remind a man of his former participation in a community that, in fundamental ways, molded his patterns of belief and conduct, creating the human he was to become."[10] When contemplating the role of restaurants in serving comfort food and establishing what I would call a *context of being comfortable*, Michael Jones's quote in this volume from John Lancaster that it is "designed to remind us of familiar things, to connect us with our personal histories and our communities and our families"

Enjoy Valois Coffee. Photo by Susan Eleuterio.

rings especially true for not only the Valois male customers documented by Duneier in the 1990s, but for the broader demographic who visit today.[11]

The traditional (at least to most Americans) foods on the menu, the cash-only policy, the plain-spoken but at the same time globally connected atmo-sphere (in addition to the connection to President Obama, one wall of the restaurant is devoted to large clocks set to the times in Athens, Tokyo, London, New York, and of course, Chicago), along with what has become a custom for a variety of people to eat together, creates an opportunity for commensality, what Leonard Mars, in writing about Jewish cultural traditions of eating and drinking, notes as "a total social fact." He references Marcel Mauss, saying, "it is a social fact which is simultaneously esthetic, economic, legal, politi-cal, religious, moral, and familial."[12] Sociologists such as Claude Fischler have also emphasized the power and significance of eating together, noting that "it counteracts the essential, basic, biological, 'exclusive selfishness of eating' and turns it into, at the very least, a collective, social experience."[13] The cafeteria's combination of comfort factors and food mimics the "local diner" found in many less urban and urbane places and permits its clients to cross a variety of barriers in order to reach commensality. At the same time, even those who eat alone at Valois or take their food to go are participating in a form of commen-sality provided by the personal sharing of cooked food directly from the line cooks to the customer, by the conviviality of Valois where each person who interacts with you offers a greeting—and, in the case of President Obama, through sharing food in a community where "everybody knows his name." As noted below, the cafeteria's practice of asking single diners to share a table reinforces both the practice of eating with others and feeling comfortable.

Charlene and Barbara note: "The older guys used to sit here and solve the problems of the world; have their coffee." Years later, all four of us used to see some of these same men gathered to play chess at a nearby Borders bookstore. Gentrification has eliminated many of the gathering places in Hyde Park; the bookstore is gone, as is the International House of Pancakes, which used to serve as another comforting breakfast place in the area for locals. Valois remains a place where, as Ron Grossman noted in an article about *Slim's Table*, "between meals, things are slower, allowing Valois's regulars to linger for hours over a cup of coffee."[14] Valois coffee cups are imprinted, perhaps ironically, "Enjoy Valois Gourmet Coffee"—and coffee is a bargain at $1.50, less than the Starbucks down the street. While Starbucks has emphasized a comforting atmosphere, what CEO Howard Schultz has called "a third place between home and work,"[15] old-school cafeterias like the Valois continue to have an important role to play (and to serve as the *third place*) for those whose budgets cannot accommodate the more expensive chain restaurants and who may not always be welcome to linger for several hours. Class and race issues, even in an integrated neighborhood like Hyde Park, continue to dictate who is made to feel comfortable in dining establishments, despite the fact that the first African American president was a local resident.

Unique to Valois is the motto *See Your Food* prominently displayed on its marquee outside. I asked Phillis, Barbara, and Charlene what they thought this might mean. Phillis: "Seeing is believing . . . that no one picked their nose or forgot to wash their hands." Charlene: "You see them cooking and making the food. A lot of African Americans don't like eating out; you don't know who cooked the food and there's a history of mistrust. They didn't want us in restaurants." Folklorist Patricia Turner has documented mistrust of restaurants by a number of African Americans in her examination of a long-standing rumor in the black community that the Church's Chicken franchise was owned by the Ku Klux Klan. She reflects on anthropologist Mary Douglas's point that "people with a minority status in their society are likely both to be suspicious of cooked food and to be protective of the body's orifices."[16] Barbara: "My brother-in-law grew up in a little town from the South; they never thought they could afford to eat in restaurants. There's also the attitude that nobody cooks the food like you. My grandmother cooked chicken and dumplings; nobody makes it like her. Some people don't like change, and some will only eat one thing at a restaurant."

Valois Restaurant, "See Your Food." Photo by Susan Eleuterio.

As with most cafeterias, the food and its preparation at Valois *is* visible, not only the cooked dishes but the cooks who are working at the grill. Today, it has become trendy to "see your food," that is, to have an open kitchen or at home to have diners sitting in the kitchen with those cooking, but in the past, this was uncharacteristic. Unlike the expensive performance art of chefs at gourmet restaurants such as Chicago's Alinea, the Valois cooks retain the no-nonsense tradition of cooking the food efficiently and without drama. The mistrust of African American diners who had to protest just to be permitted to sit at lunch counters in the South (and were not served in many restaurants in the North as well) has perhaps also contributed to the success of places like Valois where everything is out in the open. It is not only the food that provides comfort, but the atmosphere as well—the feeling that there are no secrets.

At the same time, the notion of seeing your food has been true histori-cally at most American cafeterias and its perceived value in terms of comfort is not limited to African American patrons. Lynne Olver, editor of the Food Timeline, quotes a 1998 *Los Angeles Times* article about a Los Angeles pioneer of cafeterias, Helen Mosher: "She advertised: 'All Women Cooks—Food That Can Be Seen,' and best of all, 'No Tips.'"[17] Another legendary Los Angeles cafe-teria chain, Clifton's, was sold in 2010 to nightclub producer Andrew Meieran, who noted that "[the food] had to be good because it was actually out there in front of you and customers would never pick items if they looked or smelled bad. On a normal restaurant menu, you don't have any idea what you're going to get until it finally arrives. But in a cafeteria, the food is right up front and personal. And if it don't look good, you ain't gonna buy it."[18] Olver quotes a writer in the 1925 edition of *American Cookery*:

"I am," said the woman, "a cafeteria addict. I go to the cafeteria rather than the restaurant because their coffee is hotter, it comes direct from the urn to me, and warms my heart as I drink it. The soups are hotter, too, and . . . all other

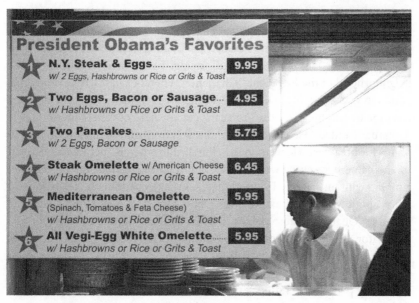

President Obama's Favorites

1. **N.Y. Steak & Eggs**........................ 9.95
w/ 2 Eggs, Hashbrowns or Rice or Grits & Toast

2. **Two Eggs, Bacon or Sausage**... 4.95
w/ Hashbrowns or Rice or Grits & Toast

3. **Two Pancakes**............................. 5.75
w/ 2 Eggs, Bacon or Sausage

4. **Steak Omelette** w/ American Cheese 6.45
w/ Hashbrowns or Rice or Grits & Toast

5. **Mediterranean Omelette**............ 5.95
(Spinach, Tomatoes & Feta Cheese)
w/ Hashbrowns or Rice or Grits & Toast

6. **All Vegi-Egg White Omelette**...... 5.95
w/ Hashbrowns or Rice or Grits & Toast

President Obama's Favorites Menu. Photo by Susan Eleuterio.

foods meant to be hot come right from the kettle to the customer without the long preambles, the waits and inspections and other performances involved in their transference form [*sic*] the hotel or restaurant kitchen to the dining room table, during which hot dishes grow cold, and cold grow lukewarm, and everything steamy gets sodden. Also, when there is a question of a "chancy" food like cantaloupe, I am able to order one from visual inspection rather than from a bill of fare which may read "Rockyford melon," and turn out to be something like a mealy potato when it comes to the cover. The same holds good for all other fruits, and for pies, cake, dishes of pickles and preserves, vegetables, salads. In the best cafeterias everything is in full view, your slice of roast beef is cut from the hot joint while you look on; your chop is offered for your inspection before it is broiled, you pick your baked potato and point to the salad of your choice.... The counter people seem to have the gift of kings and princes in remembering faces, that gift of good democrats in according them welcoming recognition, and that further gift of the born restaurateur in remembering tastes. After one or two requests for the wishbone, the short-bone, or any other bone of the roast chicken, the man will put it aside for you while you are yet three places off.... Finally, the appraiser of the contents of your tray smiles at you, welcomes you back if you have been on vacation, the cashier bids you good-day as you approach with your check, and thanks you when you pay. You leave the place comforted and feeling good." [19]

Nearly 90 years later, many of these same comments are made by patrons of the Valois. Regarding President Obama's relationship to Valois and the community of Hyde Park, Barbara noted, "I was coming here before he came here. My mother was looking at me [and] saying, 'I can't believe you live in the neighborhood of the President.'" Charlene: "When he's in town, anybody that comes in gets a free brunch, they serve them the *Obama Breakfast*. He came last time he was here." Phillis: "You can't get nowhere near here then."

Barbara added: "He used to jog on the lakefront and then come in here to Valois for breakfast. He went to my church, and when he became a US senator, he came here every weekend. He could come to shoot the breeze after running with his friends. I've read that he said it's one thing he really misses." What about Michelle? I asked. (Mrs. Obama is referred to as "Michelle" and President Obama is referred to as "Barack" by those of us who voted for him as senator.) "She was a soccer mom, the kids were younger then and her favorite is a French restaurant." In his *Chicago Tribune* article Charles Johnson did note that (owner Spiros) "Argiris remembers Sasha and Malia Obama munching pancakes on Sunday mornings, and that fitness advocate Michelle Obama was quite partial to the peach cobbler."[20]

Phillis: "This is his community, he did everything in the community, got his hair cut at Fifty-first Street." Charlene: "He's a regular guy; he'd be happy eating at a hot dog stand. He's a people person." Barbara: "This is the president's place."[21] As Charlene noted, Valois celebrated both the 2008 and 2012 presidential elections with a free or reduced-cost "Obama" breakfast, serving over 700 for his re-election.[22] Photos from the most recent election posted on the *Chicago Tribune* website featured Valois with "Barack Obama 2012" campaign signs, along with patrons in Obama T-shirts eating the designated Obama breakfast of eggs, potatoes, sausage/bacon, toast, coffee, and juice. [23] Creating community through food goes both ways at the Valois. Writes Johnson: "Jon L. Lathouris, who used to flip Obama's eggs when he frequented the restaurant, pointed to a wall next to the cash register with a photo of a smiling Obama, and said, 'Yeah, I miss him, I miss my friend.'"[24] While there is a long tradition of US presidents emphasizing their connection to the everyday comforts of familiar food,[25] the connection Barack Obama has to community members like Charlene, Phillis, and Barbara, and to me, is a mix of local pride, support for his policies, and having made a personal connection, whether through church (as in Barbara's case) or even on the campaign trail.

My own experience of eating with the president underscores Charlene's description of the president as down to earth, especially when it comes to eating. I attended a fundraiser when he was running for president in 2007, which was organized like a wedding reception dinner. Tables of ten had one empty place and then-Senator Obama moved around the room, sitting at each table for five minutes. I was the only woman at our table, and we were one of the last tables he came to. Here was my big chance to ask the future president to end the wars in Iraq and Afghanistan, but he looked exhausted and the guys (including my son) all wanted to talk basketball—which he clearly enjoyed, bragging that he made a basket when he was playing with some soldiers at a base overseas. I finally piped up and said, "Senator, you should eat something!" He laughed and went on talking about basketball, neglecting to touch the food on his plate.

In describing the appeal of Valois, Duneier wrote: "Cafeteria life offers its regulars the opportunity to participate in the reality of the wider world itself. For here is one microcosm of society existing in its natural objective form— an embodiment of power, cultural diversity, and behavioral expectations."[26] While Duneier's focus was on how Valois (and other public eating places) provides a safe entrée to the larger world, I would argue that it also offers a haven of comfort and normality to someone like the president (along with other famous Chicagoans who have frequented it). They, too, need "reality," not perhaps of the wider world, but of the world of home—a place where you can be, as Charlene says, "a regular guy"—or gal. Although Valois seems to attract more famous men than women, perhaps the next glass ceiling broken will be when women politicians can seek out comfort food without worrying about someone discussing their weight or food choices.

The six items listed as "The President's Favorites" represent a range of what traditionally would be called comfort breakfast food (steak, eggs, toast, bacon, sausage, pancakes, hash browns, and grits) and what might be labeled as "healthy breakfast food" (egg whites and Mediterranean omelettes). The First Lady's campaign for healthful food and physical activity, called "Let's Move," seems to have extended to the Valois, where you can assuage any guilt over eating toast and grits by adding vegetables or skipping the egg yolks. But this does not seem to have impacted the president. Discussing a presidential visit in the spring of 2014, Valois owner Tom Chronopoulos told a reporter, "I suggested the egg white omelet to make Michelle happy. But he refused it."[27]

Grits, rice, and biscuits (as an alternative to toast) represent Southern traditions, and grits especially are defined as comfort food. One can assume that they reflect the heritage of many of the African American residents of Hyde Park and the surrounding neighborhoods. Chicago was the destination for a number of Southern blacks who left during the Great Migration[28] from the early 1900s to 1970, particularly the South Side (with more middle-class neighborhoods like Hyde Park becoming increasingly integrated after the 1960s, with the expansion of public housing).[29] Phillis noted: "There is a sense of protection within Hyde Park's boundaries. The community commands certain public behavior with two law enforcement agencies, the university and the city's, so control is tight. Many of the surrounding communities are poor and lack flourishing and thriving businesses." At the same time, the food at Valois is not soul food or Greek food, but a mix of the influence of multiple cultures, just like the clientele of the restaurant.[30]

Grits also have a history as comfort food for presidents, especially for Jimmy Carter. Henry Haller, in the *White House Family Cookbook*, notes: "A staple dish for the Carters and their Southern visitors, grits soon became standard fare for White House guests from all over the world."[31] Other US presidents have depended on African American cooks and have expressed a preference for comfort food, both privately and at times in public. Adrian Miller writes: "This presidential love of comfort food often created tension in the kitchen between the classically trained European chefs and the 'home-trained' black cooks who consistently won the hearts of the First Diners and their guests. The White House table featured such soulful favorites as fried chicken, greens, okra and sweet potato pie next to consommé and blancmange. Many presidents chose to mediate the tension by having the black cooks make the private meals while the European chefs handled grand entertainments."[32]

Barbara noted: "My grandmother used to cook all of this. They would go out in the field, you had to have a hearty breakfast. She would say, 'Eat breakfast like a king, lunch like a prince, and dinner like a pauper.'" Phillis added: "When you eat in the morning like that, it takes you through the day." The folk wisdom of Barbara's grandmother concerning the importance of breakfast has been underscored in recent years by the Federal School Breakfast Program, which is based in part on nutritional and school-based studies showing that students who eat breakfast have better learning and health outcomes. [33] Charlene, whose family came from the South, said they would have rice for breakfast, and both she and Barbara's families would eat the rice with sugar and butter. "In the South, it's rice or grits."

Traditionally, rice, grits, and biscuits are eaten with butter, one of the key aspects of this being categorized as comfort food. Butter has survived numerous attacks by nutritionists and health experts, and has even become trendy in some diets but there remains a sense of a guilty pleasure in eating foods associated with it. [34] As Charlene noted: "Comfort food is heavy, rich, and fills you up."

All experts on biscuits, Phillis, Charlene, and Barbara were particularly critical of the rendering at Valois. Phillis: "They aren't biscuits, they're puffed up bread. They are like a cake or a roll, and too sweet. Maybe it's because they are Greeks. Real Southern biscuits are made in neighborhood kitchens."

Valois Biscuits. Photo by Susan Eleuterio.

Barbara: "I know how to make biscuits; my grandmother taught me. We used a glass to cut them and I used to sell them in the projects. They would have quarter parties (house parties held to pay the rent). You paid a quarter to come in, a quarter for a hot dog, a quarter for a pop or beer. The thing was to invite as many people as you could to make a profit. Now there also was gambling in the back room, but there was dancing and food and the kids in the front part of the house. The next day the adults didn't want to cook, so I would go around and sell them biscuits." Another African American friend of ours, James Rushing, stated: "Black folks tolerate those biscuits at Valois, they are not used to that kind of biscuit, but that's what they have. Most of the time, we take the crust off the top and bottom, and leave the insides—there is too much bread. The right kind of biscuit, you sop in butter and syrup." For me, as a non-Southerner who grew up with a Portuguese grandmother who made sweet bread, having biscuits rather than toast is a comfort in itself. It is possible that Phillis is on to something; the Valois biscuits are more like a sweet bread than a traditional Southern white flour biscuit. Perhaps there is an influence of Greek Easter bread. Nonetheless, they fulfill the requirements of comfort food both symbolically as a Southern treat and in reality by their connection with home cooking and butter. Calling them "rolls" might confuse the issue, since rolls in Chicago can be anything from dinner rolls to cinnamon rolls (another Chicago favorite comfort food renowned at Anne Sather's restaurant). At the same time, the Greek owners of Valois have repeated a practice noted by Michelle Roth in her study of Greek diners: "It was clear that each diner owner and their family were focused on sharing their culture with their clients."[35]

In addition to Barack Obama and Chicago's first African American mayor, Harold Washington, other politicians and prominent Chicagoans—especially those from the South Side, such as Jesse Jackson (activist, candidate for US president, and founder of the Rainbow/PUSH community organizing group), White Sox owner Bill Veeck, and in recent years, Mayor Rahm Emanuel—are known to have come by to press the flesh, eat, and organize. At the same time, Valois is a place where you can eat by yourself. Barbara noted: "I would come here to eat alone. If it's real crowded, they will ask you to share a table, but you can take your time and they know you. One time I saw one of the cooks, Larry, on the street, and he said, 'You're the steak [for breakfast] lady.' When I get in line, I see him pull the steak out, he knows what I want. They are cooking but paying attention." Charlene added: "It's not pretentious. You can grab a breakfast and eat and run, they're very friendly. They have a good eye for people and they know who's in here."

Valois is known as a comforting place not only to a wide mix of the population but also to the police. Glancing at a table of heavily vest-protected city police, Barbara noted: "They like a good heavy meal and they don't want to be bothered with BS. It's safe." Phillis added: "There's nothing to do with race, class, or politics here." Duneier's sociological study of Valois supports her statement, with police finding comfort at the restaurant for over twenty years. Discussing how the atmosphere at Valois "broke down barriers between groups,"[36] Duneier noted: "Valois was one of the few restaurants on the South Side that evolved into a hangout for many Twenty-first District patrolmen during their mealtime breaks." He described "the unrestricted, open nature of public space in the cafeteria" and its safety not only for the police but even, on occasion, for someone who had been arrested by one of the officers in the past.[37] "The police experienced a sort of companionship there that they rarely found in other places."[38] Other patrons today are comforted by this clientele. Chicago Yelp reviewer Jason P. noted: "My dad once told me that any place that always has some older people and police officers eating inside has to be good. Been enjoying meals since the mid 90s. Love the breakfast food. One of the few establishments that knows how to make an omelet that's not overcooked. They have good lunch and dinner too.... You get good portions and the prices are fair. Just keep in mind that it's a cash only establishment."[39]

Other items on the Valois menu include roast beef, pork, turkey, Grecian chicken, fresh catfish, steak, pot pie, BBQ ribs, mashed potatoes, macaroni and cheese, baked fish, daily specials, a soup of the day, hot sandwiches, and, of course, comfort food desserts (rice pudding, pies, cobblers, and Jell-O) featured in a glass case next to the cashier. Barbara recounted: "I used to come here every Friday for the baked halibut, mac and cheese, and broccoli. They all remind me of meals my grandmother used to make. The Greeks have a slightly different twist on their food, and, of course, my grandmother's was better!" Other diners celebrate their favorite meals at Valois on Pinterest or in reviews on Yelp and Foursquare. Kristy Sanchez focused on the hot beef sandwiches with gravy, photographed lovingly on 365 South Chicago, "Lifestyles on the South Side of Chicago."[40]

As the former center of the meatpacking industry in America, Chicago's comfort food continues to include an emphasis on meat and potatoes. Food historian Tracey Poe writes: "While food is often thought of as a feminized cultural form, conjuring images of the comforts of home and mothers cooking family meals, Chicago foodways have a brawnier, more animalistic connotation."[41] Barbara's choice of steak for breakfast is not unusual in a town still known for steakhouses, and her favorite Friday meal at Valois reflects a tradition in many Midwestern communities of fish for Friday dinner, as well as the merging of immigrant customs (Catholics eating fish on Fridays) with the availability of fish from the Great Lakes.[42] Combined with macaroni and cheese, a basic of African American soul food,[43] this meal offers comfort that is filling and healthful at the same time.

Patrons of Valois from around the country and even internationally celebrate its menu items on Yelp and other food related social media. Several mention Kool-Aid, a comfort drink from childhood; others label specific comfort foods, such as Cynthia T. from Oakland, California: "I had the baked chicken with mashed potatoes and gravy. It was yummy comfort food! I'm sleepy now!"[44] A. J. S. from Seattle was intrigued with the overall environment and especially the taste of the hash browned potatoes:

What an experience! I got looked at funny, yelled at, choices were questioned and they only took cash! I can't wait to return! . . . It is cash only, and you walk up and get a tray, cafeteria style. Everything is cheap. You can get the Obama specials, or really whatever breakfast food, steak or sandwich [sic] you feel like. We got breakfast foods and the guy at the counter yelled directions at me (not in a mean way, of course). I can't help looking like an out of place tourist sometimes, okay? They also acted upset with me that I didn't want 3 pats of butter with my oatmeal, and my dining companion did not want anything to drink or any grits to go with his eggs. This was all fine, I was mesmerized by watching a kitchen like that work—omelettes made instantly, pancakes ready to go, people calling out orders, women offering what's next for your breakfast meal. There isn't anything like this from where I'm from. The food was solid and tasty. Not too greasy, and the hashbrowns actually tasted like thinly sliced fresh potatoes. Eggs not overcooked and breakfast meats not rubbery.[45]

Whether eating alone or in a group, we go to places like Valois for the nourishment of the soul—even those who take the food home (a custom of many Valois regulars) are accessing a reward of urban life, which is often missing for suburban and rural elders. Cafeterias provide choice and convenience, and an opportunity to eat and share food which offers the comfort of home cooking, and perhaps memories of a simpler time in our lives. But as can be seen by the fact that even the president of the United States has a continued relationship with Valois, when well run, cafeterias also provide a sense of community and connection through creating a comforting context for eating familiar foods.

Notes

1. Bruce Kraig, "Restaurants," *Electronic Encyclopedia of Chicago History*, http://www .encyclopedia.chicagohistory.org/pages/1066.html, 1066; and Carol Dawson and Carol Johnston, *House of Plenty The Rise, Fall, and Revival of Luby's Cafeterias* (Austin: University of Texas Press, 2006), 23.

2. Chicagoans have a history of a flat Midwestern pronunciation of French and German names and words, for instance Goethe Street is pronounced *Go thee*.

3. Lynne Olver quotes Richard J. Hooker on the history of cafeterias in the Midwest: "Self-service took another form when the cafeteria was invented in the Midwest. The first seems to have been in Chicago in 1893, and by 1895 there were four there. Soon every major city had cafeterias where the customer picked up tray, cutlery, and napkin and proceeded down a long counter, choosing food and presenting a ticket to be punched accordingly. The diner sat at a polished wood table in a tile-walled room often in full sight, through a plate-glass window, of passers-by. On leaving, the customer presented his punched ticket at the door, paid the bill, took, a free toothpick, and departed." From Richard J. Hooker, *Food and Drink in America: A History*, quoted by Lynne Olver, The Food Timeline, 2000, last modified 2014, http://www.foodtimeline.org/restaurants.html#cafeterias.

4. Mitchell Duneier, "Slim and Bart: An Odd Urban Friendship Born at the Valois 'See Your Food' Cafeteria," *Chicago Reader*, June 6, 1992, http://www.chicagoreader.com/ chicago/slim-and-bart/Content?oid=880229; Ron Grossman, "The View From Slim's Table: Regulars at a South Side Cafeteria Dish Out a Rude Awakening for Sociolo-gists," *Chicago Tribune*, January 15, 1992, http://articles.chicagotribune.com/1992–09–15/ features/9203240318_1_mitchell-duneier-valois-first-book.

5. Phillis Humphries, interview, December 2014; video interviews with local residents in 2012, http://www.myfoxchicago.com/clip/7930767/Obama%20supporters%20in%20

Hyde%20Park%20celebrate%20re-election%20with%20free%20breakfast%20at%20; and
Linda Qui, "The Valois Hands Out Meals Fit for a President," *Chicago Maroon*, November 9,
2012, http://chicagomaroon.com/2012/11/09/valois-hands-out-meals-fit-for-a-president/.

6. John Henderson, interview with Spiros Argisis, "A Breakfast Diamond in the Rough,"
Denver Post, April 23, 2008, http://www.denverpost.com/ci_9009104.

7. Charles Johnson, "Breakfast Standards and So Much More: Valois a Community
Gathering Spot Since 1921," *Chicago Tribune*, April 18, 2013, http://articles.chicagotribune
.com/2013-04-18/features/ct-dining-0418-home-plate-valois-20130418_1_hyde-park-bank
-dining-room-eggs.

8. Charles Johnson and Mitchell Duneier, *Slim's Table: Race, Respectability, and Masculinity* (Chicago: University of Chicago Press, 1992), 51–54.

9. Johnson, "Breakfast Standards and So Much More."

10. Johnson and Duneier, *Slim's Table*.

11. John Lancaster in "Incredible Edibles," *The New Yorker*, March 21, 2011: 64–68, quoted
by Michael Owen Jones, "'Stressed' Spelled Backwards Is 'Desserts': Self-Medicating Moods
with Foods."

12. Leonard Mars, "Food and Disharmony: Commensality among Jews," *Food and Foodways: Explorations in the History and Culture of Human Nourishment* 7, no. 3: 189–202, DOI,
10.1080/07409710.1997.9962064.

13. Claude Fischler, *Commensality, Society and Culture* (Sage Publications, Social Science
Information, 2011), Sagepub.co.uk/journalsPermissions.nav.

14. Johnson, "Breakfast Standards and So Much More."

15. Stephanie Larkin, "What Makes the Starbucks Coffee Experience Special," quoting
Howard Schulz, http://www.starbucks.com/about-us/our-heritage; http://www.streetdirec
tory.com/food_editorials/beverages/coffee/what_makes_the_starbucks_coffee_experience
_special.html.

16. Patricia Turner, "Church's Fried Chicken and The Klan: A Rhetorical Analysis of
Rumor in the Black Community," *Western Folklore* 46 (1987): 305.

17. Lynne Olver, "Cafeterias," http://www.foodtimeline.org/restaurants.html#cafeterias,
quoting Cecelia Rasmussen, "LA Then and Now," *Los Angeles Times*, November 22, 1998, B3.

18. Hunter Oatman-Stanford, "L.A.'s Wildest Cafeteria Served Utopian Fantasy with a
Side of Enchiladas," *Collector's Weekly*, February 13, 2014. Clifton's was also unusual for its
time in that the owner, Clifford Clinton, welcomed African American patrons as well as
whites. He wrote, "If colored skin is a passport to death for our liberties, then it is a passport
to Clifton's." http://www.collectorsweekly.com/articles/cliftons-brookdale-cafeteria.

19. Olver, "Cafeterias."

20. Charles Johnson, http://articles.chicagotribune.com/2013-04-18/features/ct-dining
-0418-home-plate-valois-20130418_1_hyde-park-bank-dining-room-eggs.

21. In a 2012 YouTube interview with Zennie Abraham, the owner says they served
3,000 people for free the day Obama was elected. https://www.youtube.com/watch?v
=AoCHeeCbahE.

22. Video interviews with local residents in 2012, http://www.myfoxchicago.com/clip/
7930767/Obama%20supporters%20in%20Hyde%20Park%20celebrate%20re-election%20

with%20free%20breakfast%20at%20; and Linda Qiu, "Valois Hands Out Meals Fit for a President," *Chicago Maroon*, http://chicagomaroon.com/2012/11/09/valois-hands-out -meals-fit-for-a-president.

23. Nancy Stone, photo, *Chicago Tribune*, November 7, 2012, http://galleries.apps.chicago tribune.com/chi-photos-election-day-after-20121107/#chi-ilelect7eggs-20121107.

24. Qiu, *Chicago Maroon*, http://chicagomaroon.com/2012/11/09/valois-hands-out-meals -fit-for-a-president.

25. www.foodtimeline.org.presidents.html.

26. Duneier, 90.

27. DNAinfo, "President Obama Has Bacon for Breakfast at Valois Restaurant," http:// www.dnainfo.com/chicago/20140523/hyde-park/president-obama-has-bacon-hashbrowns -for-breakfast-at-valois-restaurant. 2014.

28. James Grossman, "Great Migration," *Electronic Encyclopedia of Chicago History*, 2005, http://www.encyclopedia.chicagohistory.org/pages/545.html.

29. Dominic Pacyga, "South Side," *Electronic Encyclopedia of Chicago History*, 2005, http://www.encyclopedia.chicagohistory.org/pages/1177.htm.

30. Michael Twitty carefully explicates the much longer history of soul food in his review of several works on soul food, including Adrian Miller's *Soul Food: The Surprising Story of an American Cuisine, One Plate at a Time*, http://prospect.org/article/ soul-foods-contested-history.

31. Henry Haller, *The White House Family Cookbook* (New York: Random House, 1987), 229–30, quoted by Lynn Olver, www.foodtimeline.org/presidents.html.

32. Adrian Miller, "African American Cooks in the White House. Hiding in Plain Sight," *Washington Post*, June 3, 2014.

33. "School Breakfast Program," Food Action and Research Center, 2010, http://frac.org/ federal-foodnutrition-programs/school-breakfast-program/.

34. Recent trends and fads have focused on the dangers of trans fats and on coffee with unsalted grass fed butter. See "Americans Are Eating More Butter Now Than They Have in the Past 40 Years," http://www.huffingtonpost.com/2014/01/10/butter-consumption_n_4568064.html; and Lisa Elaine Held, "Why Wellness Experts Are Putting Butter in Their Coffee," *Prevention*, www.prevention.com/food/healthy-eating-tips/ why-wellness-experts-are-putting-butter-their-coffee.

35. Michelle Roth, "Greek Diners: How Greeks Have Kept Traditional and Americanized Greek Foodways Alive in American Diners," MA thesis, George Mason University, 2014, 33, http://digilib.gmu.edu/jspui/bitstream/1920/9090/1/Roth_thesis_2014.pdfhttp://digilib.gmu .edu/xmlui/handle/1920/9090?show=full.

36. Duneier, 90.

37. Ibid.

38. Ibid. 91.

39. Jason P., Yelp, February 16, 2012, http://www.yelp.com/biz/valois-chicago?hrid=Ggysr 42G6ky6QRNw841FZQ&rh_type=attribute&rh_ident=BusinessAcceptsCreditCards.no.

40. http://365southchicago.com/2011/03/01/60-valois-restaurant/; Pinterest, https://www.pinterest.com/pin/87398048994128535/.

41. Tracy Poe, "Foodways," *Electronic Encyclopedia of Chicago History*, www.encyclopedia.chicagohistory.org/pages/470.html.

42. Janet Gilmore, "Wisconsin's Friday Night Fish Fry Tradition," *Classic Wisconsin*, 2007, http://www.classicwisconsin.com/features/fridaynightfish.html.

43. "Soul Food: A Brief History," http://www.aaregistry.org/historic_events/view/soul-food-brief-history.

44. Cynthia T., Yelp, August 3, 2014, http://www.yelp.com/biz/valois-chicago?hrid=Ggysr42G6ky6QRNw841FZQ&rh_type=attribute&rh_ident=BusinessAcceptsCreditCards.no.

45. A. J. S., Yelp, http://www.yelp.com/biz/valois-chicago?hrid=Ggysr42G6ky6QRNw841FZQ&rh_type=attribute&rh_ident=BusinessAcceptsCreditCards.no.11/27/2012.

Going for Doughboys in Little Rhody: Class, Place, and Nostalgia

Alicia Kristen

"Going for doughboys" is a Rhode Island summer tradition, and if one is already driving all the way to the ocean, a lunchtime meal of clam cakes and clam chowder is the perfect accompaniment to the sweet fried dough treat. "Little Rhody" is a small state framed on three sides by Connecticut and Massachusetts. The fourth side features bays that reach all the way into the middle of the state and create 420 miles of coastline in a state with only 1,214 square miles of area, a proportion that gives Rhode Island its nickname "the Ocean State." In spite of this, urban congestion and Rhode Islanders' conceptions of driving distances mean that for most families, going to the ocean is a holiday.

As a child celebrating summer on Rhode Island's northernmost beaches, I would enlist a crew of children to produce "doughboys" of sand. When I asked other children to help me make these imaginary doughboys, or offered them to people passing by, there were no questions about how to make these imitation treats or why they looked the way they did. We took them for granted because they are a place-based food to which our Rhode Island heritage has accustomed us through the shared tradition of "going for doughboys." Later in life, if we relayed stories of making doughboys of sand and someone from outside the area asked what doughboys were, we would take pride in explaining the complexity of their identity. In this way, the ability to recognize the "doughboy" form and the associated summer tradition of "going for doughboys" serves as a marker of insider identity and cultural pride.

The identity marked by association with doughboys may be "Rhode Islander" but more specifically, it demarcates the inland working-class Rhode Islanders who make up the majority of the state's population. The tie to class is intrinsic to the comfort value of going for doughboys; higher-class Newport residents do not have doughboy stands. Residents of southern Rhode Island, the part featured in most travel guides, typically come from similar ethnicities (French, Italian, English) but a higher class. Within a thirty-mile drive of the Newport mansions, the beacon of Rhode Island's coastal gentry, you would not find a beach stand dedicated to doughboys and clam cakes. While the foodways of clambakes may originate on the coast, the tradition of going for doughboys is rather a journey from mill cities to the nearest coast, seeking comfort in the holiday with other working-class Rhode Islanders.

Going for doughboys is thus a tradition that marks doughboys as comfort food due to a place/class context. My research deviates from current threads of scholarship on identity and comfort food in several ways. Raman discusses the importance of food in immigration;[1] while this is relevant to my study, it perpetuates a focus on ethnicity. In my study, I draw from Neustadt and Long to demonstrate how ethnic heritage plays a part in the making of the tradition, but ultimately the tradition outgrows ethnicity;[2] rather, it serves as a class-based holiday that provides "anchors" (the Rhode Island state flag!) to maintain the *Rhode Islander* identity.[3] While Locher et al.'s description of comfort foods[4] is apt in terms of anchors, nostalgia, and the connection of comfort foods to positive social experiences, they argue that one common criterion of comfort food is that it is experienced alone. I would argue that the *way* doughboys meet all other criteria of comfort foods is through their enjoyment with others. The complexity of the tradition warrants that I explore the food itself as a place-based food and the historical contexts that shape the anti-hegemonic Rhode Islander identity.[5] From the mill towns of Rhode Island to the historic amusement parks of the coasts, I aim to take you on a journey for doughboys that demonstrates the importance of community interactions in this comfort food tradition.

What Are Doughboys?

In Rhode Island, we call two distinct foods "doughboys." I am writing about fried-dough balls unique to Rhode Island, so I will refer to those as *doughboys*. Vendors in Rhode Island also sell the wide, plate-shaped fried dough that my friends throughout the country know as fried dough under signs reading "doughboys"; to distinguish between the two, I will call that product, even in its Rhode Island context, *fried dough*. Fried dough is about eight inches wide and one inch thick. It is bubbly with a golden crust and doughy on the inside; vendors serve fried dough on plates and offer granulated sugar, powdered sugar, and cinnamon/sugar in shakers to sprinkle on top. Doughboys are distinct from many fried-dough foods, such as funnel cakes and elephant ears, sold in other regions in that the dough is not at all sweet and they are never topped with powdered sugar.[6]

If Rhode Islanders talk about eating doughboys, they generally mean the doughboys available exclusively in Rhode Island, not the fried dough described above. Rhode Islanders primarily get these summer-time treats from Iggy's Doughboys and Chowder house; as such, they use "Iggy's doughboys" as a proprietary eponym, similar to how the brand names Kleenex, Band-Aid, and Frisbee are used to refer to product forms rather than to the specific brand. For doughboys, the use of a proprietary eponym is significant because it is localized to the Iggy's Doughboys restaurant on Oakland Beach. Saltzman describes how "the taste—or at least the image—of such place-[named] foods is integrally related to their preparation style and the place where they originated and cannot be separated."[7] Iggy's makes doughboys out of two-inch (roughly shaped) balls of fried dough and serves them in a paper bag filled with granulated sugar in which to coat them. As my grandmother fondly recalls: "Some looked like fat cows, some had long necks we'd crunch off!"[8] Some people describe their dense texture as comparable to *beignets* or donut holes. A Rhode Islander would describe them as nearly identical to *clam cakes*, a spherical fried-dough food with clam juice and pieces of clams mixed in. My father has made both clam cakes and doughboys out of white bread dough from local bakeries and found the texture about right, though he found issues with the authenticity of making and eating this place-based food at home.[9]

Although Iggy's doughboys may have a distinct form, that form has changed over time. Originally, they were smooth balls glazed in honey-sugar syrup. Three generations of my family know them as irregularly shaped spheres shaken in a paper bag with sugar. Current images from the Iggy's website show them as slightly flattened, formed into consistent square shapes. These changes have occurred with relatively little commentary, perhaps because the significance of doughboys lies more in the traditions surrounding them than in their form.

Place, History, and Tradition

Today, there are a handful of food establishments serving what Rhode Islanders deem as quality doughboys. Until a decade ago, however, Rhode Islanders across the state congregated at just two locations: Oakland Beach and Rocky Point.

At Oakland Beach, people wait in long lines in front of Iggy's Doughboys. This beach stand/restaurant originated as Mrs. Gus's Doughboys and Pizza in 1940, where it sold 20 million doughboys[10] until it was purchased in 1989 by Gus's employee Gaetano Gravino and was remade into Iggy's Doughboys and Chowder house.[11] Freida Gus brought the tradition from Neapolis, Lakonia, Greece, having consumed Greek doughnuts coated in honeyed sugar as a little girl in 1907.[12] She may have named them "doughboys" after a contemporary type of English dumpling resembling the modern donut to make them sound more familiar to the "Yankee" Rhode Islanders of English heritage. The beach stand came at a time of economic depression for Oakland Beach; the heyday of the Oakland Beach amusement park in the 1920s had passed. The hurricane of 1938 wrecked the small resort, originally designed as a more affordable and accessible alternative for working-class families to experience amusements at the coast.[13] Before the pieces could be picked up, World War II and the hurricane of 1954 struck the area.[14] The beach stand was one of the few structures that remained, and when the city of Warwick decided to maintain the beach as a simple picnicking park, the beach stand became the primary attraction; families who had traditionally made annual trips to the Oakland Beach amusement park started "going for doughboys" instead.

Rocky Point Amusement Park, just three miles down the road, had also been wrecked by the hurricane of 1938 but reopened in 1948 to begin its Golden Years.[15] Rocky Point clam dinners, which had been occurring since before the turn of the century, drew thousands of Rhode Islanders, all seated in one large dining hall. A meal at Rocky Point consisted of "unlimited" red clam chowder, clam cakes, doughboys, lobster for those of who could afford the pricier ticket, and steamers to take home for another meal. Until the turn of the twenty-first century, Rocky Point was the only competitor to the Oakland Beach stand for "authentic" Rhode Island doughboys. They served the niche of festival rather than family outing destination. Unfortunately, Rocky Point closed entirely in 1995, ending the tradition of Rocky Point clam dinners and making more room for clam dinners in the context of small restaurant dining.

My great-grandmother lived just down the street from Iggy's and Rocky Point during the beginning of the twentieth century and began our family's practice of going every year for clam cakes and doughboys. My father mentioned how Rhode Islanders would not normally drive so far (about fifteen miles) for a lunch, but by the time he was a boy, eating at Iggy's and Rocky Point had become a popular way for Rhode Islanders to mark the summer season, similar to making wreaths around Christmastime.[16] The menu bears resemblance to the nineteenth-century clambakes, described by modern participants as "a kind of summer Thanksgiving, 'bigger than Christmas.'"[17] Perhaps the reason that the Rocky Point drew enough patrons to fill the "World's Largest" 4,000-person capacity dining hall was that it provided access to a Rhode Island clam-themed summer holiday that inland, working-class Rhode Islanders had not previously experienced as part of their heritage.[18]

Clambakes and Ethnic Heritage

Clam cakes and doughboys go hand in hand, yet how did these two foods—nearly identical yet one savory and one sweet—come together? The origin is hard to come across, since Rhode Islanders write far more about their family experiences with doughboys than about the historical context. A few bloggers claim that doughboys began in either Italian pizzerias or Portuguese bakeries. Don Yoder points out that "viewed historically, each regional and national cuisine is a culinary hybrid, with an elaborate stratigraphy of diverse historical layers combined into a usable and evidently satisfying structure."[19] I will attempt to dig into just a few of the deep and obscure history of doughboys to uncover some of their cultural significance.

Gus's originally sold doughboys alongside pizza, not clam cakes, and their sticky glaze made them reminiscent of Italian *zeppoles*. The three decades preceding the founding of Gus's saw the immigration of Italian immigrants to Rhode Island skyrocket, tripling the Italian American population in the state the first ten years and resulting in a current demographic of 20 percent Italian American ancestry.[20] The immigrants were mainly farmers from southern Italy who came to work in the mills of Providence, Pawtucket, and the surrounding cities. One district of Providence is so concentrated in Italian Americans that the traffic lines down the middle of the street are painted after the flag of Italy, as if *festa* is occurring year-round.[21] The proximity of Greece and southern Italy make it no surprise that the doughboys that Mrs. Gus introduced from her heritage were a hit with working-class Rhode Islanders, many of whom would recognize the treat as the zeppoles of home.

In the mid-twentieth century, another ethnic group suddenly surged. Portuguese whalers and their families had been moving to Rhode Island since 1880, joining Rhode Island "Yankees" (of colonial English heritage) in coastal professions.[22] Shortly after Gus's began to take off, Portuguese immigrants settled throughout New England coastal towns, leading to Rhode Island currently having the highest percentage of Portuguese Americans of any state in the nation.

Iggy's Doughboys sign. Courtesy Courtney Roberts.

The exchange of foodways between the Portuguese settlers and Rhode Island Yankees was inevitable. Portuguese settlers joined in the traditional clambakes with "good feelings between the two groups."[23] In combination with the Italian immigrants, they created the doughboy accompaniment of Rhode Island clam chowder (clear chowder with a tomato-flavored broth). This preceded the drastically different red Manhattan clam chowder, which is more like tomato/vegetable soup with clams in it.[24] During clambakes, the women all cook together as the men tend the fire, allowing for integration through the gendered division of ethnicity-based clusters.[25] In addition to learning New England clambake foodways, Portuguese women brought their own ethnic foodways with them. Bakeries throughout the region sell a treat called *malasadas*, which are spheres of dense fried dough coated in granulated sugar.

When Gus's became Iggy's in the 1980s, the menu changed. Instead of selling pizza with doughboys resembling an Italian dessert (zeppoles, with their sticky glaze), Iggy's sold clambake foods with doughboys resembling the Portuguese dessert called malasadas. The texture and preparation of malasadas is so similar to clam cakes (exchanging the clam interior for a sugar coating) that we can imagine a Portuguese woman recognizing the similar form and introducing malasadas as a desert for clambakes; it could be that Iggy's merely commercialized that foodway.

Alternatively, the Portuguese bakeries may have preserved the tradition of malasadas through the middle of the twenty-first century, and Iggy's is responsible for joining together the Portuguese foodways of clambakes and malasadas as the new owners sought a recipe with which to continue producing the sugary fried-dough treat known as doughboys. This would have been a result of what Lucy Long describes as "menu selection," or the intentional creation of a menu to represent a cultural cuisine, celebrating a perceived shared identity.[26] While most Rhode Islanders today know doughboy as a local food divorced from heritage cuisines, those who travel outside the state bring context to their experience that confirms the correlation. In a comment on the Yelp profile for Iggy's, Karen C. writes, "Two years ago, I went to Hawaii and ate Leonard's pillowy malasadas. They are heavenly squares of fried dough covered in powdered sugar or cinnamon sugar. So good . . . I returned to Newport mourning the loss of these confections from my life. We're in Narragansett a few weeks ago and decide to finally try the famous Iggy's Doughboys. I wish we had ventured off the island and tried them earlier! Who knew doughboys are essentially akin to malasadas?!! To think that I could have been enjoying these heavenly pieces of fried dough years earlier, makes me so sad . . ." Even though Karen identifies as a Rhode Islander, not as a Portuguese American, she could recognize how distinctly similar doughboys are to malasadas. (Note also that she originates from Newport; her origin in this region perhaps explains why she had until that point missed out on the Rhode Island working-class tradition of going for doughboys.)

The integration of ethnic foods representing dominant immigrant populations with the regional foodways of clambakes would explain why the consumption of doughboys cooked in the same oil as the clam cakes form a summer ritual that unites diverse Rhode Islanders. The original form of the Oakland Beach doughboys catered to Italian Americans, the form that my family recalls catered to Portuguese Americans, and today doughboys are coming close to resembling the treats that friends across the country recognize as fried dough. They have come so far from their original honeyed form that anything in their coating besides sugar is "possibly a bit blasphemous."[27] In this way, the form that current generations recognize from their childhood memories is the one that they uphold as the epitome of "authentic" Rhode Island doughboys.

Celebrating summer by participating in a Rocky Point clam dinner or making a trip to Iggy's Doughboys was also a way for large immigrant populations to gather and celebrate a product of their food heritage. The experience provided at Rocky Point and Oakland Beach parallels that of the Catskills resorts described by Saltzman: "Going to the Catskills was about returning year after year to an idealized and recreated version of home and holiday time, complete with all the familiar food you could ever want."[28] Similarly, immigrant populations traveling from central Rhode Island to the coast could spend their vacation time taking comfort in the familiarity of zeppoles or malasadas while simultaneously enjoying the exotic clam-based foods of New England. In this way, doughboys are a place-based food grounded in the enactment of traditions that emphasize both insider identity and tourism.

A Place-Based Food

Doughboys are clearly place-based foods, even though they do not meet some common assumptions about the criteria of such. Saltzman defines place-based foods as having some combination of characteristics including being artisan prepared, having a heritage basis, and having ingredients grown in a particular locale.[29] While they are not made by a particular artisan, their authenticity is validated by the establishment from which they are obtained. Doughboys are made locally and most likely derive from local ethnic heritages, yet references to their origins are obscure and rarely mentioned. Their ingredients are not particularly local, and thus they are not affected by the soil of Rhode Island, but that is not to say their taste is not influenced by place. They are crafted on the coast and take on the smell of Oakland Beach (different from a generic "ocean" scent), and since they are cooked in the same oil as the clam cakes, they have a hint of the flavor of locally harvested clams. The relationship to the ocean was key to the authenticity of food sold at beach stands, reinforced by the sign at Gus's reading: "The fish that you ate at Gus's today, slept last night in Narraganset Bay."[30] In this way, the location, in addition to the preparation style, influences the taste.[31]

Doughboys made at home (on rare occasions, out of nostalgia for summer, and without qualifying as part of the summer ritual) are "inauthentic" in their taste, a distinction that may not be noticed by outsiders. When I asked my grandmother about doughboys, she immediately said she could not tell me much because they were not something she usually made at home.[32] My father and I discussed how online reviewers of the restaurants would compare clam cakes to fritters or hush puppies, and identify doughboys as "just" fried dough. In this way, although the flavor is noticeably distinct, outsiders may not be attuned enough to recognize the *terroir* of doughboys. The sugar (a global commodity) may mask that distinction. My grandmother, suffering from memory loss, thought at first that the doughboys must have been made of sweeter dough than the clam cakes, since they were deep-fried together but tasted so different. My grandfather reminded her that the only difference was the exclusion of clams and the inclusion of a sugar coating.[33] I found it interesting that, in her decades outside of Rhode Island, she recalled the similarity between doughboys and clam cakes in the flavor of the dough but tried to reconcile it with a reinterpretation of how they were made. This demonstrates that the terroir of doughboys is unusual because doughboys are basically a savory food made sweet only by a sugary coating that partially masks the local flavors.

"Going for Doughboys"

As described earlier, part of what makes doughboys special is the tradition surrounding them. Here, I will describe my family's experience in a way that reflects commonalities I have learned through informal descriptions of other families' experiences.

My entire family of six aligned our schedules to take a full-day trip to the beach, packing our van with coolers of snacks and refreshments for the hot humid summer and dressing in beach clothes that had been packed away all winter. After getting out of the car and lathering each other in sunblock, we headed to Iggy's for either lunch or dinner.

At Iggy's, we would begin with the savory foods, saving the doughboy desserts for last. Everyone individually decided if they wanted red or white clam chowder; as a vegetarian, I preferred the clearer red chowder so I could pick out the tasty chowder potatoes without accidentally eating clams. Our parents ordered enough bags of clam cakes to be sure everyone would get their fill. As we were finishing the meal, my dad would order the doughboys, bringing them back to the table hot within their paper bag. As children, we delighted in shaking the bag vigorously, and as we grew older, we developed techniques for maximally coating the doughboys in sugar by shaking them in a way that didn't jostle off sugar that was already stuck. Shaking the doughboys was a way in which a child could use a developing skill to serve the family and demonstrate cultural growth. Saltzman describes how, "using the wrong fork or spoon at a formal dinner, adding soy sauce to homemade (Jewish) chicken soup, serving beer in crystal glasses at a picnic, or not knowing how to use chopsticks at a traditional Chinese meal (or using them for Thai food) clearly marks one as an outsider, one who does not know the rules for culturally appropriate behavior."[34] When *Phantom Gourmet*, a regional food review show, did a three-minute segment on Iggy's, an entire minute was dedicated to the shaking of the bag (with names like "straight shake" and "flip-flop" for the different methods).[35] Rhode Islanders can identify cultural outsiders by comparing their age to their progress toward the best shaking techniques.

After shaking the doughboys, we would each take one from the bag and head for the beach to pick out a location to lay our beach towels where they would not get trampled, close enough to the water that our parents could protect our intertidal sandcastles from rascals if we went rock-climbing on jetties or played pirates on the playground, but far enough that we could linger all day without worrying about the incoming tides.

A Cultural Marker

Doughboys embedded within the context of an outing at Oakland Beach leave many ways to distinguish between insiders and outsiders. The coarse granite sand requires a special finesse for castle-building. Clam cakes are best plain, can be dipped in chowder if desired, but should not be eaten with tartar sauce. Steamers (clams) should be dipped in butter while holding the "neck" so you can pull off the gross black casing as you eat them. The sum of these learned behaviors results in "Rhode Islander" as an ethnic identity. Kalčik describes how "the continuity of ethnic groups depends on the maintenance of boundaries between groups."[36] The identity of Rhode Islander is thus created in three ways: 1) by emphasizing details of difference within the food, 2) by emphasizing the significance of place and traditions surrounding the food, and 3) through participation in rites of inclusion that only Rhode Islanders can share as long-held memories.

When outsiders hear about doughboys, their impulse is to learn what doughboys are through similarities and divergences to foods familiar to them. One of the ways outsiders separate themselves is by redefining doughboys as "just fried dough" or comparing them to other regional fried-dough foods. A Rhode Islander would correct an outsider by describing Iggy's doughboys. Emphasizing contrast with similar foods is part of how Rhode Islanders define ourselves; we take pride in clarifying to outsiders the meaning of doughboys, coffee milk (a locally produced milk flavor, not milk in coffee), Del's frozen lemonade (lemonade served as crushed ice), frappes (a type of milkshake), grinders (a type of sub sandwich), and steamers (clams). In a verbal exchange, Rhode Islanders would reject the simplified definitions I just provided. We describe doughboys on their own terms, and when someone replies, "Oh, so it is like fried dough?" we solidify our sense of identity by explaining, "No, not exactly, because ..." This discursive behavior emphasizes details of difference and the difficulty of translating those differences.

The tendency to redefine regional foods in terms of a more "universal" norm could be seen as an act of hegemony, and Rhode Islanders subvert hegemony by emphasizing the importance of place. Cultural hegemony occurs when the worldview of a dominant group is imposed as the universal norm, lowering the status of deviant worldviews. Culinary tourists who write online reviews describe their experience in terms of food quality, taste, and aesthetics. When they equate doughboys to "comparable" fried-dough foods, they foster hegemony by lowering the status of doughboys.[37] After all, if doughboys are, as numerous Midwestern reviewers claim, "just fried dough" or merely a type of beignet, how are they significant or valuable? These discursive techniques establish one food as the norm and point of comparison and the other food as "other." Sometimes, the bias is not clear until the reverse statement is proposed: fried dough (sold at fairs and festivals across the country) is *just* a doughboy that is larger and flatter. People from other regions might take offense at that statement, since it implies that doughboys are the most authentic form and the fried dough that they grew up with is deviant and substandard.

Rather than argue on behalf of doughboys as a form, resident Rhode Islanders subvert that hegemony indirectly by emphasizing the importance of place. Yelp reviewer Briana G. writes of Iggy's Doughboys: "Oakland beach is not the nicest of beaches and you certainly cannot swim in it, but it's a great place to enjoy a meal! I love sitting out in the sun by the water, it's great except for the devil seagulls that want your doughboy as badly as you do. Speaking of which, their doughboys are delicious!" She begins by mentioning place before sharing insider knowledge that other insiders would identify with from their experiences: the declining cultural status of Oakland Beach (in terms of "niceness"), the frequent announcements from state officials about closing the beach for swimming (due to algae blooms and storm water runoff), and the conflicts between beachgoers and sea gulls (unfamiliar to Midwestern visitors, for example). The fact that she does not actually describe the doughboys or contextualize them within a meal is significant. To any insider, such information is a given; it would be as preposterous for her to define doughboys as it would be for me to have defined pizza earlier in this chapter. Through this discursive technique, she undermines any notion of doughboys as exotic or "other."

Clearly there are similarities between doughboys and fried dough, but as Saltzman describes, "foods have different meanings for insiders and outsiders. Such foods are not necessarily the same ones with which outsiders are familiar or, if they are, they are often made in more traditional ways, with special ingredients and for different purposes."[38] To Rhode Islanders, the context of "going for doughboys" is critical; it represents a multi-generational tradition of celebrating summer at the coast. In 1980, the *Providence Journal* described an example of a Rhode Islander's experience: "The shore dinner that Abe Samuels of Pawtucket ate when he was a boy is no different than today's. He is 85 and remembers when Rocky Point was a place where as many as 75,000 people went for the day."[39] By that estimate, the number of people congregating in that one place on that one day equaled about one-tenth of Rhode Island's population! Saltzman argues that "the sense of unity created by sharing food is so significant and recognizable that it figures centrally in many rites of inclusion."[40] The opportunity for thousands of Rhode Islanders to partake in the tradition creates an opportunity for memories shared by an immense number of diverse Rhode Islanders.

Tourism

The trajectory I have outlined (doughboys as an ethnic heritage food that became a regional identity marker) is a common foodway narrative, but to call it the complete story would be a gross simplification. Jones writes: "Some researchers have retreated from the complexity of contemporary eating behavior in America, preferring to investigate customs historically among allegedly isolated rural and ethnic groups, [not] realizing that Americans eat what they do, prepared as it is and served and consumed on certain occasions in particular ways for a multiplicity of reasons."[41] I would add to this argument that part of the joy of research is in identifying the complex causalities that perhaps formed the foundation for current behaviors and beliefs, but if we are to look at the foodway of "going for doughboys," as folklorists we must also step back and include the most surface-level perceptions of the people who practice the tradition.

For Rhode Islanders, going for doughboys is an opportunity to do something special each year: to eat foods outside of the everyday menu in a place that is different from their everyday environments. In this way, Rhode Islanders are also food tourists: they are inlanders experiencing the coastal cuisine as outsiders. Gary Nabhan calls the area the "Clambake Foodshed" because inland residents have been flocking to the coast to consume clams since the clambakes of the mid-nineteenth century.[42] In this case, the watershed metaphor is especially apt as Rhode Islanders flow on roads that follow rivers to their outlet in the Narragansett Bay. The flow is also unidirectional, in the sense that after the inlanders flock to the coast for clam cakes and doughboys, they generally do not bring these traditions back to their inland communities.

Valene Smith defines a tourist as "a temporarily leisured person who voluntarily visits a place far away from home for the purpose of experiencing a change."[43] The Clambake Foodshed has seen three major phases of interior tourism: the coastal resorts and clambakes, the large amusement parks and community dinners, and now the family outings to small local beach stands and restaurants. Each phase also drew its fair share of outsiders, but it is important to recognize that from the mid-nineteenth century to the present, Rocky Point and Oakland Beach have served primarily Rhode Islanders. While Oakland Beach does not seem very far, it was out of the reach of mill workers until public transportation was developed, and even then only accessible on vacations. For working-class Rhode Islanders, it was far enough and different enough to seem like a holiday. Most importantly, the resorts and amusement parks of Rocky Point and Oakland Beach offered the right vibe: "Resort vacations were and are holidays. Such events are by nature brief and characterized by playfulness, excess, and exaggeration of various aspects of everyday life. Such festive occasions, like those at resorts, often included singing, playing music, and dancing; playing games and talking into the night; wearing leisure or special clothes, drinking, and of course, eating generous amounts of specially prepared food . . . resort owners were able to emphasize that food was and is such a crucial part of family celebrations and, by extension, the resort experience."[44]

Coastal establishments performed holidays every day by providing gaudy amusements and, most importantly, cheap food in plentiful amounts. Saltzman describes how "even if resorts offered rather sparse amenities in the early days, there was always plenty to eat."[45] Recall that the Rocky Point clam dinners were all you can eat, which must have been quite the joy to working-class families who struggled the rest of the year to put food on the table. Most importantly, the coastal cuisine provided an "authentic" Rhode Island meal because it utilized local ingredients and clambake foodways; in this way, the Portuguese or Greek heritages became forgotten, replaced by symbolic construction of the cuisine as unique to Rhode Island.[46]

Tourism does occur from outside the state and the region. The Iggy's website states: "Iggy's customers are not only the locals that come down regularly, but they also consist of individuals from all over. Many of Iggy's most loyal customers are the ones that have moved out of state. When they come back to visit they make sure they get a taste of Rhode Island's best!"[47] Similarly, the mass of people at Rocky Point clam dinners were not exclusively nearby residents. In this way, outsiders can experience what it is like to be a Rhode Islander, and former residents can re-enact what it means to be a Rhode Islander, as they experience a family tradition through tourism.

Tourism to the coast by Rhode Islanders cemented the clam-based and doughboy foodways through popular memory, in spite of hurricanes and economic disasters. As the popularity of doughboys spreads, however, the tradition perhaps loses some of its more specific characteristics to the pressures of commercialization.[48] When I was a child, vendors purchased fried dough carts and replaced the sign with one reading "doughboys." They sold the plate-sized fried dough I described earlier, which lacked the terroir of Oakland Beach, the heritage-derived form, and the proper context of consumption alongside clam-based foods on an ocean holiday trip. Today, Iggy's sells their doughboy mix in bags to be made at home. Their doughboys have become flatter, with a smooth-edged square shape. Did the influx of tourists from across the country cause them to change the form to something more akin to fried dough, or is the new form just part of the continuum of transformation doughboys have experienced?

To expand on this research and understand the transformations of the experience of going for doughboys, I might implement the methodology of "food mapping" as described by Lidia Marte, in which visuals (including hand-drawn maps and photographs of food and places) are generated as mini-ethnographies that trace foods through cultural contexts.[49] For this chapter, my methods included ethnographic fieldwork, in which I interviewed tradition-bearers in my own family and in friends. I also included the volunteered perspectives of online contributors to blogs and travel sites to supplement the historical perspective provided by other researchers. In some ways, I began food mapping when I searched through photos (online and from my family) that matched the experience I remembered. I came with a distinct impression of how Oakland Beach was organized, both internally and within the larger context of Rhode Island travel, and analyzing my impressions gave me leads on perspectives of Rhode Islander's that I could interview about. Food mapping with other Rhode Islanders would only increase these leads and result in more insights about how gender, class, and ethnicity shape the relationships to doughboys as a comfort food gained through small-scale food tourism.

The tradition of "going for doughboys" defines the summer experience of Rhode Islanders. The ability of Rhode Islanders to identify doughboys not just in terms of their form but their entire traditional context serves as a cultural marker by which Rhode Islanders can distinguish outsiders and take pride in their shared identity. Rhode Islanders pick up on the smells of the beach that give doughboys terroir, recognizing intuitively that clam-based meals and doughboys go hand-in-hand. Doughboys also are exclusive to the Clambake Foodshed because of the historical exchange of ethnic foodways among settlers from England, Greece, Italy, and Portugal, but they are not only defined by place—instead, they define place. Many Rhode Islanders hate to go a summer without "going for doughboys" at Oakland Beach, in spite of the concerns about water quality. The presence of doughboys on the coast fills people with memories of tastes and smells, providing them with a shared tradition for celebrating summer as Rhode Islanders. Iggy's acknowledges the role that the establishment plays in performing the summer holiday for Rhode Islanders in their TV commercial quip: "Come to Iggy's today at our year-round location in Warwick. A Rhode Island tradition—remember: it's always summer at Iggy's."[50]

Notes

1. Parvathi Raman, "'Me in Place, and the Place in Me': A Migrant's Tale of Food, Home and Belonging," *Food, Culture, and Society* 14 (2011): 165–80.

2. Lucy M. Long, "Culinary Tourism: A Folkloristic Perspective on Eating and Otherness," in *Culinary Tourism*, ed. Lucy Long (Lexington: University Press of Kentucky, 2004), 20–50; and Kathy Neustadt, "'Born among the Shells': The Quakers of Allen's Neck and Their Clambake," in *"We Gather Together": Food and Festival in American Life*, eds. Theodore C. Humphrey and Lin T. Humphrey (Ann Arbor, MI: UMI Press, 1988), 89–110.

3. Rachelle H. Saltzman, "Identity and Food," in *Food Issues: An Encyclopedia*, ed. Ken Albala (Thousand Oaks, CA: Sage Publications, in press).

4. Julie L. Locher, William C. Yoels, Donna Maurer, and Jillian Van Ells, "Comfort Foods: An Exploratory Journey into the Social and Emotional Significance of Food," *Food & Foodways* 13 (2005): 273–97.

5. Saltzman, "Identity and Food"; Susan Kalčik, "Ethnic Foodways in America: Symbol and Performance of Identity," in *Ethnic and Regional Foodways in the United States: The Performance of Group Identity*, eds. Linda Kelly Brown and Kay Mussell (Knoxville: University of Tennessee Press, 1984), 37–65; and Long, "Culinary Tourism."

6. Doughboy Recipe. Ingredients: 2 eggs, 1/2 tsp. salt, 1 tbsp. sugar, 1/2 c. milk, 2 c. flour, 2 tsp. baking powder, 4 cups of sunflower oil. Substitute with oil of choice, but be sure it has a high smoke point. Also, for more "authenticity" use oil that previously was used to cook clam cakes! 1) Combine all ingredients. 2) Fill a medium size paper bag with sugar. 3) Heat the vegetable oil in pot to about 375 F. Be sure it does not get below 350 F or above 400 F. A good starting temperature is 360 F. Oil that is too hot or cakes which are too large will cause burning or uncooked centers. Adjust temperature up or down slightly to compensate. 4) Tear off 1" diameter pieces of dough. No need to work it into a smooth ball, but you might smoosh in any dangling pieces so you do not end up with crumbles in the oil as you scrape it off your fingers and drop it into the oil. 5) The doughboys will float; turn them over gently as they rise to cook fully both sides. Do not overload the cooker, as this will reduce heat too much. Fry only a few at a time. 6) Cook until dark golden brown on the outside, then remove with

slotted spoon and let dry on a broiler pan. 7) Every six or so, drop them in the paper bag and shake to coat them in sugar.

7. Rachelle H. Saltzman, "Rites of Intensification: Eating and Ethnicity in the Catskills," in *Culinary Tourism*, ed. Lucy Long (Lexingon: University Press of Kentucky, 2004), 97–113.

8. Gramma and Grampa Roberts, discussion with the author, March 3 2014.

9. David M. Roberts, discussion with the author, February 10, 2014.

10. J. Rengigas, "Mrs. Gus's Doughboys: Originator of the Oakland Beach Doughboys Est. 1940," 2014, http://mrsgussdoughboys.com/

11. Iggy's Doughboys, 2014, www.iggysdoughboys.com.

12. Rengigas, "Mrs. Gus's Doughboys."

13. Donald A. D'Amato, *Warwick: A City at Crossroads* (Charleston, SC: Arcadia Publishing, 2001), 98.

14. Rengigas, "Mrs. Gus's Doughboys."

15. "Park History," *Theme Park Page: Rocky Point*, 2014.

16. David M. Roberts, discussion with the author, February 9, 2014.

17. Neustadt, "'Born among the Shells,'" 96.

18. Joseph Giblin, "Bigger Than 'World's Largest': 4,000-Seat Shore Pavilion Being Built at Rocky Point," *Providence Journal*, March 27, 1955, 19.

19. Don Yoder, "Folk Cookery," in *Folklore and Folklife*, ed. Richard M. Dorson (Chicago: University of Chicago Press, 1972), 334.

20. D'Amato, *Warwick: A City at Crossroads*, 100.

21. Eliot Singer, "Conversion through Foodways Enculturation: The Meaning of Eating in an American Hindu Sect," in *Ethnic and Regional Foodways in the United States: The Performance of Group Identity*, eds. Linda Kelly Brown and Kay Mussell (Knoxville: University of Tennessee Press, 1984), 195–216.

22. Neustadt, "'Born among the Shells.'"

23. Ibid., 99.

24. Christopher Martin, "The Clams of Summer: A Spirited Quest for the Clam Shack Trinity," *Edible Rhody* (Summer 2007), 38.

25. Neustadt, "'Born among the Shells,'" 102.

26. Long, "Culinary Tourism," 49.

27. Brian Rajotte, Facebook communication to author, March 20, 2014.

28. Saltzman, "Rites of Intensification," 226.

29. Rachelle H. Saltzman, "Terroir," in *Food Issues: An Encyclopedia*, ed. Ken Albala (Thousand Oaks, CA: Sage Publications, in press), 8.

30. Rengigas, "Mrs. Gus's Doughboys."

31. Saltzman, "Terroir," 9.

32. Gramma and Grampa Roberts, discussion with the author, March 3 2014.

33. Ibid.

34. Saltzman, "Identity and Food," 6.

35. Iggy's Doughboys, 2014, www.iggysdoughboys.com.

36. Kalčik, "Ethnic Foodways in America," 45.

37. Long, "Culinary Tourism," 46.

38. Saltzman, "Identity and Food," 4.

39. Berkley Hudson, "A Tradition of Food and Fun at Rocky Point," *Providence Journal,* August 3, 1980, C1–C2.

40. Saltzman, "Identity and Food," 48.

41. Michael Owen Jones, "Afterward: Discovering the Symbolism of Food Customs and Events," in *"We Gather Together": Food and Festival in American Life,* eds. Theodore C. Humphrey and Lin T. Humphrey (Ann Arbor, MI: UMI Press, 1988), 242.

42. Gary Nabhan, "Place-based Foods at Risk in New England," Place Based Foods (2008), accessed February 7, 2014, http://garynabhan.com/i/place-based-foods.

43. Valene L. Smith, *Hosts and Guests* (Philadelphia: University of Pennsylvania Press, 1989), 1.

44. Saltzman, "Rites of Intensification," 231.

45. Ibid., 229.

46. Rebecca Sims, "Food, Place, and Authenticity: Local Food and the Sustainable Tourist Experience," *Journal of Sustainable Tourism* 17 (2009): 321–36.

47. Iggy's Doughboys, 2014, www.iggysdoughboys.com.

48. Sidney Mintz, "Eating American," in *Food in the USA: A Reader,* ed. Carole M. Counihan (New York: Routledge, 2002), 27.

49. Lidia Marte, "Foodmaps: Tracing Boundaries of 'Home' through Food Relations," *Food and Foodways* 15 (2007): 261–89.

50. Iggy's Doughboys, 2014, www.iggysdoughboys.com.

Hungry for My Past: Kitchen Comfort with Fried Bread and Eggs

Jillian Gould

Here's how I make a "hole-in-the-middle": First, I tear out the center of a piece of bread—challah is best, but if it is difficult to find, any sliced bread will do. I tear the center out, and either eat it or give it to Sally Rose, my four-year-old daughter, who is eagerly waiting for dinner. I warm up the frying pan, put a large glob of butter in, and wait for it to sizzle. The bread goes in the pan, and I crack an egg over the hole; the yolk sits on top of the bread and the egg white drips into the center of the pan. I wait for the egg to cook while the bread toasts in the heat; the goal is for the bread to absorb the butter and to turn crispy golden brown—this part can be tricky, because if the heat is up too high, the bread could easily burn. With a spatula, I turn a corner to check the color before I flip it; then I add more butter to the pan so the other side gets just as buttery and crisp. The egg white should cook and the yolk should be runny—imagine an egg over easy, fried in the middle of hot buttered toast. It is served directly from pan to plate, made to order, one at a time.

A hole-in-the-middle may sound like a breakfast meal, but it isn't in my family. Lunch, a light dinner, or even an afternoon snack—it is egg and toast, but I have never actually had it for breakfast. It is a meal that I warmly associate with my maternal grandmother, my *bubby*, who died in the summer of 1987, when I was fourteen. Rose (Kravchek) Moran was born in Kryzhopil, Ukraine, in 1904, one of eight children born to Pinchas and Mashe (Veltman) Kravchek. As a young woman, my grandmother left her home with her mother and eight siblings in the dead of night, trekking through darkness to the border between Ukraine and Romania. Their father, Pinchas, had already made his way to Canada, and they were to follow. As Bubby's older sister,

Dora, recalled, they stayed in the forest "until a man came with a little canoe."[1] The older children went ahead first, and their mother held her breath each time the boat turned away, hoping each of her children would arrive safely.[2] At last, the boat came for their mother, who crossed with the youngest, Tillie. The family stayed in Romania for about six months before they were able to leave for Canada. Bubby's brothers worked odd jobs, chopping wood, "all kinds of things." They were waiting for instructions from their father, but "at that time it used to take three or four weeks until you got a letter," Dora explained. They ended up staying through a harsh winter. "We lived in one room," recalled Dora. "We struggled. It was very hard." In the meantime, Pinchas was working out arrangements to bring the family to Canada. Finally, a man arrived with their tickets. "It took us a week by train to go from Romania to Belgium. . . . From Belgium we took a small boat to England," Dora said. From England they got onto the SS *Victorian*, a Canadian Pacific steamship that was used to carry cattle. "And it was rough," said Dora. "Everybody sat on the bundle what you had, sat on your clothing, on a box. There were no benches, no nothing. It took two weeks—fourteen days." Finally, they arrived in St. John, New Brunswick, on April 10, 1921, before making their way by train to Toronto. Rose and most of her siblings worked in the needle trade. I imagine she met my grandfather, David Marantz (at some point he changed it to Moran), through work; their marriage certificate describes them both as tailors. Rose and David had three children: Harry, Lil, and Marilyn (my mother). On Sunday afternoon visits to Bubby's apartment, my siblings and I looked forward to everything she cooked for us, and hole-in-the-middles were my favorite.

Comfort in the Making

In his introductory chapter in this volume, Michael Owen Jones remarks that various definitions of comfort food highlight "family tradition, holidays, and special events in which an individual participated."[3] By and large, the connection many people have towards comfort food is through the *taste* or by the *memory* of special recipes. This chapter explores not so much the taste but the *preparation* of a particular dish through time and space. Although my family calls it a "hole-in-the-middle," it is known by many names: egg in the hole, toad in the hole, egg on the raft, man on the raft, Popeyes, and one-eyed Jack, to name a few. They were prepared for me as a child, and now I prepare them for my own children. Through auto-ethnography, this chapter considers how a simple kitchen meal—rich in memory and nostalgia—changes over time and in various contexts of my own life.[4] From childhood and teenage years, to my first apartment in graduate school, to becoming a mother and losing a mother, this little meal has remained a steady companion through various kitchens and milestones. The recipe does not change much, but the context of how or when it is made does, as well as what it means to make it. Additionally, this chapter considers how the hole-in-the-middle is embedded in the memories of many people, in many contexts. Finally, since Bubby was known for her Jewish cooking repertoire, and since hole-in-the-middles were part of her regular rotation, I relate to them in a Jewish context. And because it is unlikely that they would appear in any Jewish cookery books, I suggest framing them not as Jewish, but as *heimish*—a Yiddish word that conjures up comfort and home.

Memory, Embodiment

In *Remembrance of Repasts: An Anthropology of Food and Memory*, David Sutton encourages his readers to have a "more embodied experience" not only by reading about his research, but also by preparing an annotated recipe, so they may *"eat in order to remember!"*[5] Ingesting comfort food can be deeply connected to memory, but so too can the preparation of comfort food. When I cook a hole-in-the-middle, I am making a dish that my bubby and my mother made before me, and for me. Tearing the center from the bread, cracking the egg on the hole, I embody the memories and actions of both my mother and my grandmother, strengthening our family ties. This dovetails with what Joëlle Bahloul calls "embodied time."[6] Bahloul's study explores how the former Jewish and Muslim residents of a shared home in Algeria have various frameworks of memory. She writes: "The ritual in the street, in the food purchases preceding celebrations—all these images are assembled in memory to signify a religious and ethnic identity."[7] As Guy, one of Bahloul's interviewees, explains: "We'd feel and smell Friday nights back there. It wasn't like here in France: here you don't really *see* the *Sabbath*. But in Algeria, you'd *feel* it. . . . In households, one could smell the odour of food cooking, that good food which we wouldn't cook during the week; those dishes simmered slowly . . . we'd feel it."[8] These embodied memories are *felt*—through memory and narrative. I remember kitchen moments over the years: Sabbath and holiday rituals and everyday cooking rituals, like Bubby's hole-in-the-middle. Does the memory run deeper than other food recollections because I watched it being made from pan to plate—taking it in—both figuratively and literally? The embodied memory of eating provides comfort through taste and nourishment; the embodied recipe provides comfort through familiarity and family identity.

In *Miriam's Kitchen*, writer Elizabeth Ehrlich records and reflects upon her mother-in-law's kitchen comforts. Miriam, a Holocaust survivor and a "keeper of rituals and recipes, and of stories . . . cooks to recreate a lost world, and to prove that unimaginable loss is not the end of everything."[9] Ehrlich learns Miriam's history through her recipes, and learns from Miriam as she documents these recipes by her side. Writes Erhlich, "I have eaten apple cake for nearly twenty years, and never seen it made." When Miriam cracks an egg, she uses her thumb to clean the egg white out of the shell. She explains: "My landlady in Germany taught me to do that. She said, from six eggs, you get one egg."[10] With the sweep of Miriam's thumb, she recalls life as a postwar refugee. She carries her narrative with her, acting it out in the kitchen, a reminder of bleak and difficult times; and yet, remarks Ehrlich: "There is a glint of optimism in the gesture, too."[11] Tasty memories and difficult memories are embodied as we eat and prepare food. Through ordinary meal preparation, life narratives are told and performed in the kitchen.

2002: Graduate School

I had made hole-in-the-middles before, but when an assignment for a food-ways course required me to document and analyze a food event, I was eager to reframe this everyday meal, which, like folklorist Mary Hufford's definition of folklife, seemed to be "hidden in full view" yet played a role in revealing layers of my identity and how I "fit into the world."[12] I invited some friends over and I made hole-in-the-middles for everyone. At the time, I considered hole-in-the-middles to be "memory food"—something from my childhood that I prepared occasionally, as well as something that I had not eaten in a long while. I wanted to consciously remember Bubby, my childhood, and to connect to my past through this meal. There are only three ingredients in a hole-in-the-middle: bread, eggs, and butter/oil, all of which are common pantry items; however, in order to make it the way Bubby did, I needed to find challah, not an everyday food item in St. John's, Newfoundland. I managed to find a bakery, which made me a special loaf, by request.[13] Bubby ate other kinds of bread, but as I think about our hole-in-the-middle weekend afternoons, it occurs to me that challah may have been "essential" simply because she was trying to use up a leftover loaf from Friday night Shabbat dinners. In this way, stale bread and eggs made for an economical dish that was filling as well as delicious. Secondly, Bubby's hole-in-the-middles always were made with margarine, because in her kosher kitchen, margarine was *parve* (neutral), as opposed to butter (dairy), and therefore wouldn't interfere with dietary restrictions.[14]

I began by taking a piece of challah out of the bag, tearing a hole-in-the-middle of the bread, and quickly putting the misshapen circle of bread in my mouth. I noted to my guests that the act of eating the bread was significant, as it evoked memories of Bubby. She always ate that piece of bread, and it was important for me to eat it as well. It dawned on me, as I made one hole-in-the-middle after the other for my friends, that I did not have time to eat nor did I want to, after everyone had finished their plates. I imagined that Bubby may have felt the same way, and may have eaten those little pieces of bread to sustain her own hunger. In fact, although Bubby sat down and ate other meals with us, I do not recall ever seeing her eating a hole-in-the-middle.

Preparing the dish as Bubby did was even more meaningful to me than actually eating the results. As Barbara Kirshenblatt-Gimblett suggests, "Repertoires, whether of songs, tales, or other expressive forms, are examples of accumulations made over a lifetime. Their powers of evocation derive from the associations that accumulate with them."[15] I learned to make hole-in-the-middles from my bubby; they were part of her repertoire, and now they are part of mine. As I make them throughout my life, I am brought back to different times, spaces, and contexts. When an elderly man recites a prayer, he is brought back to various points in his life; Kirshenblatt-Gimblett uses this example to demonstrate how individuals can be aware "of the extraordinary power of a prayer, or other expressive forms, to call up in paradigmatic fashion memories of the many contexts in which a prayer or song has been performed."[16] Likewise, preparing the dish evokes various contexts in my life, and also reinforces connections with family members who were with me. I am at Bubby's apartment, waiting for my hole-in-the-middle, and my siblings—Jennifer and Jonathan—and my parents are there, too. I am in my mother's kitchen of my childhood home, making a hole-in-the-middle for my brother. I am in the large Victorian home I am subletting with two other graduate students, making hole-in-the-middles for my friends. I am brought back to these places, as well as to the people who were there with me.

Transmission

Both my mother and my bubby had natural skills and talent in the kitchen. Each could cook or bake with ease; both were creative and resourceful and did not rely on cookbooks. While they did not consciously pass these skills on to me, it was understood in my family that cooking was valued, and that my mother and Bubby had special competence to prepare delicious food. Nevertheless, when my mother was growing up, Bubby did not allow her in the kitchen—or, at least, she did not encourage her. My mother was the same way with me. Any cooking skills I have acquired over the years have been by observation or imitation, and the hole-in-the-middle—which I watched Bubby make countless times—was the first food item I ever dared to make on my own. As a folklorist, I am interested in what skills are valued and passed along in a family. Bubby worked in the garment industry and was handy with a needle and thread, yet sewing was not a skill that was passed along. In fact, I do not think my mother knew how to sew at all—not even a button. But cooking: Both were skilled and natural and wonderful cooks. I did not consciously learn from my mother or Bubby, but I watched them, and I remember their repertoires, and what they made regularly—recipes *they* embodied. Recipes that were not written down. I watched how my mother's soups always started with an onion. I watched as Bubby warmed up the frying pan enough so that the margarine would sizzle, but not so much that it would burn. When she made hole-in-the-middles, I took note of how she used a spatula to turn a corner of the bread, checking the color before carefully flipping it over. David Sutton suggests that "cooking is best learned through an embodied apprenticeship, in which what is remembered is not a set of rules, but images, tastes, smells and experiences, techniques that can only be partially articulated, or memory-jogged, through the medium of recipes."[17] While this implies that some text-based recipes are simply triggers for what is remembered, I am certain that neither my bubby nor my mother ever consulted a recipe for hole-in-the-middle. What intrigues me most are the everyday casual recipes they prepared: Meals that were off the cuff—most likely because they had never been written down—and meals that were significant parts of their repertoires. As Diane Tye suggests, "Sometimes our everyday memories are the most telling."[18] When I think about how to connect with my mother or my grandmother, the meal that I return to is the hole-in-the-middle. Not the mandelbroit my mother was so famous for making, although I make it from time to time (crunchy, not too sweet—my mother would be proud); not the cold beet borscht (beautiful fuchsia, sour cream beaten in); and not the little rolled jam cookies that Bubby made (similar to *rugelach*, I ate them by the handful with a big glass of milk). Instead, I return to the hole-in-the-middle: warm and crunchy, with rich runny egg yolk absorbed by buttery toast.

Kitchen Stories

"My bubby made these for me," I tell Sally Rose as I tear the center out of the bread. "I know that!" she replies, impatient. "Bubby was my mom's—your bubby's mommy," I say. "You were named for her." I am consciously trying to enforce a connection. "Her name was Rose." "I knooooooooow!" Sally screams. "I loved hole-in-the-middles," I continue, despite Sally's increasing lack of patience and interest. "They were one of my favorite meals growing up—both my bubby and my mommy made them for me." Sally is no longer listening, but I realize that my recollections are as much for me as they are for her. "I am more than what the thin present defines," writes cultural geographer Yi-Fu Tuan, pondering the meaning of the past on our present lives.[19] While often family folklore may be passed along un-self-consciously, other times a conscious effort has to be made to ensure continuity. I worry that my children will not have a connection to my parents so I make an effort to insert them—through photographs, stories, recipes—into our everyday lives. I was lucky to have warm and lasting relationships with my grandparents, and I put a lot of value on these special connections. The death of each of my parents so shortly after the birth of my children means that my daughter and son will only "know" their maternal grandparents through our family folklore. Sally was six months old when my mother died; and when my father died two years later, Max was only four months old. While my father lay dying in hospital, he remarked how sad he was that Sally would not remember him and that Max would never know him. An attentive nurse overheard, leaning in to tell us her own experience: Although her grandfather died when she was a baby, her parents talked about him often. "At mealtimes, at holidays—he was there," she said gently. "I didn't get to meet him, but I know him, and he is with me, always." Her words were touching and reassuring, and I hope that Sally and Max will say something similar one day. In the meantime, food is a trigger for me to share stories about my parents, and for Sally as well. "I ate my first breakfast cereal with Grandpa C. C.," she likes to tell me whenever she has Cheerios. In the months leading up to Sally's second birthday, my father, still grieving for my mother, stayed with us for a couple of weeks. It was a special time that really sealed his relationship with Sally. For one thing, Sally and my father had breakfast together every morning. She would wake him up in the wee hours and they would sit at the table while my husband and I slept. Sally could not say "cereal" and somehow my father *became* the breakfast meal; she affectionately began to call him "Grandpa C. C."—"C. C." for cereal. In *A Celebration of American Folklore*, the authors note, "For an individual family, folklore is its creative expression of a common past."[20] Our kitchen stories connect us to one another; the memories and narratives we share can be just as powerful as the food itself. The hole-in-the-middle connects me to my family. I have never seen it on a restaurant menu, and I have never eaten it outside a family home. When I make a hole-in-the-middle for Sally, I usually

tell a story about Bubby or my mother—even if she protests—because I need
to reinforce our family folklore.

Embodied Nostalgia

I am hungry for my past. Hungry and even mournful. Susan Stewart writes:
"Nostalgia is a sadness without an object, a sadness which creates a longing
that of necessity is inauthentic because it does not take part in lived experience."[21] I long to bring my past into my present. I am not particularly old, but
like the elders of Barbara Myerhoff's *Number Our Days*, I try to maintain
a "sense of continuity" with my past selves.[22] Experiencing the death of my
parents in my late thirties, while simultaneously experiencing motherhood
for the first time, has accelerated my cogs on the lifecycle, making me nostalgic for a recent past. Svetlana Boym defines nostalgia as "a longing for a
home that no longer exists or has never existed."[23] Cabbage borscht hallways
of Bubby's apartment building; warm cinnamon and toasted almonds of my
mother's kitchen; I am sad that my children will not share these experiences.
While I long for that past to meet my present, nostalgia also surrounds what
has not yet been lost. My mother cooked and baked often, making meals and
treats for family and friends. While my sister and I moved to new cities, my
brother and his wife stayed in Toronto, close to parents. As such, my brother's
son had a special relationship with my mother and father, seeing them at least
once a week for a visit and a meal. During the last months of my mother's
life, she received palliative care at home. When she became too ill to cook, my
brother surreptitiously cracked eggs on bread, making hole-in-the-middles
for his son. Jonathan recalls: "As mom got sicker she could no longer stand
at the stove. But I wanted Isaiah to have strong memories of mom, I wanted
somehow to extend the memories—to fill that three-year-old brain—so I
would cook [hole-in-the-middles] when we visited, and tell Isaiah that mom
cooked them." His anticipation of loss underscored his "sadness without an
object": by preparing the hole-in-the-middle, he confronted nostalgia head
on, thus making it tangible, before it disappeared.

Ordinary longings for what has vanished: domestic memories of childhood, everyday meals, family at the table—nostalgic memories may be shared
by members of the same family, but framed differently based on individual
experiences. My hole-in-the-middles are Bubby's kitchen and my childhood
home, but what I long for is what I never had: for my mother to make hole-
in-the-middles for my children, the way my bubby made them for me. When
I cook them today, they are infused with nostalgia.

2010: Becoming a Mother, Losing a Mother

My mother's cancer came back in 2009. She had been treated for the illness over ten years beforehand, and we thought she was done with the disease. This time the cancer was persistent; nevertheless, even while she was undergoing radiation and chemotherapy treatments, my mother insisted on carrying on life as normal. She would go from the hospital to an engagement party, to a concert, to the kitchen. She continued to cook and bake and socialize. Throughout the treatments, my mother remained optimistic and determined to ignore the cancer. Once her oncologist told me she braced herself each time she would go in to see my mother after a treatment. "I keep waiting for her to have a bad day," she said. But even after the strongest treatments, it never happened. My mother was adventurous and upbeat, and she loved to have fun. Throughout my childhood and adolescence, she often dragged my siblings and me to concerts, plays, and performances. "Stand up!" she would shout. She was not a passive audience member—she would jump up from her seat and move to the music. As a jaded preteen, I stubbornly stayed in my seat. When Chubby Checker performed in Toronto in the 1980s, my mother ran on stage and danced the twist with him. There is a Jewish saying, "You can't dance at two weddings," but somehow my mother never missed an event, a show, a *simcha*.[24] The inscription on her gravestone reads: *She danced at every wedding.*

Sally Rose was born early in the morning on February 12, 2010. She was premature and tiny, but thankfully she was healthy. She was seven weeks early, and she arrived on my mother's sixty-eighth birthday. I called my mother, who was in a Toronto hospital, to share the good news. "Mama," I said. "You're a bubby!" I told her about the birth and that baby Sally was doing well. My mother was overjoyed, "This is the best birthday present," she said. Sally had to stay in the Neonatal Intensive Care Unit (NICU) for one month. Days were long and nights were short. I was pumping every few hours around the clock, trying to nourish my newborn. Shortly after Sally was born, we received the devastating news that my mother's treatments were no longer having an effect on the cancer, and in fact, the tumor was growing. With no other options, my mother would go home, where she would receive palliative care. As I am learning how to care for my new little baby, I am grappling with how to lose my mother. I recall sitting in the rocking chair in the hospital, 1,321 miles from my childhood home, holding tiny Sally under my hospital gown, "skin to skin," and sobbing.

My mother loved cooking and documenting meals—she always carried a disposable camera in her purse and insisted on taking photographs of family restaurant meals. We would roll our eyes and poke fun at my mother, but now I treasure these captured moments and wish she had insisted on taking photos inside our home as well. Some images, however, are imprinted in my memory and reinforced by action. For example, when my mother made a hole-in-the-middle, she would tear out the center from the piece of bread, and rather than eat it, she would give it to me—perhaps to tide over my hunger while I waited. That little piece of bread always seemed especially tasty. The action of tearing the bread also evokes Friday night (Shabbat) dinners at my home growing up. After saying the blessing over the challah, we would tear pieces of bread from the loaf before passing morsels around the table, saying "Good Shabbos" to everyone. The memory remains strong each time I tear the hole from the middle.

I ate a lot of hole-in-the-middles during Sally's first month in the NICU. Long days at the hospital were filled with cinnamon buns and cold turkey sandwiches from the hospital coffee shop. At home each evening, my husband and I, exhausted, wanted something quick, nourishing, and warm. I do not even recall who made them—but they tasted so good. In the words of food writer Laurie Colwin: "When life is hard and the day has been long, the ideal dinner is not four perfect courses, each in a lovely pool of sauce . . . but rather something comforting and savory, easy on the digestion—something that makes one feel, if even for one minute, that one is safe."[25]

Shortly after Sally Rose came home from the hospital, I was packing a suitcase once again. I did not want to be so far away from my mother as she entered this last stage of her life, and I wanted her to spend time with her new little granddaughter. Baby Sally and I flew from St. John's, Newfoundland, to Toronto on a clear April day. My father picked us up at the airport and we drove to the home where I grew up. With Sally, I slept in my sister's old bedroom, a bassinet set up next to my bed. Days were spent with friends, family, and medical professionals—every morning and afternoon, people came to visit my mother, who held court right through the end. One steamy August night, there was a knock on the bedroom door. My mother's breathing had drastically slowed down. She was taking her last breaths. It was time to say goodbye. Together, my father and I held her hands and told her how much we loved her. It was devastating and surreal. At the funeral, I held Sally Rose close to my breast. Through my tears I was grateful for the time I got to spend with my mother. It took many months before I was able to see my mother in my mind's eye the way I wanted to remember her: happy, healthy, and well, rather than thin and weak, and overshadowed by illness. That memory shift occurred around the same time that Sally started to eat "real food"—of course, the first thing I cooked for her was a hole-in-the-middle. She has demanded them ever since.

A Hole-in-the-Middle by Any Other Name . . .

Informal conversations with friends, colleagues, students, and family members highlighted variations and warm memories of the dish, but it was not until I discovered the recipe on a popular food blog that I realized what a special meal it is for so many people. In 2008, food blogger Ree Drummond of *The Pioneer Woman* fame[26] posted a recipe for "egg-in-a-holes."[27] Here is how she describes learning to make the recipe in order to please her fiancé: "I had to learn to make these delicious little numbers or he wouldn't go through with the wedding. Called 'Egg-in-a-Holes' by his paternal grandmother who made them for him all during his childhood, I've learned not only to love them through the years . . . but to *need* them. They define comfort food, are painfully easy to make, and will turn any stressful, hectic morning into something entirely different." Like all of her blog entries, a photograph illustrates each step of the recipe, along with simple directions. She writes: "To begin, grab a slice of bread. You can use storebought white, wheat, or you can get fancy and use brioche or challah. But only if you live in a city." This is a homey recipe; the idea is to use whatever is available. Bubby's hole-in-the-middles were not fancy; it just so happened that challah was the bread that she had on hand. Drummond's post hit a note with her readers, who contributed 1,241 comments, significantly more than any other post in the "Comfort Food" category. Readers shared names for the dish (egg in a frame, egg in a basket, toad in a hole, bull's eye, Popeye's, sunny beds . . .) and stories about family members who made it (dad, mother, grandfather, grandmother), as well as when and where.[28] The majority framed the dish as a childhood favorite or as something they currently prepare for their children; on the other hand, some commenters did not mention children at all. "I love this stuff," wrote Chocolatechic. "So simple, so wonderful. It says 'home.'"

Although my siblings and I call it hole-in-the-middle, I wondered if my cousins also called it by the same name. Since we shared the same grandmother, I asked them if Bubby made hole-in-the-middles for them as well. They did not remember, but said their mother (my mother's sister-in-law) made them, and they were called Popeye's. "I guess the yolk looked like Popeye's large eye," my cousin Lisa said.[29] Her brother, Brian, recalls: "I don't remember that much about them but do remember that my mom would tear out a hole in the center of the bread, put it in the frying pan then drop an egg into the hole. I thought every mom made them! My memory is a bit limited but one thing I can say is that they do bring back some fond memories—a long time ago—of lunches with my family. Great memories!"[30] Their sister, Marci, also recalls the dish: "My mom used to call them Popeye's. They were yummy. She would fry one side, then flip it over, crack the egg in the middle and then finish it off with a final turn. I have yet been able to replicate the recipe. Obviously mom's lovin' is missing."[31]

Jewish or Heimish?

In the *Mensch Chef* cookbook, Mitchell Davis introduces a recipe called Jewish Spaghetti, which is "the ultimate comfort food" for every member of his family.[32] Writes Davis: "It was so much a part of our vernacular, that we thought it was a recipe shared by Jews throughout the Diaspora." In fact, Davis's great grandmother, Eva, invented the dish, which, Davis explains, "isn't really spaghetti, or even Jewish for that matter."[33] Nevertheless, for Davis and his family members, it was beloved and Jewish. The hole-in-the-middle is my Jewish Spaghetti. I imagine it in a Jewish context not only because my bubby made it, but also because it was made with challah. Nevertheless, the diversity and name variations of this simple dish cast a wide net, and like Jewish Spaghetti, other than using challah as an ingredient (which is variable), there is nothing Jewish about the dish. This leaves me to wonder how my Yiddish-speaking bubby learned to make it in the first place. When she arrived in Toronto as an immigrant from Ukraine in the 1920s, several Jewish organizations existed and offered various kitchen and domestic science classes.[34] As Barbara Kirshenblatt-Gimblett notes, "By the last decades of the nineteenth century cooking classes were a staple of public school education; they were a vocational subject in industrial-training curricula for immigrants by the 1890s in New York and other cities"[35] Furthermore, writes Kirshenblatt-Gimblett: "The Official Souvenir Booklet of the 1895 Fair in Aid of the Educational Alliance and the Hebrew Technical Institute included a photograph of a cooking class, in which uniformed young women—in aprons, armlets to protect their sleeves, and caps—were busily occupied in an instructional kitchen."[36] As a young woman, my bubby may have taken cooking classes through the Bazaar Cooking Schools, which were established by the popular Jewish women's association, Hadassah, in Toronto in the 1930s, or through the Jewish Family Welfare Bureau (JFWF), which offered a Homemaking Club for housewives and mothers, offering a series of lectures in cooking, nutrition, and household budgeting.[37] While I can only speculate at this point, this is a subject I would like to pursue further in the future.

Nevertheless, while the origins of how Bubby learned the recipe remain a mystery, I continue to imagine the hole-in-the-middle in a Jewish context, even if it would never appear in a Jewish cookbook. As Timothy Lloyd writes about Cincinnati Chili: "It is possible for new foods to be introduced, or even to be invented, and then over time to have their own system of custom and identification build up around them."[38] Some foods lose their ethnic identity, as they take on the identity of place (Cincinnati Chili or New York or Montreal bagels, for example),[39] while other foods take on the identity of those who prepare it. Like Jewish Spaghetti, my hole-in-the-middles are Jewish by association, if not by ingredients. While challah is an essential ingredient for my brother's hole-in-the-middles, for me, the type of bread I use is irrelevant. Rather, it is my *memory* of challah and Bubby that makes it Jewish, as well as the embodied memory of tearing the Sabbath challah. Finally, I would like to suggest that if hole-in-the-middles are not Jewish, then perhaps they are simply heimish—a Yiddish word that suggests home comfort. A hole-in-the-middle is an "everyday" food item prepared in home kitchens. Certainly, there is no fuss involved in the preparation.

When I began this chapter, I wanted to explore how a simple meal—preparing, eating, remembering—can not only provide comfort, but also become an important part of my family folklore. I thought of how hole-in-the-middles connected me to my bubby, my mother, and to my children. When I asked my siblings about their memories of this same dish, they were divided. Both remembered them and associated them with Bubby and Mom. My sister enjoyed them but doesn't make them for her children: "They were good," she recalls. "But I didn't love them." My brother, on the other hand, considers them very special. Unlike other family recipes, the comfort of the hole-in-the-middle—for me—is not in the taste, but rather, in the making. Tearing out the piece of bread from the center and eating it is just as meaningful as the end result: the final golden hole-in-the-middle.

I will conclude this chapter with a final anecdote: One afternoon, when Max was about six months old, I invited his babysitter to stay for dinner. It was an off-the-cuff invitation, before I realized we needed to go grocery shopping, and there wasn't much to eat. I asked if she had heard of hole-in-the-middles—our go-to easy supper and comfort meal. She smiled. We had "egg-in-a-bagel," she said. "My parents were Montrealers, and, of course, they were made on Montreal bagels." I had never considered making one on a bagel. "The bagel would get all crunchy on the outside, the inside was chewy and sweet—they were delicious!" She said her mother was quite creative and thinks she invented them. "She was always making things up," Trina said. "You know what she called fried eggs? Drop-ins!" As I cooked the hole-in-the-middles, we talked about home, mothers, and grandmothers. Trina had moved to St. John's for graduate school; we met through the Jewish Community Havura, and although she babysat Max on more than one occasion, it was the first time she had shared a meal with us. Many hole-in-the-middles later, I said we would invite her again, "next time for a real meal." She dismissed my comment and said how nice it was to have the meal we had: informal, unpretentious, delicious. From time to time, I think about that evening with Trina—we have had guests over for dinner before and since; better food, good friends—but that night was one of the warmest meals my family has ever shared. The act of making it and the love that went into it—it is the love that I carry from my parents and my grandparents. A hole-in-the-middle is not fancy, but it hits the spot. Buttery. Crunchy. Nourishing. That night with Trina was more than sharing bread—it was sharing comfort.

Notes

This chapter began as an assignment for Dr. Paul Smith's Foodways course in 2002, and my thanks to him for earliest comments. Versions of this chapter were presented at the Folklore Studies Association of Canada meeting in Corner Brook, Newfoundland (2013), as well as at the American Folklore Studies Annual Meeting in Rhode Island (2013), as part of a panel on comfort food. So much thanks to Michael Owen Jones and Lucy Long for inviting me to submit to this volume. I would also like to thank Diane Tye for many helpful comments; Barbara Kirshenblatt-Gimblett and Eve Jochnowitz for thoughtful email correspondence about Jewish food; Donna Bernardo-Ceriz of the Ontario Jewish Archives for responding to my research queries by distance; and graduate research assistant, Kari Sawden. Finally, huge thanks to friends, family, and colleagues near and far who shared comfort food memories.

1. Dora Kraft Waltman, interview with Marla Waltman, March 26, 1978, Toronto, Canada. I am grateful that my cousin Marla Waltman Daschko, Dora's granddaughter, conducted and transcribed the interview and provided me with the transcript. When I tried to confirm my bubby's birthplace, Marla said it was most likely Kryzhopil, although it may have been Zhabokrich, Vinnitsya, Ukraine, where the family had lived previously, and where Pinchas and Mashe were born.

2. I had heard this story from my mother throughout my childhood. It was fascinating to read the transcript of Dora's interview—describing our family folklore—as her own experience, in her own words. The only difference between her version and the one I remember was that in the latter, Masha went ahead first and waited for her children; in Dora's version, by contrast, Masha's children all went ahead first and she was the last to cross, with little Tillie.

3. Michael Owen Jones, "'Stressed' Spelled Backwards Is 'Desserts': Self-Medicating Moods with Foods," in this volume.

4. Folklorist Kirin Narayan defines auto-ethnography as "ethnography of one's self or one's group." As she explains: "Auto-ethnography dissolves notions of ethnography as dependent on encounters across cultural difference, instead turning a descriptive and analytic eye

on one's own experience as shaped by larger structures and processes." See Kirin Narayan, *Alive in the Writing: Crafting Ethnography in the Company of Chekhov* (Chicago: University of Chicago Press, 2012), 95. For a more in-depth introduction to auto-ethnography, see Carolyn Ellis and Arthur P. Bochner, "Autoethnography, Personal Narrative, Reflexivity: Researcher as Subject," in *Handbook of Qualitative Research. Second Edition*, eds. Norman K. Denizen and Yvonna S. Lincoln (Thousand Oaks, CA: Sage, 2000), 733–68.

5. David Sutton, *Remembrance of Repasts: An Anthropology of Food and Memory* (Oxford: Berg, 2001), 18.

6. Joëlle Bahloul, *The Architecture of Memory: A Jewish-Muslim Household in Colonial Algeria, 1937–1962* (Cambridge: Cambridge University Press, 1996), 104.

7. Ibid., 104–105.

8. Ibid., 104.

9. Elizabeth Ehrlich, *Miriam's Kitchen: A Memoir* (New York: Penguin Books, 1998), xii.

10. Ibid., 65.

11. Ibid.

12. Mary Hufford, "American Folklife: A Commonwealth of Cultures," American Folklife Center, Library of Congress, http://www.loc.gov/folklife/cwc/.

13. The bakery, Manna, specializes in Eastern European breads and made challahs occasionally as part of their rotation. As I write this piece—over ten years later—another spot, The Georgestown Bakery, makes challahs every Friday.

14. Observant Jews who follow Jewish dietary restrictions are not allowed to mix milk and dairy products; therefore, margarine, which is *parve* (neutral) is commonly used instead of butter. For discussion on Crisco in Jewish households, see Barbara Kirshenblatt-Gimblett, "Kitchen Judaism," in *Getting Comfortable in New York, 1880–1950*, eds. Susan Braunstein and Jenna Weissman Joselit (New York: The Jewish Museum, 1990), 94.

15. Barbara Kirshenblatt-Gimblett, "Objects of Memory: Material Culture as Life Review," in *Folk Groups and Folklore Genres: A Reader*, ed. Elliot Oring (Logan: Utah State University Press, 1989), 329.

16. Kirshenblatt-Gimblett, 330.

17. Sutton, 135,

18. Diane Tye, *Baking As Biography: A Life Story in Recipes* (Montreal: McGill-Queen's University Press, 2010), 4.

19. Yi-Fu Tuan, *Space and Place: The Perspective of Experience* (Minneapolis: University of Minnesota Press, 2005 [1997]), 186. Thanks to Diane Tye for pointing out this lovely phrase, which I also used to illustrate a similar point in my PhD thesis (2009).

20. Steven J. Zeitlin, Amy J. Kotkin, and Holly Cutting Baker, *A Celebration of American Family Folklore* (New York: Pantheon Books, 1982), 2.

21. Susan Stewart. *On Longing: Narratives of the Miniature, the Gigantic, the Souvenir, the Collection* (Durham: Duke University Press, 1993), 23. I use this quote when I discuss Jewish memory food in "Toronto Blueberry Buns: History, Community, Memory," *Material History Review* 57 (Spring 2003): 30–39.

22. Barbara Myerhoff, *Number Our Days* (New York: Touchstone, 1978), 222.

23. Svetlana Boym, *The Future of Nostalgia* (New York: Basic Books, 2001), xiii.

24. A happy occasion (Hebrew/ Yiddish).

25. Laurie Colwin, *Home Cooking: A Writer in the Kitchen* (New York: Perennial, 1993), 107.

26. http://thepioneerwoman.com/.

27. http://thepioneerwoman.com/cooking/2008/07/egg-in-a-hole-see-alternate-names -below/. I am indebted to Diane Tye for telling me about this blog post.

28. This dish evokes memories and elicits narrative. See also Huffpost Taste" blog entry, "Toad in the Hole, Egg in a Nest: What Do You Call It?" *Huffington Post*, October 9, 2012, http://www.huffingtonpost.com/2012/10/09/toad-in-the-hole_n_1949599.html. The blog entry begins: "One of our favorite breakfast dishes of all time has a recurring problem: no one can agree on what to call it. We have always called this genius invention—an egg fried inside a piece of toast—Toad in the Hole. Or Egg in a Nest. Egg in a Basket? You see the problem, right?"

29. Lisa (Moran) Atlas, email correspondence, June 14, 2013.

30. Brian Moran, email correspondence, June 15, 2013.

31. Marci (Moran) Vandersluis, email correspondence, June 15, 2013.

32. Mitchell Davis, *The Mensch Chef: Or Why Delicious Jewish Food Isn't an Oxymoron* (New York: Clarkson Potter, 2002), 100.

33. Ibid.

34. Thank you to archivist Donna Bernardo-Ceriz at the Ontario Jewish Archives, for providing information about these courses.

35. Barbara Kirshenblatt-Gimblett, "Kitchen Judaism," in *Getting Comfortable in New York: The American Jewish Home, 1880–1950*, eds. Susan L. Braunstein and Jenna Weissman Joselit (New York: The Jewish Museum, 1990), 98.

36. Ibid.

37. Donna Bernardo-Ceriz from the Ontario Jewish Archives provided this information via email correspondence.

38. Timothy C. Lloyd, "The Cincinnati Chili Culinary Complex," in *The Taste of American Place*, eds. Barbara Shortridge and James Shortridge (Lanham, MD: Rowman & Littlefield, 1998), 45.

39. I discuss these issues in more detail in "Toronto Blueberry Buns: History, Community, Memory," *Material History Review* 57 (Spring 2003): 3039.

Viili as a Finnish American Comfort Food: The Long and Short of It

Yvonne R. Lockwood and William G. Lockwood

During the last decade of the nineteenth century and the first decades of the twentieth, Finns immigrated in large numbers to the United States. Today, Finnish American foodways and culture are the result of multiple generations of development. Many of the daily foods found on Finnish American tables could be called "Midwestern fare," even though these foods are often cooked in a Finnish manner.[1] Some dishes of genuine Finnish origin, however, are still part of the daily repertoire. Among these is *viili*, a fermented milk product, loved and consumed on a daily basis by some and despised and avoided by a few others. There are two variants of viili: one is stretchy and called "long," the other is not stretchy but pudding-like and called "short." We will discuss viili and its role in Finnish America and explore its status as a comfort food.

The majority of emigrants from Finland settled in Michigan's Upper Peninsula and northern Minnesota. They worked as miners, lumberjacks, and Great Lakes fishermen. Some turned to subsistence farming on marginal land left after loggers had cut away the forests, leaving stumps and debris.[2] Many farmers on these stump farms, however, still had to work in mines, woods, and lumber mills several months a year to pay debts, leaving their wives to manage the agricultural work.[3] Farms also provided subsistence to those who held regular jobs in local extractive industries. Even those who settled in small mining and mill towns usually kept a garden and cow. Hunting and fishing supplemented the diet.

Michigan and Minnesota are still home to the largest Finnish American population. The region around Lake Superior is the center of Finnish America, where communities maintain close contact, traditions are strong, and many cultural activists are located and cultural activities are initiated. Other pockets of Finnish Americans are scattered between the East and West coasts and from the Canadian border to Florida.

Immigrants did not represent a cross section of Finland's population but were drawn from some regions and some social strata more than others, although the majority came from Western Finland. Some regions, social groups, and classes, each with a discrete subculture, including foodways, were more influential in shaping the new Finnish American culture than others. This developing ethnic culture also drew from mainstream America, the cultures of other ethnic groups, and Finland itself. During the last decades of the twentieth century and continuing to the present, there has been an influx of Finnish nationals.

Milk products are ubiquitous in Finland. After bread, milk products are the most important staples in the Finnish national diet and Finland has the highest consumption of milk in the world.[4] Shops sell many different kinds of milk, buttermilk, viili, quark, sour cream, and yogurt. The high consumption of milk products is interesting, because 17 percent of the population is lactose intolerant, lacking the enzyme lactase to break down the sugar in milk, which is higher than for Europeans generally. For this reason, many milk products sold in Finnish markets are treated for lactose intolerance.

In Finnish America, especially in the north country of Michigan, Wisconsin, and Minnesota, milk and milk products are more important in the diet than that of non-Finnish Americans. Many prefer to drink milk with their meals, and there are a number of dishes in the Finnish American diet that are cooked in milk, and made with sour cream, buttermilk, and lots of butter. Because lactose intolerance is a genetic condition, we can assume the intolerance rate in Finnish America matches that of Finland. Compared to Finland, however, the choice of products treated for lactose intolerance is limited.

Individual lactose intolerance varies. Some suffer from drinking just a little milk, others only after large amounts. Fermented products, however, such as viili, are more readily tolerated because much of the lactic acid bacteria has broken down much of the lactose.

Viili is an ancient food and, like other fermented milk products, is a method of preserving milk.[5] The origin of viili adds to its mystique. "How," wondered one Finnish American, "do these bacteria know they're Finnish and make *viili* and not French yogurt instead?"[6] Although rennet has no role in the making of viili, some believe that the original viili was made by "letting milk set in a freshly killed calf's stomach."[7] In his definitive work on milk production economy in Sweden, Gustav Rank attributes the origin of *lång-mjölk* in Sweden and *pitkäviili* in Finland to the use of the butterwort plant

(*Pinguicula vulgaris*), although it has not been used within living memory.[8] The origin of viili, however, is not particularly important to the community. One always makes it with a little of the previous batch, the starter, and what is important is *having* the starter. How Finnish Americans have maintained viili over generations is key to its social and cultural role.[9]

The importance of this ancient food in the diet of immigrating Finns is demonstrated by the fact that they carried viili across the ocean to their new home. Viili has been made in Finnish American homes ever since. One Finnish American describes her grandmother's method of transporting her viili to the US: "This *viili* was brought from Finland by my grandmother at the turn of the century. To transport it over the long sea journey, she spread it on handkerchiefs and let them dry, then wrapped it up and carried it with her. When she got to this country and again had access to cow's milk, she peeled the dried viili culture from her handkerchiefs and mixed it with the milk. This viili has been kept going for many years by her granddaughters."[10] We have evidence that this was not an original idea. Scientists report that "in Scandinavia, the starter culture was preserved from season to season by soaking a linen cloth in *viili* and drying it. Emigrants from Scandinavia did the same."[11] Individuals take pride in their starters. Some are handed down from generation to generation and are highly prized and carefully tended.

When making viili, a spoonful is taken from an existing batch (the starter) and mixed in a bowl with cold milk, traditionally raw or pasteurized. Those without access to either use homogenized milk, and they sometimes add a little cream to get the top layer skin. Some also use 2 percent milk or even skim milk. None of these alternatives produce what a traditionalist would call a good bowl of viili. The bowl is then placed in a cupboard until the milk is clabbered, at which point it is covered and placed in the refrigerator to cool. Depending on the temperature of the room, the process takes from twelve to forty-eight hours. When clabbered and the cream has risen to the top, the viili has a dual texture of a velvety crust or skin, which is highly favored, and a filling with a creamy, mildly acidic flavor.

There is a "long" viili and a "short" viili.[12] Finnish Americans, however, do not recognize these terms. For most, viili is viili. Both can be eaten with a spoon or whipped and drunk. The long variant (pitkäviili, which is not a term used by most Finnish Americans) is a characteristically long, ropey, viscous, and elastic texture produced by a strain of bacteria that converts the carbohydrates in milk into long chains of exopolysaccharides.[13] This is the variant said to have originated with butterwort. The short variant is almost pudding-like or gelatinous, without any stretch, and the flavor is slightly acidic, even with hints of sweetness. Some claim that stirring will increase the stringiness.

Others believe that the stringiness increases with each new batch. Generally, long viili is regarded as the real thing. It was the variant brought by immigrants and that the older generations grew up eating. When a spoonful of long viili is lifted out of the bowl, it stretches. "At its best, the viili should be so elastic," Brown jokingly writes, "[that it] requires cutting with scissors."[14] Elsewhere, it has been described as "elastic yogurt."[15] It is this stringy, slippery texture that viili lovers enjoy—even though it repulses most non-Finnish Americans and some Finnish Americans, and some children compare it with snot. Today, starters for long viili are increasingly difficult to find in both Finland and America. Some Finnish Americans bring back starters of the commercially made, short variant from Finland, believing it to be better than what is available locally or that it is the real thing, "real Finnish." A Finnish American cookbook writer makes short viili by using "buttermilk" as her starter, but the result, she says, is not as tasty as the long.[16] Having grown up on a farm eating long viili, one woman does not regard "this new" (short) viili as viili at all.[17]

Finnish Americans who love viili eat it at any time of the day or night, as a snack and as a light meal, often with rye bread and butter and salted salmon, or with or without sugar. It is made in individual bowls and eaten with a spoon. The styles of eating vary. Do you dip deeply into the bowl to get some creamy topping with each spoonful? Or do you push that creamy skin to the side and eat it last? Or do you eat it first? Do you whip it up and drink it?[18] A favorite meal of the late Jingo Viitala Vachon, a much-loved author and artist of the Upper Peninsula, Michigan, was "a big hunk of salted whitefish, a few slabs of coarse, brown, homemade *rieska* [an unleavened flat bread made from potato, barley, or rye flour] with homemade butter and a bowl of *viili*."[19] A Minnesotan asserted that to survive "you'll get along fine with fish, bread, and *viili*."[20] Younger Finnish Americans tend not to have this strong attachment to viili, but rather prefer yogurt, often loaded with sugar and jam. While lovers of viili describe it as enjoyable, flavorful, tasty (not flat like yogurt), tingly, yummy, healthy, and refreshing, those with a distaste for it use descriptors such as disgusting, the odor of vomit, slimy, snotty, and stringy. A third-generation woman recalls her childhood memory that provides a striking contrast to the fond descriptions of viili-lovers: "I think *viili* is something you need to acquire a taste for. I'm not nuts about it, but I can eat it. It seems quite bland, almost bitter, to me. I remember being kind of intrigued by the thick skin on the top. This was the cream portion of the milk that separated as it was forming; it kind of looked sick to me. The part underneath was much thinner, kind of stringy almost and would plop off your spoon if you didn't get enough mass on your spoon to cause it to break [from the rest in the bowl]."[21]

Her mother, father, and grandmother ate viili almost every day, and though she never developed the same love for it, today, as an adult, she is game to try it again.

Viili is a distinctive Finnish dish. Although similar fermented milk products are found elsewhere in the Nordic area, especially Sweden, Finnish Americans regard viili as uniquely Finnish. Like the sauna, it is even thought to have curative properties. Gustav Rank reported that milk cultured with butterwort had certain antibiotic properties.[22] A third-generation Finnish American writes that "*viili* is known to be beneficial to digestion, especially to those whose genetic makeup is Finnish. It is especially good for gallstones (a common Finnish ailment) and can neutralize gastric distress. [My cousin says] daily consumption of *viili* can make a person live longer."[23] Another tells of the healthful benefits she witnessed: "My husband loves *viili*. About twenty years ago, my mother died and my dad brought all her *viili* ready-made to my husband. He started eating it every day and it cured his stomach. He was eating a few rolls of Tums every day."[24] Hangovers are also said to be cured by drinking whipped viili.[25] In addition, viili is believed to promote strength. At the festivities of the annual St. Urho's Day[26] celebrations in Farmington Hills, Michigan, a Finnish American customarily brings in a large batch of viili and urges others to have some because "viili is what made St. Urho strong."

Out of the large repertoire of foods brought by Finnish immigrants, those to have survived have great symbolic value. To consume them, even to discuss them, is to affirm one's ethnic identity. Food, like few other cultural features, is a strong symbol of who we are. Viili serves this cultural function, just as do other foods in the contemporary Finnish American diet.[27]

Viili also serves a social function. It is not sold in local markets and has only recently become available over the internet. The social aspect of viili has to do with the network of people necessary for its distribution. Inevitably, the starter is lost; one forgets to save some for the next batch or a bad batch may be produced. Thunderstorms are believed to spoil viili, and more than one person has panicked during a storm, not knowing how to protect the starter. For decades, the only way one could have viili was to get a starter from family, friends, or neighbors. People in the western Upper Peninsula would just pick up the telephone when it rang for someone else on the party line and ask whether someone had a viili starter. An Italian American in the same area offered to exchange grappa for a viili starter. Sharing is still prevalent. This is a problem, however, for those Finnish Americans who have migrated beyond the Finnish American settlements, as many were forced to because of economic circumstances. If they have lost sustained contact, and no longer have access to a viili starter, it may mean losing one more attribute of their

Finnishness. When a former editor of a Finnish American newspaper offered to send *viili* starters to readers, she was buried with requests stating the offer "was a dream come true." One recipient wrote: "Thank you for the *viili* culture you sent me. You have no idea of the joy in our home when we had a bowl of 'feelia'—that wonderful flavor and strings [meaning the elastic stretch]." Several others responded that it was just what they remembered.[28]

Perhaps the most obvious aspect of viili as a comfort food is its base in ethnicity. It is a familiar Finnish food that evokes Finnishness, memories, and ties to Finland. Viili is eaten by all ages but especially by older Finns, most of whom have eaten it all their lives and look forward to every satisfying bowlful. Younger generations who choose to eat it, rather than yogurt, may add jam and sweetened fruits, such as in yogurt, or sugar and cinnamon. Nonetheless, they are eating it because it is Finnish.[29]

We cannot discount the revival of viili. Finns who did not grow up with viili, or who have not had it for years, are now seeking starters. They are motivated to familiarize themselves with viili and other Finnish foods, because of recent consciousness of their heritage, or in the case of those who have not had viili for years, nostalgia. At the annual FinnFest USA conference and festival in 2013, a demonstration on viili-making caused the room to overflow.[30] Giving away 100 starters, the lecturer ran out of viili. Food culture is an ongoing negotiation of likes and dislikes of tradition and Finnish food traditions continue to be discovered.

Food is bound up with cultural meaning and through foodways people connect to their past. We attribute terms such as "comfort food" and "food nostalgia" to feelings evoked by certain foods. The *Merriam Webster Dictionary* defines comfort food as "food prepared in a traditional style having a usually nostalgic or sentimental appeal." Comfort food inevitably evokes nostalgia, a longing for the familiar, and is a reminder of childhood, places, and past experiences.[31] It is said that nostalgia often suggests a false sense of an idealized place or past.[32] Finnish Americans have a sense of nostalgia for some poverty foods that were eaten when money or ingredients were scarce and times were tough.[33] These foods may be craved and occasionally consumed even after poverty is no longer an issue. The potato sausage, for example, consumed by Finnish Americans during the war years of the 1940s into the 1950s, consisted mostly of potatoes with only enough pork to flavor. Today, this same sausage consists of more pork than potatoes. It is, however, the wartime sausage that evokes a sense of nostalgia and memories of childhood and past experiences. Its modern version is a different food. The Finnish American stew called *mojakka* can also be regarded as a poverty dish of the past. Traditionally, it is made with fish or beef, potatoes, carrots, and maybe onion in a water base. It often is a thin, soupy-like stew. Many still make it in this style, because that is what mojakka is to them, while others have adapted their recipe into a thicker, heartier stew. Another dish very much like mojakka is potatoes cooked in milk and served like a soup. Recalling his childhood, one Finnish American explained that one day his family would have potatoes cooked in milk and the next day, milk with potatoes.[34] This is what poor Finns often ate. Today, these are both comfort and nostalgic foods, reminders of a past when life was much tougher.

Remembering and transmitting the past is an essential aspect of the building of individual and community identities.[35] Food can evoke mutual memories in those who are feeling nostalgic, and sharing those foods maintains community. For Finnish Americans, the nostalgia is for a childhood, family, or experiences in the midst of a dense ethnic community as existed up to World War II and just after, for a time that no longer exists. Today, serving mojakka at community events is de rigueur; sharing it together reinforces Finnish American identity.[36]

There are abundant examples of food serving similar functions in other immigrant and ethnic communities. For immigrants in foreign lands, food evokes memories and nostalgia for a distant homeland, absent family and friends, and all that is familiar. For Pieds-Noirs in France, for example, Algerian food is a tool that sustains community memory and their piece of the past.[37] To cope with their liminality, Salvadorans in the United States crave rich Salvadoran foods that remind them of home and make them feel connected.[38] In Miami, where Cuban nostalgia is dominated by memories of pre-revolutionary Cuba, more recent immigrants have nostalgia for Russian products, especially canned beef (*carne rusa*). One recently arrived Cuban American stated: "We are remembering our youth and having a good time. What do politics have to do with eating a can of Russian beef and drinking vodka?"[39] Food for Ecuadorans in Queens, New York, provides a means to reconstruct their identity and frame their feelings about citizenship and immigrant life.[40] Indians in Silicon Valley go to an Indian store for the sights, smells, and sounds that contribute to the creation of a virtual community.[41] However, in these cases, too, food nostalgia tends to reify the past, glossing over conflict and constructing a false, harmonious past.[42]

One restaurant reviewer commented that comfort food is "familiar, flavorful and filling.... No matter the ethnic origin, it invariably involves a degree of nostalgia; a familiar component that resonates with your past."[43] This fits viili.

Notes

1. Yvonne Lockwood, "Finnish American Foodways," in *Ethnic American Food Today: A Cultural Encyclopedia*, ed. Lucy Long (Lanham, MD: Rowman & Littlefield, 2015).

2. Cf. Alanen, "In Search of the Pioneer Finnish Homesteader in America," 72–92; and Gough, *Farming the Cutover: A Social History of Northern Wisconsin, 1900–1940* (Lawrence: University of Kansas Press, 1997).

3. A. William Hoglund, "Flight from Industry. Finns and Farming in American," *Finnish American. A Journal of Finnish American History and Culture* I (1978): 1–21.

4. Ulla Käkönen, *Natural Cooking the Finnish Way* (New York: Quadrangle, 1974), viii; Aini Rajanen, *Of Finnish Ways* (Minneapolis: Dillon Press. 1981), 104; www.maitojatervesys.fi/www/en/milk_in_finland.php; www.maataloustilastot.fi/en/what_was_eaten_finland-2012_en.

5. Harold McGee, *On Food and Cooking: The Science and Lore of the Kitchen* (New York: Charles Scribner's Sons, 1984), 31–36. According to Harold McGee (7–8), humans are exceptional among mammals, because they drink milk after they begin to eat solid food. Even among humans, those who drink milk after infancy are the exception. This is not just a matter of taste or of custom. Most humans lose the lactose-breaking enzyme, lactase, by the age of three-and-a-half. This inability to digest milk sugar became known only in the late 1960s, because of a strong Eurocentric bias and because most Westerners, particularly those of northern European background, are capable of digesting lactose into adulthood. Only about 10 percent of white Americans are lactose intolerant, as compared to 70 percent of black Americans. It has been suggested that a genetic trait of continuing lactase production arose in northern European people, because it conferred the advantages of increased intake and improved absorption of calcium on a group whose dark, cold environment developed little vitamin D in the skin. Finns, on the other hand, seem to be an anomaly; a sizable percentage of them do not have this genetic trait, presumably because their ancestors migrated to the Nordic region more recently.

6. Lynn Marie Laitala, "Sharing the Culture," *The Finnish American Reporter* (January 1996): 3.

7. Mrs. Edward Lassila, interview from the Wayne State University Folklore Archive, accession no. 1952 (42).

8. Gustav Rank's work on milk fermentation (*Från mjölk till ost. Drag ur den älder mjölkhushållningen i Sverige* [Nordiska museets handlingar 66, 1966]) is summarized in a review by Brita Egardt, "Early Milk Production Economy in Sweden," *Ethnologia Scandinavica* (1971): 196–97, and is the source used here. Cf. R. Fondén, K. Leporanta, and U. Svensson, "Nordic/Scandinavian Fermented Milk Products," in *Fermented Milks*, ed. Adnan Tamime (Oxford: Blackwell, 2006), 158. In her article about butterwort, Ruth MacFarland in the *Finnish American Reporter* (2009: 21) cites the Swedish scientist, C. Linnaeus, who wrote, in 1732, about his observation of preserving milk: "In the neighborhood (of Umea) grows *pinguicula*. When the inhabitants of these parts once procure this plant, they avail themselves of it throughout the whole year; for they preserve it dried during the winter, and use it as a kind of rennet till the return of spring" (quoted by Ruth MacFarlane,

"Research Uncovers Connection between Butterwort, *Viiliä*," *Finnish American Reporter* 23, no. 7 [2009]).

What is now Finland was originally part of the Swedish Kingdom, from the thirteenth century until 1809. Many milk cultures in this region share origins and similar cultural traditions in foodways and other material folk traditions.

9. Joyce Koskenmaki, "Sharing the Culture," *The Finnish American Reporter*, January 1996, 3.

10. R. Fondén, K. Leporanta, and U. Svensson (2006), 159. There are many websites about cultured milk products, including viili. Armenian Americans report that they, too, brought their *madzoon* (or *mahdsoon*) starters to the United States in the same way.

11. Käkönen, *Natural Cooking the Finnish Way*, 187; and Brown, "The Vigorous Diet of Finland," 139.

12. R. Fondén, K. Leporanta, and U. Svensson, "Nordic/Scandinavian Fermented Milk Products, 166–67, report that the primary bacteria producing the slippery quality is a specific strain of *Lactococcus lactis Subsp. Cremories.*

13. Brown, "The Vigorous Diet of Finland," *The Cooking of Scandinavia* (New York: Time Life Books, 1968), 139.

14. Anna Maria Tanttu and Juha Tanttu, *Food from Finland* (Helsinki: Kustannuso- sakeyhtiö Otava, 1988), 24.

15. Käkönen, *Natural Cooking the Finnish Way*, 187. Käkönen uses the term "buttermilk," which is confusing. Does she mean buttermilk sold in the United States or Finnish *piima,* which is often translated as "buttermilk"? In either case, the bacteria is different from that in viili.

16. A Finnish American resident of Greater Detroit, January 2015.

17. In the early 1900s, in rural Finland, viili was made in large shallow bowls resulting in lots of the creamy crust.

18. Jingo Viitala Vachon, *Tall Timber Tales* (1973), 81.

19. Anne R. Kaplan, Marjorie A. Hoover, and Willard B. Moore, "The Finns," in *The Minnesota Ethnic Food Book* (St. Paul: Minnesota Historical Society, 1986), 151.

20. Szyszkoski, interview, 1999.

21. Egardt, "Early Milk Production Economy in Sweden," 196–97.

22. Koskenmaki, "Sharing the Culture," 3.

23. Berg, interview, 1999.

24. Rajanen, *Of Finnish Ways*, 99.

25. St. Urho is a fictitious Finnish American hero and protagonist of legend, fabricated in 1950, who is said to have saved Finland's grape vineyards from grasshoppers. Modeled after St. Patrick's Day, St. Urho's Day is celebrated across the country on March 16. For more details, see Hilary Virtanen, "Forging a Leader for a New Heritage: Finnish Americans and St. Urho," in *Pyha Urho: Fakeloresta folkloreksi* (*St. Urho: From Fakelore to Folklore*), eds. Anne Heimo, Tuomas Hovi, and Maria Vasenkari (Turku, Finland: University of Turku, 2012), 63–83; and Joanne Asala, compiler, *Finnish American Folklore: The Legend of St. Urho* (Iowa City: Penfield Books, 2001).

26. Cf. Y. Lockwood (in press). For a more detailed discussion on the social and cultural roles of both viili and *leipäjuusto* (cheese) in Finnish America, see Yvonne R. Lockwood

and William G. Lockwood, "Finnish American Milk Products in the Northwoods," in *Milk: Beyond the Dairy*, proceedings of the Oxford Symposium on Food and Cookery 1999, ed. Harlan Walker (Devon, England: Prospect Books, 2000), 232–39.

27. *Finnish American Reporter*, January 1997, 3. Viili is widely known as "feelia," in Finnish America. It is an example of Finglish. Cf. Dawkins for a discussion on the affects of food on memory and nostalgia, and Coakley on the emotional affects of food on the body. Nicole Dawkins, "The Hunger for Home: Nostalgic Affect, Embodied Memory and the Sensual Politics of Transnational Foodways," *Undergraduate Journal of Anthropology* 1 (2009): 33–42.

28. Linda Coakley, "Polish Encounters with the Irish Foodscape: An Examination of the Losses and Gains of Migrant Foodways," *Food and Foodways: Explorations in the History and Culture of Human Nourishment*, 20, no. 3–4 (2012): 307–325, DOI: 10.1080/07409710.2012.715968.

29. Commercial viili in Finland is available with sugary fruit.

30. FinnFest USA has had significant influence on the maintenance, diffusion, and reintroduction of traditional Finnish and Finnish American foods in Finnish America.

31. Cf. Julie L. Locher, "Comfort Food," *Encyclopedia of Food and Culture*, accessed Febraury 11, 2015, http://www.encyclopedia.com. Most scholars would agree that ethnic foods bring both a sense of comfort and nostalgia.

32. Cf. Mark Swislocki, *Culinary Nostalgia: Regional Food Culture and Urban Experience in Shanghai* (Palo Alto: Stanford University Press, 2008); and Anita Mannur, "Culinary Nostalgia, Authenticity, Nationalism and Diaspora," in *Culinary Fictions: Food in South Asian Diasporic Culture* (Philadelphia: Temple University Press, 2010), 27–78.

33. Cf. James L. Watson and Melissa L. Caldwell, "Introduction," in *The Cultural Politics of Food and Eating* (Malden, MA: Blackwell Publishers, 2005), 1–10; and Penny Van Esterick, "From Hunger Foods to Heritage Foods: Challenges to Food Localization in Laos," in *Fast Food/Slow Food: The Cultural Economy of the Global Food System*, ed. Richard Wilk (Altamira Press, 2006), 83–96.

34. Michael Loukinen, *Finnish American Lives*, UP North Films, 1982.

35. Amy Hubbell, "(In)Edible Algeria: Transmitting Pied-Noir Nostalgia Through Food," in *Edible Alterities: Perspective from La Francophonic*, special issue, eds. Angela Giovanangeli and Julie Robert, *Portal. Journal of Multidisciplinary International Studies* 10, no. 2, 3.

36. Novelists and poets evoke memories and nostalgia among their co-ethnics through their writing. Food for Finnish American writers provides a language by which to evoke memories and a sense of Finnishness. Titles such as "Blueberry Season," by Jane Piirto, and *Blueberry God,* by Reino Hannula, evoke memories of berry-picking and blueberries that have a special place in Finnish and Finnish American culture. Other titles are a story "Kalja" (a slightly alcoholic beverage) by Finny Lager, and poems such as "Mojakka," by Jim Johnson, "Coffee Talk," commemorating the importance of coffee time in Finnish American culture, by Kathleen Halme, "Reikäleipä and Viili," by Bernice Rednick, and "Amerikan Pie," by Mary Kinnunen, about her mother's berry pies. Short stories by the late Jingo Viitala Vachon are "Old Time Berry Picking," "Frog in the Kala Mojakka," and "Old Finnish Cooking," about fish-head and tail stew, rieska (a type of bread), blood cake, and homemade caviar. A cheer that was once shouted at Suomi College basketball games also used food to

provoke community spirit: "Silakka, mojakka, hardtack too, come on Suomi, we're for you!" (Herring, stew, crisp rye bread. . . .)

37. Hubbell, "(In)Edible Algeria."

38. Stowers, "Gastronomic Nostalgia."

39. Nora Gomez Torres, "Cubans Finding Comfort, Nostalgia in Russian Products," *Miami Herald*, November 14, 2014, accessed February 10, 2014, www.miamiherald.com/news/ . . . /article3936801.html.

40. Maria Amelia Viteri, "Nostalgia Food and Belonging: Ecuadorans in New York City," in *Ethnicity, Citizenship, and Belonging: Practice, Theory, and Spatial Dimensions*, eds. Sarah Albiez, Nelly Castro, Lara Jüssen, and Eva Youkhana (Vervuert: Iberoamericana, 2011): 221–236, accessed February 19, 2014, http://www.academia.edu/nostalgia.

41. Purnima Manekar, "India Shopping: Indian Grocery Stores and Transnational Configurations of Belonging," *Ethnos* 67, no. 1: 75–80.

42. Mannur, "Culinary Nostalgia: Salvadoran Immigrants Craving for Their Ideal Meal," *Ecology of Food and Nutrition* 51, no. 5: 374–93, accessed February 19, 2015, DOI: 10.1080/03670244.2012.696008.

43. Brad Japhe, "Japanese Comfort Food," quoted by M. O. Jones in this volume.

Comfort Food in Culinary Tourism: Negotiating "Home" as Exotic and Familiar

Lucy M. Long

Comfort food usually brings to mind familiar foods that represent security, home, and cherished grandmothers. The phrase emerged in the US in the late 1970s and '80s, and has been embraced by mainstream American food culture, where it usually refers to foods associated with a generic and stereotypical but mythic national past grounded in home and family and represented by hearty dishes heavy on carbohydrates, sugar, and salt, or by cooking and eating styles that emphasize quantity, relaxation, and lack of any physical or psychological or emotional stress. The category appears in restaurants, cooking shows, recipe books, magazines, and advertising, and is becoming a global phenomenon.[1]

It is not the type of food, however, one expects to find in culinary tourism, "eating out of curiosity," or traveling primarily for a food experience, a popular emerging niche within the tourism industry. Culinary tourism, also known as food tourism and gastrotourism, usually emphasizes novelty, exoticism, and even a slight bit of danger in trying new experiences. Industry producers tend to promote upscale, gourmet, and "memorable" foods and dining experiences—qualities that are seemingly the opposite of comfort food. The two trends appear to be contradictory, yet there are now instances of comfort food being incorporated into culinary tourism, not just as a descriptor of foods being offered in restaurants as part of hospitality services to tourists, but as the main attraction and destination of culinary tours. Furthermore, they are appearing not only in regions usually associated with comfort food, such as the Midwest and the South, but throughout the country and in urban areas as well—and not only in the US, but also around the globe.

For example, in 2009, a newspaper in New Mexico, the *Albuquerque Journal*, carried the headline, "New Tourism Department Initiative Seeks to Create Culinary Trail for Famous Comfort Food." Several years later, a website for tourism in Indiana announced a culinary tour offering "Southern comfort, German heritage and locally grown produce" in the southwestern part of the state. Similarly, the description for "Authentic Ohio Amish Country Tours" boasted that "on one tour, guests can share a private meal with an Amish bishop and his family, learning about their life story and traditions while you relish Amish comfort food." Yet another tour advertisement promises to provide the "sweet warmth of hearty meals to fill your heart with gastronomic joy," and concludes by asking: "But where will you find the best comfort food in London?"

How do these tours bridge the contradictions between these two categories? How do they define comfort food? What audiences are they trying to attract? And how successful are they? Do they change the food itself in any manner, or impact our perceptions of either comfort food or culinary tourism? Does this convergence have broader significance? What does it mean for "familiar" foods generally associated with home and family to be presented as an attraction for tourists? Whose home and whose families are being presented? Is home a "real" and physical space, or is it metaphoric, evoked by images? And what of those who do not find memories of home nurturing and affirming? Are other associations offered through these tours that allow for the temporary relief from stress expected from "comfort foods"?

I address these questions by focusing on examples in the American Midwest. I draw upon personal experiences and ethnographic research as well as advertising and publicity by providers within the tourism and hospitality industries. I also examine the concepts of comfort food and culinary tourism, defining the terms and identifying points where they might converge.

Definitions—Comfort Food

The first use of the phrase "comfort food" seems to be from Dr. Joyce Brothers in a 1966 newspaper column titled "Psychological Problems Play a Part in Obesity." Therein, she writes: "Studies indicate that most adults, when under severe emotional stress, turn to what could be called 'comfort food'—food associated with the security of childhood, like mother's poached egg or famous chicken soup."[2] A better known and apparently more influential appearance, however, was in an article in the magazine section of the *Washington Post* on December 25, 1977, in which restaurant critic Phyllis Richman called upon it in describing shrimp and grits—not a dish that would immediately come to mind for many Americans as a comfort food. In 2013, Richman revisited the term, illustrating it with an anecdote of an occasion in which she was sick and wanted chicken noodle soup. She observed that the concept existed; it simply needed a name, and even though the specific foods illustrating that concept differ for each of us, we all seem to understand it.[3]

Richman's claim seems accurate since the term has since been widely adopted into American foodways vocabulary, used in the commercial food scene of restaurants, cookbooks, and domestic and cooking magazines as well as in everyday speech. According to the *Oxford English Dictionary*, comfort food is now defined as "food that comforts or affords solace."[4] These foods usually—but not always—tend to be high in fat, sugar, and carbohydrates, are oftentimes convenient or easy to prepare (not stressful), provide physical warmth and emotional nurturing, and carry positive memories of the past and feelings of familiarity and security.

Sociologist Julie Locher offers a definition based on her research with college students: "Comfort food may be best thought of as any food consumed by individuals, often during periods of stress, that evokes positive emotions and is associated with significant social relationships."[5] Locher points out that the phrase came into vernacular speech in the 1990s, becoming particularly popular after the events of September 11, 2001, a time of social upheaval on a global scale, perhaps relevant to understanding its usage in culinary tourism.[6] In further study of the concept, Locher and several colleagues identify a number of characteristics of comfort food gleaned from surveys of undergraduates.[7] These foods displayed several patterns: they evoked a sense of familiarity, were eaten when "feeling down" or needing "an extra boost," and were often consumed when alone. From this research, the authors also identify four categories of comfort foods according to the primary characteristic of bringing about relief from stress: nostalgic, indulgence, convenience, and physical comfort foods. The specific foods representing these categories differed according to each individual, but there has since developed a popular consensus of what comfort foods are, and these tend to be "all-American"[8] ones associated with home cooking, such as meatloaf and mashed potatoes, macaroni and cheese, fried chicken, pies, cakes, and so on.

The research by Locher and colleagues has ramifications for understanding how comfort food is used in culinary tourism. They note that familiar foods are turned to for stress relief and comfort because new and unfamiliar ones tend to cause anxiety (2005: 21).[9] "Familiar" tends to be understood in terms of home, family, and childhood, and those concepts are frequently invoked in reference to comfort food: "homemade," "home-cooked," "family-style," or "just like grandmother made" are typical descriptions. For many of us, this nostalgia romanticizes the past, but its role in allowing us to participate in those idealizations perhaps helps to explain why comfort food has been embraced by the general public. While later studies have questioned the efficacy of comfort food's power to comfort, one study claims that it fulfills a need to belong and to alleviate loneliness.[10] Home ideally represents a place where a feeling of belongingness is nurtured.

Furthermore, because of its primary function being the relief of stress, comfort food has become a recognized genre that is evaluated differently from "regular" food. Rather than being judged for its nutritional, health, or other qualities, it is judged for its psychological and emotional benefits.[11] Reframing a food as belonging to that genre means that it will then be judged accordingly—and the consumption of it can be justified on the basis of needing those benefits. Presenting a food as comfort food, then, means that the usual concerns for health, nutrition, convenience, expense, environmental sustainability, or other factors motivating our food choices can be suspended while we focus on the emotional and nurturing aspects of the food.[12] For example, a bowl of ice cream after a relationship dissolves, a carbohydrate-loaded meal when back home from college or visiting family, or high-fat and sugar-fried dough for various holiday celebrations could all be deemed physically unhealthy, but can be justified because of a need for comfort.

That comfort food has come to be equated with unhealthful eating is evident in newer trends in comfort food that attempt to bring it in line with current concerns over nutrition, health, the industrial food system, and environmental sustainability. The internet, cookbooks, magazines, and cooking shows frequently push recipes for stereotypical comfort food dishes (macaroni and cheese, meatloaf, fried chicken, mashed potatoes and gravy, desserts, and so on) that use ingredients considered healthier, more nutritious, and prepared in ways that use less fat or that help retain or boost the nutrients.[13] Locally and organically grown, seasonal, and native ingredients are also being promoted, particularly in replacing the frequently heavily processed ingredients in many comfort foods, such as cream of mushroom soup in green bean casserole.[14] Comfort food has also been appropriated by the "foodie" movement that approaches cooking and eating as recreation, entertainment, and artistic expression, so that updated versions of classic comfort foods—"comfort food done with a twist"—are now popular. Furthermore, the cultural diversity and the individualism of American society are reflected in the recognition that the specific foods providing comfort differ from person to person and group to group.[15]

Definitions—Culinary Tourism

Food has always been a part of hospitality services offered to travelers, but it was generally not treated by American or British society as an attraction in itself.[16] A niche within tourism that focused on food only started to develop in the 1990s, with tourism scholars and industry partners in England, New Zealand, Australia, and Canada leading the way, and the US joining these efforts in the mid-2000s. Termed "gastrotourism," "food tourism," and "culinary tourism," it grew initially out of wine tourism and has generally emphasized higher-end, gourmet, distinctive, and exotic foods. By the latter part of the first decade of 2000, the global tourism industry had discovered culinary tourism. It now thrives as one of the most popular types of international and domestic tourism and is perceived as a significant contributor to economic development.[17] As an industry, culinary tourism focuses on the commercial viability of particular dishes, cuisines, and venues, evaluating them on their potential for drawing tourists away from home and spending money on products and experiences. The emphasis is on offering foods that will motivate travel and consumption, which usually translates into higher-end, gourmet foods that are exotic in some way and not available at home.

Comfort food, because of its associations with home and the familiar, would not seem to be a suitable category of food to offer; it might be appropriate for those tourists not particularly interested in food, but culinary tourists are generally seeking foods that are distinctive and unfamiliar or prepared in a manner that is new to them.[18] Yet comfort food is being incorporated into these tours. Approaching culinary tourism as a cultural activity helps shed light on how and why comfort food might fit in. Tourism, in general, can be seen as a negotiation of novelty and familiarity, or, as the motto for tourism in Hawaii stated, "exotic but safe."[19] A destination has to be exotic enough to stir curiosity and to draw people away from home, but it needs to offer enough safety so that people are not afraid to visit. Culinary tourism similarly is a negotiation between the exotic and the familiar. The food needs to be novel, strange, or different enough to stir curiosity, but familiar enough to be recognizable as an edible substance. Such "eating out of curiosity," as I first defined culinary tourism, is a constant balancing act between what is new to an individual or group and what is familiar, as well as between palatability and individual experiences.[20]

A more extensive definition of culinary tourism as "the voluntary intentional participation in the foodways of an Other" opens up more possibilities for types of foodways experiences and types of Others or novel foods.[21] Within this formulation, foodways includes the total range of activities and processes around food, expanding tourism to more than the consumption of food to its production, procurement, preservation, preparation, presentation, and even cleanup and disposal. Also, foods considered exotic can represent different times, regions, places, belief systems, classes, occupations, ages, and personal tastes, not just the more common cultural or ethnic Other. This expands the range of foods and food experiences that can be included as attractions for culinary tourism, and the industry is slowly recognizing that. Regional foods, for example, have become a highly marketable destination, and heritage tourism now celebrates dishes and menus recreated from the past. Other aspects of foodways are also being explored—especially preparation, with cooking classes being popular destinations and "add-on's" to tours which sometimes even include shopping for ingredients in another country. Agritourism—tourism focused on agriculture—is also recognizing that eating food might be connected to raising it, so that orchards, dairies, farms, and vineyards now frequently include tastings or dinners along with tours of their vicinities.

Comfort food within the culinary tourism industry may reflect marketing strategies that constantly search for something new to offer customers. It also demonstrates the expanding notions of food as foodways and of what foods are edible and palatable. Within this more cultural-based understanding of culinary tourism, though, it may also represent a turning inward to recognize and celebrate what has been overlooked "at home," so to speak, or it may represent a shift of what is familiar to be something only accessible as a tourist. To better understand the meanings of these trends, we need to look at what types of tours are featuring comfort food, what audiences they seem to appeal to, what types of foods are included, and what associations are attached to them.

Examples of Comfort Food in Culinary Tourism

I explore here three tourism projects. Each represents different approaches being used within culinary tourism, and highlights different themes of comfort as well as types of Other. The first features the Amish, an ethnic group historically considered outside the American mainstream culture—exotic—who have been the object of a thriving tourism industry. Their foodways reflect their history and includes some unique dishes, but actually shares many commonalities with standard "American" fare, making the cuisine a relatively familiar one for culinary tourists that can represent nostalgia as well as an ethnic Other. The second example is a much more recently developed tour in a part of Ohio popular for outdoor recreation whose natural environment and seasonal changes to that environment are prime tourist attractions. The food offered is familiar "classic comfort foods," and these are presented as offering physical comfort that is necessary and well deserved after braving the cold weather and natural hardships of winter. The third tour features restaurants in a section of Indiana offering a range of foods representing different types of comfort and different types of Other. This last has undergone several name changes, suggesting that the place of comfort food is still being worked out within the tourism industry. All three are in the same region—the Midwest— and thus share broader expectations surrounding their food and culture.

The Cultural Context—the Midwest

The Midwest generally designates the eastern interior of the country, including the states of Illinois, Indiana, Iowa, Michigan, Minnesota, Missouri, Ohio, and Wisconsin. The Great Plains states (Kansas, Nebraska, North Dakota, Oklahoma, and South Dakota) are sometimes included.[22] Although vast differences occur in topography, settlement history, and ethnic makeup, the area shares features that have shaped a common culinary culture—pioneer heritage, agriculture as the historical basis of economies and society, strong ties to industrial agriculture, social and political conservatism, significant cultural divisions between urban and rural, and an emphasis on family as the central unit. The region generally also displays an interesting contradiction of embracing of mass-produced, corporate foods—many of which are produced there, so technically are "local"—while also emphasizing family foodways traditions and home cooking.

Midwestern food is the epitome of comfort food—lots of carbohydrates and starches, fats, and sugar, a "meat and potatoes" menu, and large quantities. It is a "no surprises," straightforward, and plain style of cooking in terms of ingredients and methods, but it is felt to be prepared attentively and cooked "with love." A recipe site describes it in the following way: "Prepare for hearty fare: we're heading to the Heartland! When we say 'American food,' we mean the soothing comfort foods of the Midwest: fare that's hearty and simple, not fancy or frivolous."[23]

That attitude makes it difficult to sell Midwestern food to culinary tourists, who tend to look for more gourmet, upscale dishes that are unique and require culinary skills. It is not a food culture that emphasizes curiosity and the exotic. Instead, it is pragmatic in that people want to know exactly what they are getting for their money and know that they will like it. Food is also used more to bring people together than to demonstrate individuality and innovation, so that standard Midwestern comfort food does not offer the kind of cultural capital that tourists oftentimes seek. In general, this means that the food needs to be "fancied up" in order to attract those consumers interested in fine dining or gourmet cooking. That is what usually happens in marketing and advertising for restaurants. A restaurant in Indianapolis, Indiana, for example advertises "Midwestern comfort food with a culinary twist."[24] Its menu is a mixture of old and new, local and international, offering items such as "Grilled cheese nostalgia," "brat burger," fried chicken, hand-cut noodles.

These attitudes towards the food of the Midwest carry over to tourism in the area in general, which is sometimes referred to as "the fly-over region" of the US because of its apparent lack of holding anything of interest to tourists. Aside from a few major cities, particularly Chicago, it is not usually a destination for international tourists, but it emphasizes domestic tourism within the region with a focus on outdoor recreation, family activities, "staycations," and smaller city attractions. It is within this context that the comfort food culinary tours are being developed.

Example 1: Amish Comfort Food and Culinary Tourism

The Amish have long been a tourist attraction, a fact that they have manipulated for profit and, to some extent, cultural sustainability. They originated in Switzerland in 1525 with roots in the Protestant Reformation. A group split in 1693 and became Mennonite, which explains some of the overlaps and confusions between the two groups in the US. Religious persecution forced the Amish to leave their homeland and they no longer exist in Europe. They came to North America in two waves, first in the mid-1700s and again in the early 1800s, establishing farming communities, particularly in central Ohio and eastern and northern Indiana, the two states that today have the largest populations of Amish out of the total of around 261,000 individuals. Amish communities can now be found in twenty-eight states and the province of Ontario in Canada, with significant populations in Iowa, Michigan, Missouri, New York, and Wisconsin.

In the US, the Amish adapted the ingredients available in colonial and pioneer America, particularly, corn, molasses, apples, cabbage, and meat and other products from pigs, cows, and chickens. Amish cuisine today features potatoes, noodles, hearty soups, sausages, root vegetables, sauerkraut and other pickled vegetables (beets, green beans, cucumbers), bread, and cheese. Cream-based gravies moisten the food, and sweet and sour (sugar and vinegar) flavors appear frequently in pickles and salads. Pies, both savory and sweet, are popular. Chicken "pot pies" are common, as are a molasses pie, called "shoofly pie," and a dried apple one known as *snitz* pie. Pickles and relishes are standard accompaniments to meals, and "chow-chow" has become an iconic Amish dish, as have apple butter, sweet and sour cabbage, and such meat products as bologna and scrapple (a "pudding" made from ground beef and pork heart), liver, and kidneys mixed with cornmeal. The Amish diet includes plentiful sweets—cakes, sweet rolls, and specialties, such as the regional Pennsylvania "whoopee pie" (two rounds of small chocolate cake around a crème filling).

This is quintessential comfort food. It is fattening, and full of things that are not considered healthful or nutritious by Americans. Marketing of these foods and tourism projects, though, make no apologies for that. The food offers a way to experience a lifestyle from the past that is seen as a needed antidote to the stress of modern living. Although the Amish are exotic, they are a relatively "safe" Other, and so is their food. It embodies the values of the past, a past that comforts on the basis of nostalgia for "simpler" times.

A website for Ohio "Amish country" explains their food this way:

Amish Country Dining

You might call it comfort food. We just call it "dinner."

Amish Country attracts people for many reasons—scenery, crafts, quilts and furniture, to name a few. But at the heart of it all is the food. The outside world calls it "comfort food." We just call it dinner. Amish cooks have been blending simple ingredients into delicious treats for generations, and now you can enjoy them too, whether it's sharing a family-style meal reminiscent of grandma's house, or sinking your teeth into a cream-filled "whoopee pie."[25]

The site then goes on to list venues, including restaurants (Dutchman restaurants, inns, and bakeries run by the Dutchman Hospitality Group), wine cellars, a gourmet market, a cheese-maker/shop, a flea market, Schmucker's store and café, and Amish Door village (a restaurant, Victorian inn, bakery, and shops). It makes no attempt to try to appease guilt for consuming these rich foods although they are stereotypically hearty and heavy fare. Instead, they offer them as a window into another way of life, so that being a tourist with them helps one escape to the past. Another tour site emphasizes the educational aspect of culinary tourism:

A tour of Amish Country is a fantastic way to learn about the rich history of the determined, hardworking, and tight-knit community.

Amish Heartland Tours offers several tour options that lend a closer look at the Amish way of life. On one tour, guests can share a private meal with an Amish bishop and his family, learning about their life story and traditions while you relish Amish comfort food. Knowledgeable guides lead all of the Amish Country tour options, . . . You may even have the option to stop at a home bakery, where the smell of fresh apple fritters, cheese tarts, and glistening donuts will tempt you into a midday feast.[26]

Interestingly, another site points out that what is nostalgia for tourists is everyday and contemporary life for the Amish:

All that stuff about "local," "seasonal" and "artisanal" is nothing new for the Amish. Of course "new" is hardly what the Amish are about, as a two-hour drive to Holmes County from Columbus engrossingly verifies.[27]

This could be read as bringing comfort food into the contemporary food scene. It addresses issues that are of current concerns surrounding sustainability, appealing to both environmentally and ethically aware consumers as well as "foodies." In this way, it offsets the nostalgia also carried in comfort food. Home, then, is updated—still familiar, but able to address modern concerns.

Tourism among the Amish has included a range of formats, beginning with classic tours in which busloads of tourists are taken to Amish communities, usually ending in restaurants and shops. The Amish themselves have also developed an extensive hospitality and tourism industry, with tourist "villages" consisting of restaurants, inns, bakeries, stores, and special events. Among these is one of the most immersive forms of culinary tourism: dinners in an Amish home, prepared and served by an Amish family. These dinners are problematic because of rules limiting interactions with "outsiders," but some Amish families have created such tours, developing strategies for presenting the food without actually sharing in its consumption with tourists. These dinners are set up in advance with prepaid registrations, which can be quite high, and a set menu. The number of tourists that can be accommodated is fairly small, lending an air of "family" and authenticity to these dinners, although there frequently is little actual communication with family members. Even so, the events tend to involve the entire family as well as some community members. The women and girls prepare the food, help serve, and clean up; the boys and men assist by killing chickens, bringing in ingredients, as well as setting up tables. Usually furniture has to be removed so that one long table could be set up to simulate family-style eating.

I attended one such dinner in Pennsylvania in 2008. The father, the patriarch of the clan, explained the food, gave a brief history of the Amish, and talked about his family and how they grew and prepared the food themselves. The women served heaping platters of fried chicken, beef and noodles, mashed potatoes and gravy, beans, coleslaw, biscuits, lots of pickles, and pies for dessert. Platters were passed around, and guests served themselves family-style. I say "guests" with hesitation since we were paying customers and did not know the family or have any connection to them beyond what they offered as part of the tour. The event definitely emphasized home as the central space in which a rural and idyllic notion of family was being performed.

The food represented several aspects of comfort: nostalgia, in that it represented a past prior to modernity, and indulgence, because of the high fat, sugar, salt, and starch content. Convenience also was present for me and the other tourists, although the inconvenience of its preparation was emphasized by the tour operators and in the descriptions of it by the family patriarch. The food itself seemed to be an authentic representation of Amish foodways, but we had no way of knowing what this particular family actually ate at daily meals. Consuming it in this context gave a sense of participating in the everyday lives of this group of people. It also gave us a point of connection with the Amish as well as with each other; we could talk about the food, discussing similarities with other familiar dishes. The family-style dining enabled us to overlook the fact that welcoming strangers into one's home was generally not an accepted part of the culture and that we were definitely outsiders. The familiarity of most of the dishes, though, helped us feel "at home" and can be interpreted as offering a sense of safety and security rather than the danger associated with exotic foods.

Example 2: Classic Comfort Food in Central Ohio

The second example comes from the Hocking Hills area in south central Ohio, an hour's drive at most from the capital city of Columbus and known primarily for scenic drives and outdoor recreation. The ad reads as follows:

2015 Comfort Food Cruise

The tastiest event in Hocking Hills spans the next two weekends—January 31–February 1 and February 7–8

Whether it feels like home, or it's your first time in our neck of the woods, there's no better way to explore the region than on a cruise through the Hocking Hills. Enjoy the beauty of winter while indulging in some of your favorite comfort foods. For six days, you can taste these dishes all around the region. Go for the gusto and try to taste all ten in a day or take a leisurely tour and take as long as six days. Best of all, there are plenty of things to do in Hocking Hills. At the first guilty twinge, just set out for a hike on one of our trails . . . In addition to using some of that comfort food fuel, you will be treated to a feast for the senses as you pass cave walls covered with ice beards and waterfalls frozen in suspended animation.

Tickets: $15/person. $5 of every ticket sold will benefit local food pantries.[28]

The Hocking Hills is not an area celebrated for its food, but food is usually part of hospitality services, along with lodging and transportation. Tourism executer Karen Raymore, of ExplorehockingHills.com, came up with the idea of the comfort food trail as a way to attract more tourists.[29] Organizers felt that local culture could not boast unique dishes, but it could claim a variety of items usually described as comfort foods. Although these might be considered boring to some tourists, since they are not necessarily exotic, gourmet, or high-end, they represent the local culture. They then used social media to survey what people thought of as comfort food, identifying some specific dishes. They then took that list to the ten participating restaurants that chose items to add to their menu. The recipes, ingredients, and manner of presentation were left up to the restaurants themselves, doing the best they could and using their own understandings of comfort food and what customers might be looking for. There were guidelines, however, pertaining to the local identity of the dishes. One restaurant had a Scottish theme and wanted to offer a Scottish dish. The organizers decided that it did not fit: "If it's something you've never heard of, it's not comfort food."[30] The types of food listed in the announcement would be familiar to most residents of the area as well as to mainstream American food culture: biscuits and gravy, breakfast burrito, mac and cheese, baked steak sliders, pizza, meatloaf, mixed berry cobbler, spaghetti, chicken and noodles, and chocolate ice cream.

The ten restaurants initially offered those dishes as a sampling, but some also developed them into larger servings and part of the menu. Tourists purchased tickets for the samplings and set their own driving schedules during the weekend of the tour. It was extremely successful. Tourists raved about it, and restaurants were delighted with turnout. They expected 100 tourists the first year (in 2014), and got 400. The second year, they had over 700 people. For 2016, more restaurants want to participate, and three weekends at the end of January are being set aside for the tour instead of two. According to the organizers, tourists came from in state and surrounding regions, but also some international tour companies picked up on the marketing.

The tour highlights several elements of comfort food. The dishes offered are ordinary, everyday fare for many people in this region, and could even be called all-American. Pizza and spaghetti are Americanized to the point that they have lost their ethnic associations; so has the burrito, which has been adapted from southwestern and Mexican American foodways to American tastes and incorporated into the national and commercial foodscape. Meat-loaf, macaroni and cheese, and steak are also standards in mainstream menus. The dishes include meat and starch combinations with plentiful dairy and sugar—classic American comfort food familiar to many Americans. Two of the dishes—biscuits and gravy and chicken and noodles—could be associated with region (the first with the South) or even ethnicity (the latter with the Amish or German settlers), but they tend to represent "pioneer" cooking in this region, thus falling into the nostalgia category.

The tour also connects this food to natural surroundings and to the seasons. Winter tends to be the usual time for comfort food, when our bodies want something warm and perhaps need more carbohydrates to keep us warm. These dishes belong to Locher's category of physical comfort food. They also suggest that the normal division of the year is into four seasons. American culture is founded on that expectation and on the resulting moves of social life from indoors to outdoors, reflecting the historical geography of the settlement of the nation in areas such as New England and the Mid-Atlantic states, which have four distinct seasons. Also, the idea of tying comfort food to natural sites and outdoor activities could suggest that the food itself is less "cultivated"—the simpler, plainer style of cooking associated with comfort food is better suited to the enjoyment of nature. This, perhaps, represents nostalgia for simpler times.

The third category of comfort food utilized here is indulgence foods. Ice cream obviously fits this category, but so can other items because of their heartiness and high fat, sugar, and salt content. The tour recognizes indulgence—even offering that as one of the attractions—but, in its reference to a "guilty twinge" after eating, suggests that such indulgence can be offset by hiking. The comfort food then becomes fuel, so that indulging in it is actually physically necessary.

The "classic" comfort foods featured in this tour were expected to be familiar to most tourists. They were not being presented as exotic in themselves nor was the area in which they were found; however, they represented the lack of stress expected to be discovered in this region where appreciation of nature and participation in outdoor recreations were possible. That possibility contrasts with the everyday circumstances of modern living, and therefore is the exotic Other drawing the tourists. As such, the familiarity of the food balances the exoticism, grounding tourists in nostalgic comfort.

Example 3: Region, Ethnicity, and Ambiguity:
Southwest Indiana Comfort Food Trail

The third example is from Indiana, a state representing the "heartland" of the nation. As such, its food would be expected to be quintessentially American, reflecting historical patterns and aesthetics. Interestingly, the trail references other regions and ethnicities, almost as if in recognition that the heartland is not exotic enough to elicit tourists' curiosity.

Southwest Indiana Comfort Food Trail

Southern comfort, German heritage and locally grown produce.

From fried biscuits at Joe Huber Family Farm and Restaurant in Borden to spatzle at the Gerst Haus in Evansville, the region's beloved foods reflect Southern influences from Kentucky, German and Swiss roots and the rural heritage of farms and orchards. You can pick your own fruit at Bryant's Blueberries in New Salisbury, visit goats at Cabriole Farmstead Goat Cheese in Greenville, try local wines at Huber's Orchard, Winery and Vineyards and enjoy artisan beer at the New Albanian Brewing company. You'll also find treats that have been favored for more than a century, such as buttery sweet caramels and spicy Red Hots at Jeffersonville's Schimpff's Confectionery or the astonishing crunch of Tell City Pretzels.[31]

This tour offers more variety than the previous one, listing quintessential comfort foods—biscuits, noodles (spatzle), cheese, fruit, sweets, "treats"—but adding wine and beer, items that can be considered comfort foods associated more with adulthood than childhood. It also points to cooking processes associated with comfort (fried) as well as ones that show care (artisanal). The "pick-your-own" fruit allows individuals to personalize the food while also evoking a rural past in which everyone participated in harvesting their food. Perhaps most important is the assertion that these are "beloved" foods in the region, suggesting that they are both familiar and hold an emotional attachment for native eaters.

Interestingly, the tour also references another region of the US—the South—that is commonly associated in the public imagination with comfort food, treating it as if that regional food automatically will be an attraction to tourists. It also mentions specific ethnic groups—Swiss and German—which would be considered exotic to some Americans, but it includes their culinary traditions as a familiar part of the Midwestern region's comfort foods. The trail highlights the nostalgia category of comfort food by speaking of heritage and roots. It points out that some of the foods have been regional favorites for more than a century, solidly connecting them to the past. Some of the imagery is also placed in the past—local, farm, orchard, rural—adding to nostalgia. The tour also suggests that these comfort foods fit the indulgence category in referring to some of the offerings as "treats."

The trail, however, seems to be problematic and not entirely successful. It also suggests that the phrase "comfort food" did not seem to work since the name of the trail was changed in 2015 from "Southwest Indiana Comfort Food Trail" to "A Southern Comfort Food Trail" and then to "Tour, Taste, Traditions: Your Guide to Indiana's Full Bounty."[32] It turns out that the trail itself was not a local initiative, nor organized as a cohesive tour, but designed by a commercial magazine, *Midwest Living*, that picked out restaurants and designated them as part of the trail. The local and state convention and visitor's bureaus and tourism offices seemed unaware of the trail and even the local restaurants listed had no knowledge of it. When I spoke to the co-owners of one restaurant that was described specifically as offering comfort food, neither one had heard of the trail. One of them was hesitant to accept the comfort food label, saying that they preferred to describe their offerings as "real food," like one would find at "your grandmother's table."[33] She also noted that, of course, everyone's grandmother might serve different things or might not even cook at all.

These responses suggest the fluidity of the category of comfort food as well as the associations of it with being not "exciting" or exotic enough to draw tourists. After all, many people in that region still eat these foods on a daily basis and would not need to leave home for them. In fact, the big draw in the region, according to one tourism provider, was a fall festival in Evansville that boasts that it is the second largest street fair in the country after New Orleans' Mardi Gras. Lasting three days and drawing 200,000 people each day, it definitely does not promote comfort food. Instead, according to its website: "You can certainly find standard festival fare, but more adventurous eaters should look for exotic choices like alligator stew, chocolate-covered grasshoppers and brain sandwiches. Spend a day or two to enjoy all the fun: live music, parades and midway."[34]

Observations: Converging Genres

Comfort food and culinary tourism seem to be contradictory, if not conflicting, in their emphasis on the familiar and exotic, yet they also share some key features. In their points of similarities, however, they are able to converge and fit together in a way that does not seem incongruous.[35] Both involve an individual's perspective of what foods fit into those categories. That is, what is comforting to one person might not be to another, and what is exotic to one group of people might be familiar to another. This fluidity of boundaries means that tourism and hospitality providers need to constantly negotiate the specific dishes or foodways experiences being offered with the experiences and tastes of the anticipated consumers. In doing so, those providers are also defining what constitutes those categories, so examples both reflect and shape individual and cultural perceptions.

Both categories of food experiences play with balancing the familiar with the exotic, with the familiar providing the baseline, the norm, in a way, for the defining of other experiences. Culinary tourism, in general, can be seen as a negotiation between the exotic and the familiar, as well as the between edibility and palatability.[36] A place, event, group, process, or artifact needs to be different enough to entice people away from their homes (either physical or metaphorical), but it needs to be familiar enough that the potential tourist feels safe trying it out.[37] Comfort food, in contrast, emphasizes familiar food experiences that will not cause surprise, alarm, or stress. In theory, and by definition, it is the opposite of "eating out of curiosity." In reality, consumers oftentimes act upon curiosity in how a familiar food will taste in a new context, made with new ingredients, and with new preparation techniques, but the edibility or palatability of the dish itself is usually not in question, as it might be in tourism. I suggest here that culinary tourism providers use comfort food to create a sense of familiarity and safety, similar to the observation by tourism researchers Quan and Wang, that continuing daily routines of food consumption can create an "ontological comfort of home" that "helps overcome anxieties and unfitness caused by unfamiliar environments on journey."[38]

Both categories also utilize the idea of home as either an actual physical space or a metaphor. Culinary tourism, according to industry definitions, requires literally leaving home in order to travel to another location to experience food.[39] In comfort food, home is referenced through production style—with frequent claims of being "homemade"—and is frequently conflated with family—as in serving a group at a table with communal dishes and being called "family-style" or "home-style" service. Also, recipes are frequently identified as coming from or imitating those made by grandmothers and mothers, calling upon the traditional gender role of women as rulers and purveyors of the kitchen, the home, and other domestic areas of life. The appearance of comfort food in culinary tourism suggests that the qualities of comfort food—representing tradition, relief, security, and, above all, home—are no longer a regular part of our lives and can therefore be presented as exotic, as Other, and as an object of curiosity. If comfort food represents Home as a metaphorical space of security, perhaps Home is now exotic. The sense of belonging that is associated with home, similarly, is no longer found literally at home, but is exotic and sought elsewhere.

Also, both comfort food and culinary tourism are genres—categories carrying their own evaluative guidelines and expectations—that are simultaneously invented ones for commercial purposes and "native" ones that resonate with the general public. An essential theme in both is the opportunity to consume food that is either out of the ordinary or that would otherwise be considered unhealthful. Framing an eating experience as either of those categories, then, means that the food will be evaluated according to how well it fulfills the expectations of those genres.

In this sense, both categories can be seen as offering spaces in which the usual rules of behavior are suspended, "allowing" us to eat foods we might not normally consider consuming. Such spaces can be thought of as liminal, from the French folklorist Arnold van Gennep, who coined the term "liminality" in *Rites des Passage* (1909), which was also described by anthropologist Victor Turner as a condition of being "betwixt and between." Another definition of liminality comes from Alessandro Falassi, who refers to it as "time out of time" in regard to festivals, namely a state of suspension separated from a previous condition and not yet incorporated into the new one. "[F]or me the essence of liminality is to be found in its release from normal constraints, making possible the deconstruction of the 'uninteresting' constructions of common sense, the 'meaningfulness of ordinary life'. . . . Liminality is the domain of the 'interesting,' or of 'uncommon sense.'"[40]

Tourism scholars have borrowed the concept of liminality to explain behaviors tourists exhibit that they would normally find offensive or even immoral.[41] Applied to culinary tourism, it suggests a psychological frame of mind in which tourists consume—or, at least, taste—foods they would normally see as inedible or unpalatable. But not all culinary tourism needs to be that extreme. A tourist might consume foods he or she normally considers unhealthful or outside their usual dietary restrictions, such as large quantities of fat or sugar, larger portions than usual, or different preparation techniques that frequently characterize comfort food. Any type of Other is available for culinary tourism, although the tourism industry tends to highlight the cultural Other.

Similarly, the category of comfort food offers a psychological space in which we eat for emotional reasons rather than nutritional, health, economic, convenience, fuel, or other pragmatic factors. Reframing foods that are frequently considered unhealthful and non-nutritious as comfort foods allows us to justify indulging in them, suspending the normal rules for consumption. Comfort food, then, offers liminality, outside of our usual, everyday lives. From this perspective, both culinary tourism and comfort food can be seen as liminal categories in which we can explore and consume what is exotic or familiar, comforting or discomforting. As one individual responded in an informal query about these tours: "Calling it comfort food is just an excuse to eat stuff that's usually unhealthy for me; putting comfort food in culinary tourism is a double excuse!"[42] Unfortunately, the reality of "coming home" to scales and clothes that no longer fit all too often demonstrates that what we eat during those liminal periods does stay with us.

One final thought is that tourism itself, according to scholars who study it as a cultural phenomenon, is not just a matter of travel—as the tourism industry defines it—but involves a different way of looking at the world. John Urry proposed the concept of the "tourist gaze," in which tourists look with curiosity, with an openness to see wonder, in objects, activities, places, and people.[43] Individuals can be tourists in name only, in that they can travel without being curious about their surroundings. My own formulation of culinary tourism recognizes that the tourist gaze can be turned towards food anywhere, that it involves looking at food with curiosity, with a questioning of its edibility, palatability, functions, aesthetics, history, or meanings. That gaze can also be turned inwards onto our own familiar or everyday foods. In this sense, it looks at what we take for granted as if it is exotic to us, as if it is brand new, and also looks more deeply into it, recognizing its potential to carry meaningful connections. In this sense, comfort food is an ideal subject for the culinary tourist gaze, since it tends to be rich in personal memories and emotional associations.

Conclusions

In conclusion, these tours—and other examples—suggest that culinary tourism highlights different categories of comfort food, depending on the food culture being featured and the relationship of the anticipated tourists to that culture. Nostalgia and physical comfort are emphasized in certain settings, but indulgence is a common denominator. These tours give us an opportunity to indulge in foods that we normally would not. Interestingly, the convenience category of comfort foods seems to be implicit in all of these tours; after all, eating away from home means that someone else is doing the cooking and cleaning; the experience is therefore convenient for the tourist regardless of how inconvenient it is for the producers. In fact, the more inconvenient foods are, the more they seem to affirm the status of the tourist as being in a position to indulge.

Furthermore, comfort food seems to play several roles in culinary tourism, again depending on the relationship of the tourists to the food culture being presented. For cultures that are exotic to the tourist, the category of comfort foods offers a sense of familiarity and safety. It then allows tourists to experience someone else's familiar foodways and feel secure while doing so. This might explain why such tours seem to be successful now in large urban areas or in international destinations—both of which would be exotic to many Western tourists. The former tend to focus on neighborhoods within cities and feature restaurants there that serve the local community; while the latter frequently offer eating in a home or in a family-type atmosphere. Framing the food as comfort food defines it as edible and palatable, suggests that the setting is safe, and highlights the commonalties of humanity's organization into families. As Quan and Wang suggested in reference to routine food habits continued during tourism experiences, perhaps the idea of comfort food, whether one's own familiar food or someone else's, creates a "psychological island of home."[44]

On the other hand, culinary tourism can exoticize the familiar. By definition, comfort food is familiar, but featuring it in tourism positions it as an object of curiosity. The simple act of identifying it opens it to new ways of looking at it—as a carrier of memories, a representation of heritage and culture, an artistic statement by a chef, or as a meaningful expression of an individual's beliefs and experiences. Some tours identify the various connections and deeper meanings comfort food offers, while others treat it as needing to be up-dated in some way—such as incorporating local ingredients, new cooking techniques, or more gourmet presentations. The latter approach tends to be the trend within the hospitality and tourism industry, partly because such adaptations can then command higher prices, while the former is found more in projects by educational or cultural organizations.[45] This might explain the ambiguity of the Indiana comfort food tour. Providers were not entirely comfortable with the idea of their food being termed "comfort food." Calling it such seemed to suggest that the food was lacking in some way, perhaps in creativity or skill on their part as chefs, or in the healthfulness of the food or distinctiveness of it as a culinary tradition.

Culinary tourism in these instances seems to be affirming the usual understandings of comfort food as representing home and the familiar while also changing the genre by adapting it to more upscale and healthy eating trends. Both culinary tourism and comfort food are also reflecting and perhaps even driving some trends in the larger Western food cultures.[46] Both are highlighting local and sustainable foods that meet ethical concerns. Both are incorporating the shift from treating food just as fuel to recognizing it as expressive of identity and a medium for personal creativity and innovation as well as a social domain. Both also seem to encourage consumption of foods that normally would be suspect in terms either of health and nutrition or of edibility and palatability. At the same time, these tours reflect changes in tourism itself, in which tourists are seeking deeper and more meaningful experiences with other cultures.[47]

The role of home in these categories may also reflect larger patterns within Western and even global society. Stress has increased; fear of the Other has, too.[48] Home is both a place and a metaphor for familiarity and security, but more of us are no longer tied to "Home." Contemporary technologies have simultaneously "shrunk" the world and isolated individuals, who perhaps spend more time with their computers and cell phones than with other people. Mobility has taken many of us to new environments, so that home as a place grounded in our past and family literally does not exist for many. Perhaps home in the modern world has now become exotic, the Other, so that it is now an object of curiosity—a destination and attraction for tourism. As anthropologist Richard Wilk pointed out in *Home Cooking in the Global Village*, cooking and eating at home now incorporate those dichotomies.[49] If comfort food gives us the sense of belonging that is traditionally associated with home, incorporating it into culinary tourism offers a powerful way to find our way home while literally away from home.

Notes

1. Two examples of popular media featuring comfort food are *Slow Cooker Recipes* (Lincolnwood, IL: Publications International, 1997), with the blurb on front: "Come Home to Comfort Foods"; and *Better Homes and Gardens Comfort Food* (Des Moines, IA: Meredith, 1992), with the subtitle: "Yesterday's and Today's Favorite Dishes." Another example is discussed in a review by Linda Negro, "A Tasty Journey Around the World; Book Offers International Comfort Foods," *Evansville Courier & Press*, June 27, 2012, accessed May 15, 2015, https://www.questia.com/newspaper/1P2–33124264/a-tasty-journey-around-world -book-offers-international.

2. The column appeared in many papers across the country, including the *Des Moines Register*, November 6, 1966, accessed February 2, 2015, http://www.newspapers.com/news page/1131300/. This usage was noted by Michelle Rhea in a comment added to an online version of the Merriam-Webster dictionary that dates the term to 1977.

3. Richman revisits the term "comfort food" in another essay published in the *Washington Post* on December 17, 2013, in which she observes that some of the current trends in food

seem to be the antithesis of comfort food, such as trying potentially dangerous foods, such as the *fugu* fish or apricot seeds, accessed February 2, 2015, http://www.washingtonpost .com/lifestyle/food/comfort-food-she-may-not-have-coined-the-term-but-shes-an-expert -nonetheless/2013/12/16/eb32c150–61c5–11e3–8beb–3f9a9942850f_story.html.

4. http://www.oxforddictionaries.com/us/definition/american_english/comfort-food.

5. Julie L. Locher, "Comfort Food," in *Encyclopedia of Food and Culture*, ed. S. Katz (New York: Charles Scribner's Sons, 2003), accessed February 9, 2013, http://www.encyclopedia. com/doc/1G2–3403400153.html.

6. Also see, "Nation Turning to Comfort Food," Associated Press, November 6, 2001, accessed February 2, 2015, http://www.msnbc.com.

7. Julie L. Locher, William C. Yoels, Donna Maurer, and Jillian Van Ells, "Comfort Foods: An Exploratory Journey into the Social and Emotional Significance of Food," *Food & Food-ways* 13 (2005): 273–97.

8. This, of course, raises questions about what defines American food culture and whether there is an American cuisine, per se. Comfort food has actually been used in popular media (magazines, cookbooks, televised cooking shows, advertisements for specific foods or restaurants) to characterize an identifiable national cuisine.

9. She refers to Fischler's concept of the "omnivore's paradox," in which humans have constantly sought both the new and the familiar. Claude Fischler, "Food, Self, and Identity," *Social Science Information* 27, no. 2 (1988): 275–92.

10. The original study was Jordan D. Troisi and Shira Gabriel, "Chicken Soup Really Is Good for the Soul: 'Comfort Food' Fulfills the Need to Belong," *Psychological Science* 22, no. 6 (June 2011): 747–53, http://pss.sagepub.com/content/22/6/747.short. Published online before print May 2, 2011, DOI: 10.1177/0956797611407931. A continuation of that study is J. D. Troisi, S. Gabriel, J. L. Derrick, and A. Geisler, "Threatened Belonging and Preference for Comfort Food among the Securely Attached," *Appetite*, July 1, 2015, 58–64, DOI: 10.1016/j. appet.2015.02.029.

Also see L. S. Ong, H. I. Jzerman, and A. K. Leung, "Is Comfort Food Really Good for the Soul?: A Replication of Troisi and Gabriel's (2011) Study 2," *Front Psychol* 6 (2015): 314. More on the intersection of nostalgia, loneliness, and comfort food can be found in Karen Stein, "Comfort Foods: Bringing Back Old Favorites," *Journal of the American Dietetic Association* 108, no. 3 (March 2008): 412, 414, accessed May 15, 2015, http://www.sciencedirect.com/ science/article/pii/S0002822308000692; and Cari Romm, "Why Comfort Food Comforts," *The Atlantic*, April 3, 2015, accessed May 15, 2015, http://www.theatlantic.com/health/ archive/2015/04/why-comfort-food-comforts/389613/.

11. Some studies of comfort food have questioned its efficacy and point to the misuse of the concept to justify unhealthy eating. Heather Scherschel Wagner, Britt Ahlstrom, Joseph P. Redden, Zata Vickers, and Traci Mann, "The Myth of Comfort Food," *Health Psychol-ogy* 33, no. 12 (December 2014): 1552–57, accessed May 15, 2015, http://dx.doi.org/10.1037/ hea0000068.

12. For discussions of motivations for food choice, see Michael Owen Jones, "Food Choice, Symbolism, and Identity: Bread-and-Butter Issues for Folkloristics and Nutrition Studies (American Folklore Society Presidential Address, October 2005)," *Journal of American Folklore* 120 (2007): 129–77.

13. For example, Hannah Agran, "Comfort Food That's Good for You (Veggie Playbook)," *Midwest Living*, January/February 2015, 30–35.

14. Green bean casserole also demonstrates how a food can have different associations at different layers of society (national, regional, family, and individual). For more on its meanings as a regional family tradition, see Lucy M. Long, "Greenbean Casserole and Midwestern Identity: A Regional Foodways Aesthetic and Ethos," *Midwestern Folklore* 33, no. 1 (2007): 29–44.

15. A popular website, Allrecipes.com, featured comfort food, asking its readers to identify their comfort foods and send in recipes. The response? "In a matter of just a few days, more than 60 people had offered their ideas on the perfect comfort food. And wouldn't you know it? No two tastes were exactly alike." As illustration, readers sent in recipes for items such as Singapore noodles and Indian *tikka masala* as well as the more stereotypical mashed potatoes and chicken fried steak. Accessed February 2, 2015, What's%20Comfort%20 Food%3F%20Article%20-%20Allrecipes.com.html.

16. Tourism as an industry is considered to have started in England. Some European countries that are renowned for their cuisine—specifically, France, Spain, and Italy—were part of the "grand tour," commonly taken by upper-class Americans and Europeans as a standard part of education in the 1700 and 1800s. They were ostensibly a part of that tour, however, because of their historical role in the development of Western civilization. Domestic tourism within those countries recognized those cuisines as worthy of travel. Excellent introductions to the history and issues surrounding tourism include Erve Chambers, *Native Tours: The Anthropology of Travel and Tourism* (Prospect Heights, IL: Waveland Press, 2000) and Sharon Gmelch, ed., *Tourists and Tourism: A Reader* (Prospect Heights, IL: Waveland Press, 2004).

17. A summary of the history of culinary tourism can be found in Lucy M. Long, "Introduction," in *Culinary Tourism*, ed. Lucy M. Long (Lexington: University Press of Kentucky, 2004), 1–19; and Lucy M. Long, "Culinary Tourism," in *The Oxford Handbook of Food History*, ed. Jeffrey M. Pilcher (Oxford: Oxford University Press, 2012), 389–408. Seminal works in the scholarship of culinary tourism include Anne-Mette Hjalager and Greg Richards, eds., *Tourism and Gastronomy* (London: Routledge, 2002); C. Michael Hall, Liz Sharples, Richard Mitchell, Niki Macionias, and Brock Cambourne, eds., *Food Tourism around the World: Development, Management and Marketing* (Boston: Elsevier Butterworth Heinemann, 2003); and Lucy M. Long, ed., *Culinary Tourism* (2004). For a perspective from the tourism industry perspective, see Erik Wolf, *Culinary Tourism: The Hidden Harvest: A Dozen Hot and Fresh Reasons How Culinary Tourism Creates Economic and Community Development* (Dubuque, IA: Kendall/Hunt, 2006).

18. Tourism scholar Mark Hampton points out that the demand for familiar foods is usually associated with mass tourism, and references Stanley Plog, whose 1974 model for categorizing tourists characterized conservative, "risk-averse mass tourists" as psychocentric and "more risk-taking, adventurous" and "independent" as allocentric. In his study of backpackers, Hampton suggests that backpackers, who are usually thought of as adventurous, go out into the street for authentic experiences, but return to the "backpacker bubble," where there is a sense of familiarity and stability. There they create enclaves with other backpackers in which they then indulge in comfort foods common to their culture of heritage. He gives

an example of Israeli backpackers eating falafel and pita bread together. Mark P. Hampton, *Backpacker Tourism and Economic Development: Perspectives from the Less Developed World* (London: Routledge, 2013).

19. The source for my use of the phrase was a documentary shown in classes on the history of tourism at Bowling Green State University, 2009–2011. The video no longer seems to be available.

20. There is actually much discussion on whether tourists seek novelty or familiarity in their food consumption, or to contrast with or provide an extension of their daily lives. For example, N. Cohen and N. Avieli, "Food in Tourism: Attraction and Impediment," *Annals of Tourism Research* 31, no. 4: 755–78.

21. The first published use of the phrase "culinary tourism" was in Lucy M. Long, "Culinary Tourism: A Folkloristic Perspective on Eating and Otherness," *Southern Folklore Quarterly* 55, no. 3 (1998) and then in *Culinary Tourism* (2004).

22. For this listing, see *Encyclopedia of the Midwest*, eds. Joseph W. Slade and Judith Yaross Lee (Santa Barbara, CA: Greenwood Press, 2004), and its article by Lucy M. Long, "Food Traditions," 281–322. Also see Lucy M. Long, *Regional American Food Culture* (Santa Barbara, CA: Greenwood Press, 2009).

23. http://allrecipes.com/howto/cuisine-of-the-midwest/.

24. http://www.1001fooddrink.com.

25. http://www.ohiosamishcountry.com/listing/guide/dining /.

26. http://www.innathoneyrun.com/authentic-ohio-amish-country-tours/.

27. G. A. Benton, "Road Trip: Comfort Food in Holmes County," *Crave: The Columbus Dining Magazine*, Spring 2014, http://www.columbuscrave.com/content/stories/2014/02/ issue/road-trip-comfort-food-in-holmes-county.html.

28. http://www.explorehockinghills.com/comfortfoodcruise.aspx.

29. Phone call, Audrey Martin, May 20, 2015.

30. Ibid

31. https://visitindiana.com/trip-ideas/9745-southwest-indiana-comfort-food-trail.

32. https://visitindiana.com/trip-ideas/9745-a-southern-comfort-food-trail.

33. Phone call, Joe Huber Farm Restaurant, Starlight, IN.

34. http://www.visitevansville.com/ events/10–05–2015/94th-annual-west-side-nut-club-fall-festival.

35. Anthropologist Claude Levi-Strauss's concept of synthesis can be applied here in that two oppositions are being merged, from which something new arises. The question here is whether comfort food culinary tours then represent a category distinct from either of the two "parent" categories.

36. Long, "Culinary Tourism," 1998.

37. For tourism theory about exotic and familiar as motivations for attracting culinary tourists, see C. Michael Hall and Liz Sharples, "The Consumption of Experiences or the Experience of Consumption?: An Introduction to the Tourism of Taste," in Hall, Sharples et al., *Food Tourism around the World* (2003), 1–25.

38. Shuai Quan and Ning Wang, "Towards a Structural Model of the Tourist Experience: An Illustration from Food Experiences in Tourism," *Tourism Management* 25, no. 3 (June

2004): 297–305. They adapt Giddens's 1984 concept of "ontological security" to explain how familiar food can give tourists a sense of safety.

39. Definitions of tourism set mileage for how far from home one needs to be in order to be called a tourist.

40. Victor Turner, "Process, System, and Symbol: A New Anthropological Synthesis," *Daedalus* 106 (1977): 68.

41. Scholars have looked at the idea of tourism being liminal in relation particularly to explaining sex tourism. See, for example, Denise Brennan, "When Sex Tourists and Sex Workers Meet: Encounters within Sousua, the Dominican Republic," in Gmelch, *Tourists and Tourism* (2004), 151–64.

42. Stated by a friend of the author's during an informal discussion.

43. John Urry, *The Tourist Gaze: Leisure and Travel in Contemporary Societies* (London: Sage Publications, 1990).

44. Quan and Wang, "Towards a Structural Model of the Tourist Experience," 297–305.

45. For example, tourism initiatives in Canada tried to find ways to present what was considered the bland food culture of much of Ontario. John Selwood, "The Lure of Food: Food as an Attraction in Destination Marketing in Manitoba, Canada," in Hall, Sharples et al., *Food Tourism around the World* (2003), 78–191.

46. By "Western cultures," I refer to Canada, Australia, New Zealand, Great Britain, and the US. Culinary tourism in the continental European countries has a different emphasis since many of those cultures have recognizable and renowned cuisines as well as long histories of domestic culinary tourism.

47. Tourism research demonstrates that more tourists are seeking immersive and educational tourist experiences. This reflects a number of factors, including the shift in priorities from possessions to experiences as an indicator of success and social status. See B. Joseph Pine II and James H. Gilmore, *The Experience Economy* (1999).

48. Locher points out that global events created stress that was then translated into more consumption of comfort foods. "For example, immediately following the 11 September 2001 terrorist attack on the World Trade Center, restaurateurs across the United States reported increased sales of comfort food items, such as soup, mashed potatoes, puddings, and macaroni and cheese" (Julie L. Locher, "Comfort Food," in *Encyclopedia of Food and Culture*, ed. Solomon Katz [New York: Charles Scribner's Sons, 2003], retrieved January 23, 2015, from Encyclopedia.com: http://www.encyclopedia.com/doc/1G2-3403400153.html). Similarly, see Bret Thorn, "Seeking Comfort, Diners Indulge in Feel-Good Fare," *Nation's Restaurant News*, October 15, 2001, http://www.findarticles.com.

A Nielsen survey of grocery stores reported a significant increase in the sales of both snack foods and instant potatoes ("Nation Turning to Comfort Food," Associated Press, November 6, 2001, accessed February 2, 2015, http://www.msnbc.com).

49. Richard Wilk, *Home Cooking in the Global Village: Caribbean Food from Buccaneers to Ecotourists* (Oxford: Berg, 2006).

"Newfie Steak": Boloney as Tradition and Play in Newfoundland

Diane Tye

Reading the label on a piece of bologna is not for the faint of heart: "Mechanically separated meats (chicken, pork, beef, turkey), pork, beef, bacon, beef by-products, wheat flour, modified corn starch, salt, soya protein, water, modified wheat flour, sodium phosphate, potato starch, sodium erythorbate, spices, smoke flavour, sodium nitrite, flavour, potassium chloride, artificial maple flavour, smoke."[1] A glance at the list of ingredients and nutritional breakdown is enough to make even the moderately health conscious person cringe. The 8 percent of recommended daily intake of iron and 2 percent of calcium in a 100 g suggested serving size do not offset the high amount of saturated and trans fats, cholesterol, and sodium. Most of the 250 calories come from fat; there are 50 mg of cholesterol and even more salt—750 mg of sodium, or 31 percent of an adult's recommended daily intake. That sodium nitrate in cured meats like boloney has been connected to the formation of carcinogenic nitrosamines raises further concern.

Yet bologna, sometimes referred to as "Newfie Steak," is wildly popular among Newfoundlanders, both those living in the province and many who have moved to other locations. Atlantic Canada, and Newfoundland and Labrador[2] in particular, accounts for the majority of Canada's bologna consumption. Sixty percent of Maple Leaf's national sales (and for many Newfoundlanders it *must* be Maple Leaf bologna) are in Atlantic Canada, and the province of Newfoundland and Labrador accounts for 60 percent of those. More than 2.1 million kilograms of boloney, as it is known in Newfoundland, are eaten here each year.[3] This amounts to 4 kilograms, or nine pounds, of boloney for every man, woman, and child.[4] If the entire country ate boloney at the rate of Newfoundlanders, sales would total 141.1 million instead of the 6 million kilograms currently sold per year.[5] When interviewed by a local journalist in 2012, Warren Scott, manager for Maple Leaf, added that one third of the product weight coming to Newfoundland is bologna; sometimes it is the whole truck.[6] Many Newfoundlanders who have moved away from the island remain heavy consumers. In 2013 *Land and Sea*, a popular television program produced by CBC (Canadian Broadcasting Corporation) Newfoundland, devoted an episode to boloney. It included an interview with Dick Stoyles, owner of the Newfoundland Food Store in Cambridge, Ontario, where a large number of Newfoundlanders relocated in the 1960s after the closure of the iron ore mine on Bell Island. Stolyes reported selling ninety-five cases (equaling approximately 836 kilograms, or 1,843 pounds) of boloney per week.

Here I explore an aspect of boloney's popularity for Newfoundlanders: its identification as a comfort food. A 2012 CBC radio documentary on boloney consumption in the province sparked a host of online responses demonstrating that many Newfoundlanders see boloney this way: "bologna, beans, and home-made bread. What a treat!!!!!"; "Grilled cheese and bologna. . . . .Yum!!!!"; and "Comfort food at its best."[7] Suited to any meal and a favorite for cooked breakfasts, it is one of the most common foods to cook outdoors or on trips to hunting and fishing cabins.[8] For John Breen, owner of a popular delicatessen in St. John's, its popularity is easily explained: people think it tastes good. In a newspaper article, Breen is quoted as saying: "It's good, and tasty. It's not very healthy for ya, y'know, it's full of cholesterol and all that stuff because there's lots of fat but it's really tasty."[9]

The *Oxford English Dictionary* defines "comfort food" as "food that comforts or affords solace; hence, any food (frequently with a high sugar or carbohydrate content) that is associated with childhood or with home cooking." In her entry in the *Encyclopedia of Food and Culture*, Julie Locher stresses comfort food's associations with "significant social relationships,"[10] an aspect she expands on in a coauthored article exploring food's social and emotional significance. Locher, Yoels, Maurer, and Van Ells note comfort food's ability to both "knit persons together into the collectivity, while simultaneously differentiating them from others with differing food practices" and to enable people "to mange difficult and troubling emotions by recalling past experiences of warmth and intimacy with others."[11] Both types of connection are key to boloney's role as a comfort food for Newfoundlanders. In fact, boloney touches on all four principles that Locher et al. identify with comfort food. Calorically rich and conveniently prepared, boloney is a food that provides both physical comfort (it is filling, often fried, and served warm) and emotional comfort (it is nostalgically linked to the past).

According to the *Oxford English Dictionary*, the history of bologna sausage (first made in Bologna, Italy) dates from 1596; the term "boloney" has been in use since at least 1907. Close relatives include polony and mortadella, the English name for a type of large pork sausage, originating in Bologna, made from pure pork with peppercorns and (optionally) pistachio or olives, which is served as a cold meat and in thin slices. Davidson traces the history of bologna in his *Penguin Dictionary of Food*, linking it to mortadella. He writes that "mortadella has been much copied as 'Bologna sausage' or 'bolony' (it is possible that the latter form was corrupted to give the word polony, but this may have other origins). It has been associated with the Italian city of Bologna, a place known for excellence in food since the Middle Ages. It was already being made in 1376 when the Bologna sausage-makers' guild was established." Davidson continues: "The attractive, reasonably long-keeping sausages are much copied outside Italy. However, the general conception in other countries of what a Bologna sausage should be like was not necessarily close to that of the original mortadella." The writer concludes: "The name Bologna for copies of mortadella is almost obsolete except in the USA. American Bologna is usually made mainly from beef and some pork, and mildly spiced, then smoked and steamed."[12] Davidson describes polony as "a sausage known throughout Europe and North America. In England it is made of a pork and beef mixture, highly seasoned to suit regional tastes. Other meats can be used.... Polonies appear so often in early English cookery books from the 17th century onwards, as to give the impression that they were for a long time the best-known sausages in England. The spelling varied. Rabisha (1682) had a recipe 'to Make Polony Sassages to keep all year.' Hannah Glasse (1747) had Belony, but in later editions of her book this was changed to Bolognia. The name is usually said to derive from boloney, a corruption of Bologna, the city which has long produced sausages which were much admired and copied outside Italy (see mortadella); but some supposed that it came from Polonia, the old name for Poland, also an area with a strong sausage-making tradition."[13]

It is possible that boloney has been eaten in Newfoundland and Labrador since shortly after its invention. English mathematician and writer John Collins's 1682 publication *Salt and Fishery*, which describes various ways of producing and using salt, includes both a chapter on Newfoundland's salt cod fishery and a recipe for "Bononia Sawsedges."[14] Whatever the exact date of its first appearance in the province, boloney consumption is part of a long reliance on imported foods. As Carla Wheaton writes, "For nearly four hundred years all economic activity in Newfoundland centered around the prosecution of the fishery. West Country merchants in England funded the expeditions of the migratory fishing vessels, outfitting and supplying them with provisions and men. With the growth of a resident population along Newfoundland's coast, West Country merchants, and later local Newfoundland merchants, supplied the resident fishing families with the goods and equipment necessary in their pursuit of the fishery. Where merchants had once organized and supplied the fishing vessels heading to the waters surrounding Newfoundland, they now provisioned settlers on credit at the start of the fishing season, being repaid at the end of the season with the fisherman's produce, dried cod."[15] Fishing families raised their own vegetables, but a harsh climate and geography limited what could be grown. When shipments began to include highly processed and manufactured foods is in question, but some items, such as Caramel Logs (a confectionary produced by the Scottish company Tunnock) have been distributed throughout Newfoundland by G. J. Shortall Ltd since around 1940. Food products were eventually manufactured on the island; for example, since its establishment in 1924, Purity Products Ltd. has produced a line of products (cookies, crackers, biscuits, candies, jams, and syrups) that have become heavily identified with Newfoundland.[16] The result is that boloney is one of many processed foods (including Tunnock's Caramel Logs, Purity syrup, roast chicken flavored chips, and pineapple crush soft drink) popular here, but not widely available elsewhere, which expatriate Newfoundlanders report missing most.[17]

In Newfoundland, boloney's popularly was partly tied to its affordability. As a St. John's deli owner, John Breen, remarked, "Years ago it was a cheap meal. It was a household thing basically. When I grew up we had bologna pretty much every day because it was a cheap meat."[18] Hilda Chaulk Murray also remembers eating bologna frequently in Elliston, Trinity Bay, during the first half of the twentieth century, although in her family it was more often served at the evening meal with leftover vegetables: "These vegetables were usually all mashed together, perhaps with onion added, and heated in a frying pan, for the main supper dish, 'has' [hash]. Any leftover meat or fish would be eaten with the hash or there might be some tinned meat or bologna."[19] Marie Phillips from Cape St. George on Newfoundland's west coast recalls her reliance on boloney when raising her family in the 1950s: "We could afford to buy it then. And, you know, if we didn't have no, like lamb or beef, we'd go to boloney, see. And boloney was a big thing in our family."[20] Bologna's consumption speaks of the poverty that held earlier generations of Newfoundland communities tightly in its grip. Even today, though prices are rising, boloney's affordability continues to be an important factor in its popularity.

In earlier decades, boloney made from cheap cuts of pork and beef and from meat byproducts fit into a diet that incorporated relatively little meat.

Rural families depended on salt beef and salt pork, as well as game such as moose and rabbit, to supplement their diet of fresh and salt fish, including offal: cod tongues and cod cheeks. John Omohundro notes that, in the past, meals on Newfoundland's northern peninsula relied heavily on bread and potatoes. In his study, Carl, born during the war years, describes the diet he ate growing up as consisting of "lots of bread. Mother and my brother and I could make a meal of a tin of sardines or a slice of bologna."[21] Marie Phillips's son, Kevin, a chef who now lives in Oakville, Ontario, recalls, "I remember when my Dad and my father-in-law ran their general stores at Cape St. George and Degrau in the early '50s; they sold more bologna than any other meats. Each week they would bring in bologna by the 100s of pounds. It came in the quantity of twelve, in a hard cardboard box with the interior waxed and metal strapped on the exterior."[22] Kevin Phillips hints at the complexities that can be tied to the consumption of seemingly straightforward, mass-produced, economical foods:[23] "Today, this magnificent sausage is part of our culture and is coined 'Newfoundland Steak,' which the name was forced on us back then and now we willingly accept with pride."[24] His comment suggests that, similar to the way pasties in Michigan's Upper Peninsula have become "a public, regional symbol that recalls the past, speaks of the present, and implies the future,"[25] the consumption of boloney links past and present generations of Newfoundlanders in an articulation of regional identity.

Boloney's long shelf life—a piece I purchased on June 4, 2013, had the "best before" date of August 28—made it practical for residents in communities in the past who relied on coastal boats for the delivery of supplies, which could be cut off during the winter months. Salt was the main method of preservation, and boloney supplemented a limited rotation of meals based on local game, such as moose and rabbit, as well as a little locally raised chicken, lamb, and beef, in addition to lots of salt cod, salt beef, and salt pork. John Prescott argues that the food we like is anchored in a few basic tastes: sweet, sour, salty, bitter, and umami,[26] and in Newfoundland and Labrador salt arguably forms the backbone of the "flavor principle."[27] It helps determine what constitutes "tasty" food. Boloney fits into this flavor principle; for generations, it was a staple in isolated coastal outport communities and it remains a common food. Writing of her childhood, Candice Walsh, now in her twenties, declares with tongue-in-cheek: "My diet as a child was restricted to white bread, fried bologna, orange pekoe tea loaded with condensed milk and boiled Sunday dinner. It was freaking delicious."[28]

A diet low in protein as well as fruits and vegetables, and disproportionately heavy on white bread and tea, resulted in nutritional deficiencies that led to such diseases as beriberi.[29] Further, boloney, combined with dishes like salt cod and potatoes, salt cod fishcakes, fish and brewis (salt cod, hard bread, and fried pork fat), and Jigg's dinner (vegetables boiled with salt beef or salt pork), result in a diet high in sodium. Although statistics differ on exactly how high in sodium Newfoundlanders' diet was, or is, Canadians on average consume approximately 3,400 mg of sodium per day, more than twice the recommended intake for adults (1,500 mg per day) and far in excess of the upper tolerable limit of 2,300 mg per day.[30] Some studies indicate that New-foundlanders consume 2,994 mg of salt daily, just below the national average[31] while others, such as the Community Sector Council of Newfoundland and Labrador, claim that Newfoundland has a "history of having the highest lev-els of salt consumption in the world."[32] Given the link between high sodium consumption and chronic diseases, including heart disease and hypertension, it is no accident that Newfoundland and Labrador has the highest age-stan-dardized death rate for cardiovascular (heart) disease in women, the highest death rates in the country for heart attacks, strokes, and colorectal cancer, and a high rate of diabetes.[33] Boloney's high fat content also presents a concern given that Newfoundland has the highest overweight (40 percent) and obe-sity (29 percent) rates in the country.[34]

Rather than rejecting boloney as part of an outdated, unhealthful diet, however, Newfoundlanders generally remain enthusiastic. Kevin Phillips comments: "I call it magnificent because you know it has everything. It has protein. It is a filler. It has good taste. And a lot of people like it. You can't go wrong. It has everything."[35] Perhaps this is not surprising given that, for some people, comfort food by definition should be "unhealthy." Boloney's high fat content aligns it with other comfort foods high in sugar, starch, and fat that studies suggest may increase the availability of tryptophan, which increases the level of serotonin in the brain and results in a better mood state.[36] Locher et al. note that, for many people, comfort food should be quickly prepared and provide "effortless gratification."[37] Boloney that is usually fried, if not eaten unheated, requires little if any preparation. Its comfort can be administered quickly and with little investment of time or money. Justification is not that difficult. Kevin Phillips continues: "They say it is high in sodium, high in fat, high in nitrates. That's true to a point. But you know you're not going to sit down and eat five pounds of boloney in one sitting. You'd eat probably a cou-ple of ounces. And you get the taste. You get the protein and you're OK."[38]

Boloney's appeal is more complex than its convenience, however. As Locher et al. write, comfort foods are deeply embedded within larger social and cul-tural systems,[39] and for many, boloney is intricately connected to memories of childhood. Phillips, whose family ate boloney at breakfast, lunch, or dinner a couple of times a week when he was growing up on Newfoundland's west coast, describes boloney as being "always a treat.... It was always there. And it was always a Newfoundland dish.... I call it a taste of home."[40] As mentioned earlier, Locher et al. argue that two types of relationships give meaning and emotional significance to comfort food; Phillips's memory locates boloney in both. It ties the individual to the collectivity—in this case, Newfoundlanders—at the same time it differentiates them from outsiders, and it recalls past experiences of warmth and intimacy with others.[41] Boloney is served at home, or perhaps shared with others at a cabin or around an open fire. Marie Phillips insists that "you cannot have boloney [in a restaurant] the way a person can do it in their kitchen." She clearly prides herself on the quality of her boloney fried in a little chicken fat and served with onion gravy.[42] For these reasons, boloney speaks of reconnection. It can be something expatriate Newfoundlanders seek out, either in their new communities as a taste of home or as part of the ritual of homecoming when in the province visiting family. No longer eaten as a staple because it is the only food available, it commemorates earlier times. A YouTube video documents a middle-age woman's last meal marking the end of her visit with aging parents in Newfoundland before leaving for the airport: at her request, her father fries up boloney.[43]

Many consider boloney to be "traditional," supporting Lin T. Humphrey's findings that these foods are usually connected to family and/or holidays.[44] Todd Perrin, one of St. John's top chefs, may refuse to serve any dish made with bologna, characterizing it as a local favorite rather than a local food,[45] but others see things differently. For example, several people surveyed in Pamela Gray's 1977 study of Newfoundland foodways identified boloney as traditional.[46] At the time, Gray observed that "the infiltration of convenience foods into traditional food habits is often as subtle as serving frozen or canned green peas and cauliflower with the Sunday roast. Traditionally, the vegetables that would have most likely been served were potatoes, turnips, carrots and cabbage.... Another fact of food consumption in Newfoundland, also determined by the Department of Health, is that approximately thirteen percent of all meat that is presently purchased is processed bologna. Fried bologna and chips (French or pan-fried potatoes) is a common supper meal."[47] Two decades later, Omohundro reached the same conclusion in his study of traditional foodways on the northern peninsula: "New food items arrive to dilute the old ones in the weekly meal schedule, but the novel has not squeezed out the traditional. Bologna, salt meat, and tinned meats are the most common on Main Brook tables, followed by poultry, fish, moose, and rabbit. Bologna was estimated to be 13 percent of all meat purchases in the province a decade ago."[48] Now, more than thirty-five years after Gray's study, what was once a modern convenience food has become traditional. In an online forum, the *Newfoundland Quarterly* asked, "What foods would you associate with a typical Newfoundland meal?" Most replies referred to Jigg's dinner (boiled dinner with salt meat). Nonetheless, boloney was the first meal that came to mind for one respondent, self-identified as a thirty-five year-old engineer: "Newfoundland steak of course, good old bologna. We'll fry it, make a stew of it, sandwiches, eat it raw, take it hunting, cut it and put it with fries, I mean what can't we do with bologna? That's what I want to know."[49] Echoing Timothy Lloyd's observation that Cincinnati-style chili became an important regional food in the Cincinnati area "not simply because it is made and eaten within a particular area, but also (and perhaps primarily) because it has been adapted to suit general local taste,"[50] bologna is prepared in ways that are similar to other foods so that if the food itself cannot be considered traditional, its method of preparation certainly is. It is baked, stuffed, stewed, and most often fried. A forty-year-old welder commented: "Something that's very traditional is to make a stew out of something. Like I think we could make a stew from just about anything. Bologna stew being my favorite but I think some people see whatever is left over and think 'I could make stew out of that.'"[51] While this Newfoundlander thinks of stewing, frying was also a common cooking method, and these modes of preparation tie eaters to earlier generations of Newfoundland cooks and the dishes of stewed or fried fish and game they prepared.

Just as authors have pointed out how mass-produced, economical foods such as ramen noodles, Spam, and Jell-O may be prepared in a myriad of ways,[52] boloney also offers cooks creative potential. Kevin Phillips encourages Newfoundlanders to move beyond frying or even stewing: "I think we didn't give boloney a chance. All we did was fry it and eat it raw. So I said we got to give boloney a chance." Phillips, author of a website[53] and cookbook[54] featuring boloney recipes, has created many dishes, from burritos and pierogies to stuffed mushroom caps and cake. He reports that his goal is to prepare boloney "the way no one has ever seen it or eaten it before."[55] Just as in Hawaii, where the industrial food Spam has been repurposed, "fried, baked, steamed, marinated, wrapped in wonton or barbequed,"[56] the more than 100 recipes for boloney on Phillips's website devoted to "rediscovering Newfoundland cuisine" cover every occasion: breakfast, lunch, appetizer, and main course. Bologna wrapped scallops, bologna-stuffed mushroom caps, tempura bologna rings, bologna and garlic butter pancakes, bologna fillet with lingonberry sauce, pan-fried pierogies with bologna chunks, sweet and sour bologna, cream of broccoli and bologna soup, and bologna cordon bleu.[57]

His efforts extend an already present tendency in Newfoundland to see traditional meats, like moose and bologna, as fitting media for creative adaption and transformation. Community cookbooks across the province contain recipes such as baked bologna, bologna strips with sliced round cheese, dressed bologna,[58] boloney cups,[59] barbecued bologna,[60] bologna stew,[61] and bologna casserole.[62] This kind of innovation conforms to what Gerald Pocius discovered about the use of new items and old houses in Calvert: "Incorporation of new objects into a culture did not necessarily mean that they would have a negative impact, and in fact, they were often accepted because they appropriately coincided with existing values."[63] Just as Newfoundlanders live in new houses in old ways and adopt new objects and new technologies, they incorporate processed food like boloney into traditional dishes and adapt it to traditional cooking methods. What is tradition is reinvented.

Although boloney has not yet attracted the widespread derision of some other economical foods like Spam[64] and Jell-O,[65] boloney recipes often reflect an element of play. Having "a bit of fun" fits with constructions of Newfoundlanders as a people who do not take themselves too seriously. For example, Phillips's recipes include at least two named in honor of local CBC radio announcers: Ted Blade's Sandwich and Ramona Dearing's Bologna Cupcakes.[66] The playfulness inherent in many of the new dishes parallels boloney's place in local narrative traditions. Similar to the wild haggis tradition in Scotland are tall-tale accounts of the wild bologna in Newfoundland that some trace back to two bolognas that escaped Columbus's ship.[67] According to Edward McGrath, "The wild baloney (bologna) is found only on the island of Newfoundland. Early settlers called this animal the gommel; it was renamed to the bologna in 1927 in honour of Guglielmo Marconi who was born in Bologna, Italy."[68] McGrath goes on to identify two main types of wild baloney in Newfoundland—Zingers and Zungers—which are distinguished by the sounds they make moving through the woods.[69] Others describe the wild bologna as "a nocturnal creature common in the interior of the island of Newfoundland, Canada. It looks exactly like a bologna except when alive it has its arms and legs, and sports a ridge of hair that can only be described as a mohawk on its head."[70] These narratives are still shared orally with children.[71]

Chef Phillips plays with notions of elite cuisine as he transforms one of the most inexpensive meat products into a dish symbolic of French cuisine like cordon bleu or into Japanese inspired Tempura Boloney Rings.[72] More often, as suggested by tales of the wild boloney or recipes in community cookbooks for dishes like stuffed boloney, the play insists that boloney is not artificial. The pretense is that boloney is not made from meat byproducts but, in fact, is real meat. As Sallie Tisdale writes, "In the kitchen, nostalgia and rebellion meet,"[73] and recipes for boloney and stories about it defend Newfoundlanders' preference for a food that is under increasing fire in the media and from health professionals as outré and unhealthful.

That today tall tales of the wild bologna are found on websites directed at expatriate Newfoundlanders suggests that the most important play associated with boloney is tied to identity; it can be an expression of both class and region. What masquerades as a simple, home-cooked meal holds many meanings. Boloney may have been a food of poverty and a contributor to the high rate of chronic diseases in the province, but today many Newfoundlanders and expatriate Newfoundlanders believe that to enjoy a "feed of boloney" is the sign of a "real Newfoundlander." Undoubtedly, some Newfoundlanders continue to eat boloney for the reasons it has always been popular: despite rising prices, it is still inexpensive, it is convenient to store and prepare, and it is part of a flavor principle that is familiar in the province. However, for many, boloney also represents a comfort food, a kind of treat they reward themselves with on a weekend morning with a full breakfast, at the cabin, around an outside fire while hunting or berry-picking, for a mug-up, or for expatriates on a trip back home. It joins other foods, like homemade white bread and molasses, which were once the backbone of the Newfoundland diet but today are often eaten selectively as purposeful and positive reminders of past times and places. Because traditional food is less nourishment than symbol,[74] Newfoundlanders—at least those of middle or upper income, who can afford other choices—will occasionally turn a blind eye to grim ingredients, a failing grade regarding nutritional content, and the related health issues that might ensue. For them, eating boloney can provide comfort "by conjuring up images of a familiar and soothing way of life."[75] Because of its connection to a past and place that no longer exists, boloney transports Newfoundlanders back to this earlier way of life that, despite economic limitations, was culturally rich and bound people tightly together. Whatever its downfalls, boloney, from this perspective is, as Chef Kevin Phillips claims, "a taste of home."[76]

Notes

1. "Maple Leaf Waxed Bologna," Maple Leaf Foods, accessed June 21, 2014, http://www.discovermaleleaf.ca/products/by-brand/big-stick/maple-leaf-wax-bologna/.

2. In 2001, the province of Newfoundland officially changed its name to Newfoundland and Labrador. Here I draw almost exclusively on the experiences of residents of Newfoundland, the island portion of the province.

3. Tobias Romaniuk, "Hunting the Origins of 'Newfie Steak,'" *Telegram*, April 4, 2012, B1.

4. Heather Barrett, *In the Pink*, Canadian Broadcasting Company Radio (CBC), December 16, 2012.

5. Romaniuk, "Hunting the Origins of 'Newfie Steak,'" B1.

6. Barrett, *In the Pink*.

7. Ibid.

8. Heather King, "Remote Wilderness Cabins on the Avalon Peninsula: Male Spaces and Culture," MA thesis, Memorial University, 2012; and John Warren, "Moose Hunting in Heart's Content, Trinity Bay, Newfoundland," MA thesis, Memorial University, 2009.

9. Romaniuk, "Hunting the Origins of 'Newfie Steak,'" B1.

10. Julie L. Locher, "Comfort Food," in *Encyclopedia of Food and Culture*, ed. S. Katz (New York: Charles Scribner's Sons, 2002), 442–43.

11. Julie Locher, William C. Yoels, Donna Maurer, and Jillian Van Ells, "Comfort Foods: An Exploratory Journey into the Social and Emotional Significance of Food," *Food and Foodways* 13, no. 4 (2005): 294.

12. Alan Davidson, ed., *The Penguin Companion to Food* (New York: Penguin, 2002), 617.

13. Ibid., 739–40.

14. John Collins, *Salt and Fishery* (London: A. Godbid and J. Playford, 1682).

15. Carla Wheaton, "Trade and Commerce in Newfoundland," Heritage Newfoundland and Labrador, 1999, accessed September 7, 2015, http://www.heritage.nf.ca/articles/economy/trade.php

16. Purity Factories Ltd, accessed September 7, 2015, www.purity.nf.ca.

17. Staff, "Treats from Away?" *Telegram*, January 25, 2008, accessed September 7, 2015, http://www.thetelegram.com/Living/2008-01-25/article-1451124/Treats-from-away?/1

18. Romaniuk, "Hunting the Origins of 'Newfie Steak,'" B1.

19. Hilda Chaulk Murray, *More than 50: Woman's Life in a Newfoundland Outport, 1900–1950* (St. John's, Newfoundland: Breakwater Books, 1979), 125.

20. Land and Sea, *That Magnificent Sausage*, CBC Television, October 20, 2013.

21. John Omohundro, *Rough Food: The Seasons of Subsistence in Northern Newfoundland* (St. John's, Newfoundland: Institute of Social and Economic Research, 1994), 217.

22. Kevin Phillips, "Newfoundland Recipes," Saltjunk.com.: Everything Newfoundland and Labrador with its Culture, Cuisine and Traditions, 2000, accessed June 21, 2014, http://saltjunk.com/?page_id=5642.

23. For studies of Jell-O, ramen noodles, and Spam, see Sarah E. Newton, "'The Jell-O Syndrome': Investigating Popular Culture/Foodways," *Western Folklore* 51, no. 3–4 (1992): 249–67; Sojin Kim and R. Mark Livengood, "Ramen Noodles & Spam: Popular Foods, Significant Tastes," *Digest: An Interdisciplinary Study of Food and Foodways* 15 (1995): 2–11; and George H. Lewis, "From Minnesota Fat to Seoul Food: Spam in America and the Pacific Rim," *Journal of Popular Culture* 34, no. 2 (2000): 83–105.

24. Phillips, "Newfoundland Recipes."

25. Yvonne R. Lockwood and William G. Lockwood, "Pasties in Michigan's Upper Peninsula: Foodways, Interethnic Relations, and Regionalism," in *Creative Ethnicity: Symbols and Strategies of Contemporary Ethnic Life*, eds. Stephen Stern and John Allan Cicala (Logan: Utah State University Press, 1991), 17.

26. John Prescott, *Taste Matters: Why We Like the Foods We Do* (London: Reaktion Books, 2012), 29.

27. Elizabeth Rozin, "The Role of Flavor in the Meal and the Culture," in *Dimensions of the Meal: The Science, Culture, Business, and Art of Eating*, ed. Herbert L. Meiselman (Gaithersburg, MD: Aspen, 2000), 134–42.

28. Candice Walsh, "An Experiment in Newfoundland Gross Cuisine," *Candice Does the World*, February 18, 2011, accessed June 21, 2014, http://www.candicedoestheworld.com.

29. James Overton, "Brown Flour and Beriberi: The Politics of Dietary and Health Reform in Newfoundland in the First Half of the Twentieth Century," *Newfoundland Studies* 14, no. 1 (1998): 1–27.

30. Institute of Medicine of the National Academies, "Dietary Reference Intakes: The Essential Guide to Nutrient Requirements," National Academies Press, 2006, accessed December 3, 2014, http://www.iom.edu/Reports/2006/Dietary-Reference-Intakes-Essential -Guide-Nutrient-Requirements.aspx.

31. Didier Garriguet, "Sodium Consumption at All Ages," *Health Reports* 18, no. 2 (2007): 47–52.

32. Community Sector Council of Newfoundland and Labrador, "Take It without a Grain of Salt," 2010, accessed June 23, 2014, http://communitysector.nl.ca/csc-programs/ without-grain-salt/about.

33. Public Health Agency of Canada, "Chronic Disease Statistics for Newfoundland and Labrador," accessed May 20, 2013, http://www.phac-aspc.gc.ca/canada/regions/atlantic/Pub lications/Tool_kit/21-eng.php.

34. Statistics Canada, "Health Indicator Profile, Age-Standardized Rates Annual Esti- mates, by Sex, Canada, Provinces and Territories (CANSIM Table 105–0503)," 2014, accessed December 3, 2014, http://www5.statcan.gc.ca/cansim/a05?lang=eng&id=1050503&pattern=1 050503&searchTypeByValue=1&p2=35.

35. Land and Sea, *That Magnificent Sausage*.

36. Locher, "Comfort Food," 442.

37. Locher et al., "Comfort Foods," 286.

38. Land and Sea, *That Magnificent Sausage*.

39. Locher et al., "Comfort Foods," 277.

40. Land and Sea, *That Magnificent Sausage*.

41. Locher et al., "Comfort Foods," 294.

42. Land and Sea, *That Magnificent Sausage*.

43. Beverley Caddigan, "Last Newfoundland Breakfast HAD to Be Bologna!" May 20 2012, accessed June 21, 2014, https://www.youtube.com/watch?v=dGJ72d5gfEc.

44. Lin T. Humphrey, "Traditional Food? Traditional Values?" *Western Folklore* 48, no. 2 (1989): 163.

45. Barrett, *In the Pink*.

46. Pamela Gray, "Traditional Newfoundland Foodways: Origin, Adaptation and Change," MA thesis, Memorial University, 1977, 157.

47. Gray, "Traditional Newfoundland Foodways," 129.

48. Gray, "Traditional Newfoundland Foodways," 129; and John Omohundro, *Rough Food*, 217.

49. *Newfoundland Quarterly*, "What Foods Would You Associate with a Typical New- foundland Meal?" 2011, accessed May 7, 2013, http://www.newfoundlandquarterly.ca.

50. Timothy Charles Lloyd, "The Cincinnati Chili Complex," *Western Folklore* 40, no. 1 (1981): 39.

51. *Newfoundland Quarterly*, "What Foods."

52. See Sojin Kim and R. Mark Livengood, "Ramen Noodles and Spam"; George H. Lewis, "From Minnesota Fat to Seoul Food"; and Newton, "The Jell-O Syndrome."

53. Phillips, "Newfoundland Recipes."

54. Kevin Phillips, *The Bologna Cookbook* (St. John's, Newfoundland: Flanker Press, 2014).

55. Land and Sea, *That Magnificent Sausage.*

56. Julie Harrison, "Spam," in *Fat: The Anthropology of an Obsession*, eds. Don Kulick and Anne Meneley (New York: Jeremy P. Tarcher/Penguin, 2005), 191.

57. Phillips, "Newfoundland Recipes."

58. ACWA [Anglican Church Women's Association], *What's Cooking. ACWA-Fogo Island Cook Book* (unpublished, 1993).

59. Rosalind Crocker, *Newfoundland. Taste of Home: Cookbook and Travel Guide* (Trinity, Newfoundland: Blueberry Press, 1997).

60. Longside Club, *The Longside Cookbook. Recipes from Newfoundland and around the World* (Overland Park, KS: Classic American Fundraisers, 1989).

61. Dave Hoddinott, *500 Years of Newfoundland Cookery* (St. John's, Newfoundland: M. Printer, 1997).

62. Magda Taor and Aneitha Sheaves, eds., *Gateway Goodies Recipe Collection* (Port aux Basques, Newfoundland: Dr. Charles L. Legrow Health Centre Inc. Foundation, 1995).

63. Gerald L. Pocius, *A Place to Belong: Community Order and Everyday Space in Calvert, Newfoundland* (Montreal: McGill-Queen's University Press, 2000), 11.

64. See Lewis, "From Minnesota Fat to Seoul Food."

65. See Newton, "The Jell-O Syndrome."

66. Phillips, "Newfoundland Recipes."

67. Liz Feltham, "Hunting the Wild Bologna," Food for Thought: Ramblings from a Food Writer and Former Professional Cook, April 2014, accessed June 18, 2014, http://lizfeltham. files.wordpress.com.

68. Marconi was responsible for sending the first transatlantic wireless message from Newfoundland in 1901.

69. Ed McGrath, "Wild Baloney," Upalong.org, 2007, accessed May 7, 2013, http://www. upalong.org/archive_full.asp?id=60.

70. Unsigned, "Wild Bologna (pronounced baloney) (Newfoundland Folklore)," h2g2, *Hitchhiker's Guide to the Galaxy: The Earth Edition*, 2009, accessed June 21, 2014, www.h2g2. com/entry/A49771551.

71. For example, in 2013 a student in my Folklore 1000 class reported that her father had regaled her with stories of the wild boloney when she was growing up in rural Newfoundland.

72. Phillips, "Newfoundland Recipes."

73. Sallie Tisdale, *The Best Thing I Ever Tasted. The Secret of Food* (New York: Riverhead Books, 2000), 4.

74. Lin T. Humphrey, "Traditional Food? Traditional Values?" 163.

75. Locher et al., "Comfort Foods," 277–78.

76. Land and Sea, *That Magnificent Sausage.*

"I Know You Got Soul": Traditionalizing a Contested Cuisine

Sheila Bock

A Cuisine at the Intersections of Comfort and Discomfort

In January 2013, African American filmmaker Byron Hurt's documentary *Soul Food Junkies* premiered nationwide on PBS. Following Hurt's travels around the United States in his quest to make sense of African Americans' relationship with soul food, this film is structured around what Kimberly Nettles has called the "dueling narratives"[1] surrounding this cuisine in the present cultural moment. "On the one hand," Nettles explains,

> contemporary memories of soul food or black southern cuisine are linked to notions of family, love, and community—to the idea that black people struggling under the yoke of slavery and the post-slavery experience of sharecropping, Jim Crow racism, migration north, and discrimination could at least rely on the comforts of the traditional foods that solidified their relationships with one another in the face of adversity.[2]

At the same time, a second narrative has emerged reflecting "the fear that the foods black people consume are prime culprits in [the black community's] rising rates of obesity, Type II diabetes, coronary heart disease, and hypertension."[3] In other words, soul food is constructed as a source of both comfort and *dis*comfort at individual and community levels.[4]

Early in the film, Hurt raises the question, "Is soul food good or bad for you?" While Hurt's focus on his father's obesity and death from pancreatic cancer, as well as on health problems faced within the African American community more broadly, indicate that he sees the dangers of traditional soul food outweighing the benefits, the film also includes multiple voices expressing positive associations with the cuisine. For example, in response to the question, "What is it about soul food that is so appealing?" viewers of the film encounter answers such as these:

> Soul food is a great part of our culture because it is a time of coming together, it's a time of cooking together, talking together, sitting down, and consuming together. (Norma Jean Darden, owner of Spoonbread Restaurant)

> Soul food is a repository for our history and our dreams, and it's this memory of comfort. Soul food represents *black*. (Michaela Angela Davis, image activist)

The presence of the dueling narratives in this film situates *Soul Food Junkies* as one of the latest examples of public negotiations over the value of this popularly recognized comfort food within the African American community. That is, the documentary reflects and participates in broader conversations taking place around this contested traditional cuisine.

The labeling of food as traditional usually indicates approval,[5] but not always, as the case of soul food reveals. The meanings of soul food are shaped by different regimes of value,[6] and as Danille Elise Christensen reminds us, systems of value "are established by contextualizing culture goods (and the people and processes they index) as worthy of notice, by implicitly and explicitly situating them relative to other objects and ideas. Thus, where value hierarchies are concerned, talk *about* things is as important as practices *with* things."[7] Taking heed of this reminder, this chapter attends to the discursive role that tradition has played—and continues to play—in ongoing negotiations over the value of soul food, particularly in relation to the widespread health problems within the African American community.

The first section below offers a brief overview of how the marked traditionality of soul food among African Americans materialized in the middle decades of the twentieth century, and how soul food came to be infused with many different meanings, including racial pride, cultural achievement, survival, comfort, oppression, filth, and danger. The African American community has never been a monolithic one, and as Doris Witt notes, "The range of African American cookbooks now published reflects the multiplicity of African American culture, including the inadequacy of a still-common tendency to equate black culinary traditions with soul food."[8] Indeed, the popularly recognized soul food cuisine—including such foods as collard greens, black-eyed peas, cornbread, fried chicken, chitterlings (or chitlins), and fatback—is certainly not the only (or even the primary) tradition informing African Americans' eating habits in the present day. However, the traditionalization of soul food has served as a powerful tool in public articulations of community identity.[9] As a result, critiques of this cuisine become much more than just critiques of food. They become critical negotiations over what it means to be part of a strong, resilient black community.

The following section turns attention to cookbooks to examine how such critical negotiations over the relationship between soul food and community are currently playing out in the midst of the significant health problems in the black population.[10] Heart disease is the leading cause of death among African Americans,[11] and African Americans have the highest mortality rate from coronary heart disease of any ethnic group in the United States.[12] African Americans are also twice as likely to be diagnosed with diabetes as non-Hispanic whites, and they are significantly more likely to suffer from diabetes-related complications.[13] Obesity is a significant factor contributing to these chronic diseases, and blacks have 51 percent greater prevalence of obesity than non-Hispanic whites.[14] In the discussion below, I will identify how African American cookbook authors have sought to re-conceptualize the "traditional" nature of soul food as they present "healthful" recipes as tools of intervention in these alarming community-wide health problems.

Recognizing that claims about tradition are part of a dynamic, interpretive process that connects the past to the present,[15] this discussion will build on classic works in folklore studies that show how tradition works as a process and as a means of authentication or authorization.[16] Tom Mould's work—which uses the term "traditionalization" to label emic references to "the traditional," a value-laden concept that "indicates a conscious bestowal of status"[17]—is particularly helpful in understanding the complex discursive role of tradition in negotiations over the value of soul food. Mould illuminates how conscious acts of traditionalization by individuals not only invoke idealized pasts but they also "can open up discourse for critique rather than [inherently] affirming a general consensus about 'the traditional.'"[18] When applied to rhetorical framings of soul food constructed *by* African Americans *for* African Americans, this understanding of traditionalization helps make visible how the "traditional" nature of soul food, while widely recognized, does not have one stable meaning. Thus, as my analysis of African American-authored "healthful" cookbooks will show, conscious references to "the traditional" create opportunities for African Americans to engage with both

communally recognized visions of a shared history and individual interpreta-
tions of how this shared history should be recognized in the present day. I put
the term "healthful" in quotation marks here as a reminder that, much like
the label "traditional," this label does not refer to some inherent quality that
exists independently of discourse. Different cookbook authors interpret differently what constitutes eating healthfully (at times, for example, referencing
the amount of fat in a dish and at other times referencing the extent to which
the ingredients in a dish are all-natural instead of processed). In addition, the
"healthful" label involves a conscious bestowal of status, and, like "traditional,"
can carry different meanings within different regimes of value.[19] Ultimately,
by examining discourses of tradition in these cookbooks, this chapter illuminates how African Americans are actively working to re-present, revise, and
remix the connections among food, health, and community in the midst of a
health crisis.

The Emergence of a Self-Conscious Tradition

The Southern black diet began to shift from the category of the self-evident to
that of the self-conscious amidst the Great Migration of blacks from the rural
South to cities in the North following World War I.[20] At this time, migrants
faced resistance from the established and integrationist black middle-class,
who feared the newcomers would threaten their respectability with the white
community. As Tracy Poe has shown, Southern foodways took on symbolic
importance within these intra-racial conflicts, and the perceived "backward"
food habits the migrants brought with them received much criticism.[21] A
good deal of this disapproval was framed in terms of health in publications
like the *Chicago Defender*, a nationally circulated African American newspaper. For example, in 1920, Dr. A Wilberforce Williams's column on health
"regularly criticized eating habits associated with southern food, remarking
that heavy meats, excessive carbohydrates, and especially hot sauces and con-
diments were deleterious to the liver and would cripple the digestive system
of anyone over forty."[22] Such framings of Southern food as problematic and
in need of civilization worked to reinforce the distinctions between the native
blacks and the newcomers amidst struggles over "respectability" and status.

At the same time, as Poe points out, "migrants could not understand what
the problem was. Southern food was simply dinner. It tasted good and it
was traditional. It was a way of preserving something that reminded them
of home and family when they moved into the unfamiliar urban environment."[23] In response to the criticism from the middle-class blacks, they began

to look at "down-home cooking" as distinct and special, and continuing communal meals at family dinners and community gatherings, along with emerging businesses such as grocery stores and restaurants to meet the demand of this customer base, strengthened their symbolic identification with Southern eating traditions. Due to the influence of migrant business owners, as well as an increasing sense of racial solidarity between migrants and natives over time, Southern foodways became more normalized within urban African American communities. In fact, Southern African American cuisine eventually shifted from a mode of distinction between black community members to a mode of unity that centered on their shared heritage as Africans, slaves, sharecroppers, and industrial workers.[24]

During the civil rights and Black Power movements of the 1960s, this cuisine structured around the principles of Southernness and commensality took on the name it is popularly recognized as today: soul food. This was the culinary incarnation of "soul," a term used "to valorize the cultural forms created through a history of black oppression."[25] Initially associated with black music, the term "soul" came to refer to a range of black cultural expressions, including dress and food. Used as a means of cultural self-definition, soul was, in the words of historian William Van Deburg, "the folk equivalent of the black aesthetic,"[26] one that exemplified the cultural resilience of African Americans in the face of oppression.

"The edible form of the emerging Black is Beautiful and Black Power ethos,"[27] soul food gained its symbolic significance through its connections to blacks' experiences with slavery. This distinctive cultural form showcased the cultural achievements of ancestors who, despite being forced to live "low on the hog," were able to transform scraps into delicious food that nourished the community and helped them survive. "Like wearing African attire or sporting an Afro," Frederick Douglass Opie writes, "eating soul food in the 1960s and 1970s represented a political statement for those with a new black consciousness."[28] The role of soul food in sustaining blacks through a history of oppression made it a symbol of racial pride, a symbol of blackness.

In addition to becoming a source of racial pride, soul food came to be recognized as the quintessential comfort food in the black community, marked by familiarity, kinship, and love. For example, Amiri Baraka's (then LeRoi Jones) "Soul Food," part of a collection entitled *Home: Social Essays*, described the experience of tasting a classic soul food dish that extends well beyond physical pleasure: "Sweet potato pies, a good friend of mine asked recently, 'Do they taste anything like pumpkin?' Negative. They taste more like memory, if you're not uptown."[29] Bob Jeffries, one of the many authors of soul food cookbooks published between 1969 and 1971, explained, "the word soul, when applied to food, means only those foods that negroes grew up eating in their own homes; food that was cooked with care and love—with soul—by and for themselves, their families, and their friends."[30] The consumption of soul food, then, was not just "downright good eating"[31]—though it was this, too—it was the embodiment of the care, love, and memories infused in the familiar dishes.

At the same time, there were those who contested the value of these symbolically significant comfort foods by framing them as acute sources of *discomfort* within the black community, specifically due to their associations with slavery.[32] As Opie explains, for many, "breaking away from soul food became another way of resisting the white man's culture and returning to an idealized African culinary heritage."[33] One prominent critic was Elijah Muhammad, leader of the Nation of Islam, who saw this traditional Southern cuisine connected to slavery as unclean and detrimental to the physical and spiritual health of blacks. In his published works, Muhammad urged blacks to stop eating traditional slave foods: "Peas, collard greens, turnip greens, sweet potatoes and white potatoes are very cheaply raised foods. The Southern slave masters used them to feed the slaves, and still advise the consumption of them. Most white people of the middle and upper class do not eat this lot of cheap food, which is unfit for human consumption."[34] He also asserted that whites were promoting the consumption of unhealthful foods among blacks in order to weaken and ultimately eliminate them. For Muhammad, the traditional cuisine so celebrated in the Black Power movement was actually an artifact of the destructive culture imposed by whites during slavery and extending into the present day. Continuing to consume this cuisine characterized by filth and waste, thereby aligning themselves with an oppressed identity, would not only weaken their bodies but also inhibit the establishment of a black moral citizenry. According to Carolyn Rouse and Janet Hoskins: "To become a moral citizen meant only one thing for Elijah Muhammad, and that was the reclaiming of an authentic Asiatic essence lost in slavery and Jim Crow. Muhammad thought that this essence, which included race consciousness, industriousness, dignity, and resistance to white domination, was obscured by the figurative and literal digestion of white supremacy."[35] To free themselves ideologically from white oppression, blacks had to "stay off that grandmother's old-fashioned corn bread and black-eyed peas"[36] and distance themselves from these familiar, comforting, yet dangerous tools of degradation.[37]

Another prominent critic of traditional Southern soul food was African American comedian and civil rights activist Dick Gregory. Gregory did not frame the rejection of soul food as an act of faith as Muhammad did, though his message did converge with Muhammad's as he denounced soul food because of its contaminating effects, both physically and politically, on the black community. During an interview with reporter Vernon Jarrett from the *Chicago Tribune*, Gregory identified soul food as "the worst food that you can eat. Nothing but garbage."[38] In his 1973 book *Dick Gregory's Natural Diet for Folks Who Eat: Cookin' With Mother Nature*, he likened the widespread promotion and consumption of a soul food diet to genocide. Despite this severe criticism, Kimberly Nettles notes that his description of the origins of soul food in his book does emphasize the "industriousness and creativity of black cooks," reinforcing "the idea of soul food as a cultural creation that illustrates black people's 'adaptive response' to their environment."[39] Even for those calling for the rejection of soul food, tradition carried multidimensional meanings within the different regimes of value shaping this highly symbolic cuisine.

Muhammad, Gregory, and other "food rebels"[40] did have an impact on the eating habits of many African Americans. For political or health reasons (or both), many shunned either the cuisine as a whole or certain parts of it, such as pork. As the Black Power movements declined, the debates surrounding the relationship between African Americans, food, and identity have carried on into the following decades. Though food no longer serves as strongly as "a battleground of identity"[41] within the African American community, where the food choices one makes constitute particular political stances, it has remained a site of contention where questions of blackness still come into play. In more recent discussions about soul food that focus on its health implications, it is rarely talked about as something that should be wholly embraced or wholly rejected. Rather, it is most often constructed as good *and* bad, valuable *and* dangerous, comforting *and* discomforting, in need of preservation *and* in need of change. The following section will turn attention to how negotiations over these multiple meanings have played out in healthful cookbooks published by African Americans between the early 1990s and the present day, and the critical discursive role that "the traditional" plays within them.

Re-presenting/Revising/Remixing the "Traditional"

The 1990s and 2000s saw a proliferation of cookbooks aimed at helping African Americans to eat in more healthful ways, authored by a wide range of African American individuals including chefs, dietitians, celebrities, food writers, activists, food scientists, and people who just like to cook.[42] In this section, I will identify different strategies of traditionalization found within four of these texts: *Ruby's Low-Fat Soul Food Cookbook* (1996), *Patti LaBelle's*

Lite Cuisine (2003), *Vegan Soul Kitchen* (2009), and *Afro-Vegan* (2014). I have
selected these texts for their differences as much as for their similarities.
While all of these cookbooks employ strategies of traditionalization to mediate the competing impulses of preservation and change, they each construct
different ideal visions of how the past should be recreated in the present and
employ different strategies of traditionalization to do so. Neither these ideal
visions nor the strategies of traditionalization employed are unique to these
particular texts; bringing them together here, though, highlights the different
forms and meanings "the traditional" can take on as people grapple with the
issue of how best to enact their connections to the black community in the
face of ongoing community-wide health issues, honoring the past and looking ahead to a healthier future.

In 1996, Ruby Banks-Payne, mother of three and self-proclaimed "potato
salad specialist" who went to college in New Orleans, Louisiana, and then
moved to the North, published *Ruby's Low-Fat Soul Food Cookbook*. This
book begins with an introduction that is guided by the question, "What Is
Soul Food?" In the opening paragraph, she offers this answer: "African Americans refer to soul food as 'food that sticks to your ribs,' food that makes you
pull back from the dinner table completely satisfied. Soul food includes the
traditional dishes that native Africans brought to the New World. Soul Food
is part of our heritage, a mainstay in our rich culture to this day."[43] She goes
on to discuss briefly the history of this cuisine, beginning in 1619, when the
first Africans landed at Jamestown, Virginia, through the 1860s, when Creole
and Cajun cooking were developed and into the years following the Civil War,
when foods now commonly recognized as soul food—"candied yams, black-
eyed peas, pig's feet, okra, fried chicken, and chitlins"[44]—were introduced into
African American culture.

Moving into the present day, she identifies the role that these foods have
played in African Americans' health problems and introduces her book as a
tool of intervention into these issues: "The goal of this book is to allow each
of us to maintain good health while exploring our food heritage. Traditional
soul food recipes use far too much fat, sugar, and sodium for good health.
By reducing fat, sugar, and sodium (traditional, but unnecessary components
in these dishes), we can truly nourish our souls with a rich culinary history
while also nourishing our bodies with healthful and delicious foods."[45] Here,
Banks-Payne draws a stark line between "healthful" and "traditional" foods,
and a recurring idea running throughout this introductory section is that the
value of the "traditional" label, while important, is secondary to the value of
the "healthful" label. The main strategy she uses to reconcile this difference
is to revise the classic recipes and discard specific ingredients that interfere

with the categorization of "healthful"; in other words, she urges her readers to identify and eliminate the dangerous aspects of the tradition.

For the most part, she identifies dangerous ingredients that need to be reduced significantly, such as fat, sugar, and sodium, but at one point, she points to actual foods that must be eliminated completely:

> Although this book was developed to keep the tradition of African American cookery alive, there remain certain foods that are simply not nutritional. These foods are:
>
> chitlins
> ham hocks
> neckbones
> pig's feet
>
> These foods have been eliminated from this book. To share traditional foods that are high in fat with our children's children is OK. A single celebratory meal yearly (preferably during Kwanzaa) is enough to let them know what and how earlier generations cooked.[46]

Interestingly, while these foods are explicitly marked as not present in the book, Banks-Payne does describe a proper context for serving them. Specifically, she frames the ideal preparation and consumption of these historical soul food dishes as part of a cultural performance that benefits children by educating them about their past. It is important, though, for these performances to be marked as special and explicitly extracted from everyday living. Ideally, they will be presented as part of a scripted exhibition of cultural heritage, where the consumption of these foods would be part of a high-context ritual that attaches its meaning firmly to the distant past. Here, she constructs soul food dishes as sites of remembrance, an idea echoed in dedicating the book to her children: "I hope that through healthy eating habits that include traditional 'soul foods' their heritage will not be forgotten."[47] As constructed within this text, her desire to help her children maintain a connection to their past conflicts with her desire to instill healthful eating habits. Her framings (and reframings) of the traditional in this cookbook illustrate her attempts to resolve this tension.

A different articulation of/engagement with the traditional is visible in *Patti LaBelle's Lite Cuisine*, published in 2003, which constructs a less-stark distinction between healthful and traditional dishes. Written in response to the singer Patti LaBelle's diagnosis with diabetes, this book is a sequel to her *New York Times* bestseller *LaBelle Cuisine: Recipes to Sing About*. Both cookbooks present recipes and stories about the singer's life, and in her first cookbook, she presents a wholly positive perspective on the African American Southern cooking tradition within which she situates herself, framing the preparation and consumption of traditional foods as a source of comfort and community: "Cooking is really about love. . . . Cooking is as much about nourishment for the soul as it is the stomach. Especially the kind of cooking I grew up on. We're talking Southern, country cooking. Authentic, down-home Southern country cooking is a generation-to-generation pass-it-down-gift."[48] *Patti LaBelle's Lite Cuisine* certainly complicates this narrative by including, for example, LaBelle's reflections on her mother's double-leg amputation and eventual death due to complications from diabetes, the early deaths of each of her three sisters from cancer, and her own feelings about being diagnosed with diabetes.[49] At the same time, although the recipes in the two books differ—with the latter book calling for ingredients such as egg substitutes to cut down on cholesterol, sugar substitutes to cut down on sugar, low-sodium broth and minimal salt, and smaller amounts of fat to improve their nutritional value—she frames these recipes as being part of the same nourishing food traditions introduced in her first book, traditions grounded in "the triad of love, family, and community."[50] In other words, she constructs her second cookbook not just as an intervention in or revision of tradition, but also as a continuation of it.

One way she does this is through the evaluative names she gives her dishes, including "Oven (Tastes Like Southern) Fried Chicken" and "Tastes-Just-Like-Mom-Used-to-Make-It Chicken Pot Pie," which work to minimize intertextual gaps[51] between these dishes and those already valued as traditional because of connections to the past. The text that often accompanies these recipes further reinforces this idea. For example, next to her recipe for "No-Fuss Blackened Fish Fillets," she writes, "I've found it cooks best in the big old cast-iron skillet—the kind Grandmother Ellen used to fry her famous fried chicken."[52] In her introduction to her recipe for "Awesome Apple Pie," she invokes the voices of her aunts, two women she references often and positively in both of her cookbooks as active tradition bearers who personify the "food=love school of thought"[53] and have taught her much of what she knows about cooking: "Years of listening to the baking advice of my aunts Hattie Mae and Joshia Mae—'For sweets you want dry, crisp surfaces, so bake uncovered; half-and-half won't whip; if you must use something from a box or a bag, *puhleeze* doctor it up with plenty of homemade touches'—make this pie truly awesome."[54]

She also demonstrates recognition that traditionalization is a process that is enacted in social contexts of eating, identifying strategies readers can use to frame the dishes they cook and serve as traditional, thereby adding to the value of and ultimately authorizing the healthful recipes included in the cookbook as they move from the text of the cookbook into social contexts. For example, when she introduces a recipe for "Savory Shrimp Scampi," she encourages her readers not to tell anyone it is a "lite version" of the dish. Instead, she urges her readers to "tell everybody it was passed down to you from your great-great-grandmother on your daddy's side. And while you'd love to share the recipe, before it was passed down to you, you had to take an oath of secrecy to keep it in the family. That little story will make it taste even better."[55] Here, she approaches traditionality as not necessarily an inherent trait but as something that is enacted, providing a traditionalizing script for others to employ to make their dishes as appealing as possible to others. These constructed appeals to tradition are very much rooted in the family, imagining a continuous relationship between the past and the present.

More recently, chef and food justice activist Bryant Terry published two cookbooks presenting vegan recipes grounded in black culinary traditions: *Vegan Soul Kitchen*, published in 2009, and *Afro-Vegan*, published in 2014. The majority of recipes in *Vegan Soul Kitchen*, according to Terry, were inspired by his experiences growing up in Memphis, Tennessee, living in New Orleans, and traveling through the South, though he also includes his reinterpretations of dishes he tasted while traveling in Africa and the Caribbean. Terry explicitly distinguishes this book from so-called "healthy cookbooks" offering low-fat, low-calorie, or low-sodium versions of traditional dishes, explaining that "rather than counting calories, sacrificing flavor-enhancing ingredients like salt and 'good' fat, and recommending unhealthy industrial ingredients, *Vegan Soul Kitchen* offers animal-product-free recipes . . . that use fresh, whole, best-quality, health-supportive ingredients with an eye on local, seasonal, sustainably grown real food."[56]

Afro-Vegan focuses less on regional Southern cuisine and more on Afro-diasporic food. In describing his goals for this book, Terry writes, "I see this book naming and solidifying a new genre of cooking and eating, if you will— extending farm fresh, compassionate food to include foods of the African diaspora."[57] Responding to the discursive prevalence of whiteness in alternative food movements and the resulting exclusion of people of color,[58] both of his books speak back to the commonly held idea (found both within and outside the black community) that veganism—an alternative food practice rooted in ecological sustainability, compassionate consumption, and social justice—is a "white thing."[59]

In articulating the relationship between traditional and healthful eating practices in the black community, both books frame the highly recognized symbol of soul food as a product not of tradition, but of modernity. In *Vegan Soul Kitchen*, for example, Terry connects popular conceptions of African American and Southern cooking—"meals organized around fatty meats with overcooked vegetables and fruits playing a minor supporting role"—to "the widespread industrialization of food in this country [the United States]."[60] He also references an essay he previously published online entitled "Reclaiming True Grits," in which he argues that the "instant soul food" popularized in the 1960s is actually a "dishonest representation" that stands in the way of reclaiming "real soul food"[61] in the present day. In *Afro-Vegan*, Terry once again constructs the soul food cuisine as a product of industrialization, asserting that "plant-focused meals are nothing new to traditional African and Caribbean diets, and prior to the industrialization of U.S. food, even the oft-maligned diet of African-Americans in the Southern states placed heavy emphasis on locally grown vegetables."[62] Through these framings, he constructs the conventional vision of soul food as a disrupting force in the more authentic (and healthful) traditions foregrounded in his books.

While Terry explains that anyone can benefit from these books, it is clear that he is reaching out to black readers in particular. In *Afro-Soul*, he gives a great deal of attention to the connections between healthful eating and the ancestral roots of the black community: "More than anyone else, people of African descent should honor, cultivate, and consume food from the African diaspora. Afro-diasporic foodways (that is, the shape and development of food traditions) carry our history, memories, and stories. They also have the potential to save our lives."[63] For Terry, working for food justice means working "to reclaim our ancestral knowledge and embrace our culinary roots" (2014: 2) by growing and cooking ingredients commonly used by ancestors in the past, including vegetables, fruits, legumes, seeds, and grains.

Terry does not just point to ancestors of the distant past to traditionalize the consumption of healthful plant-based meals within the African American community. He also points to his own memories of a more recent past, memories of time spent with family:

> When I reflect on my childhood (I grew up in Memphis, Tennessee, and spent summers in rural Mississippi) during the late 1970s and 1980s, I think fondly of gardening with my family, growing collards, mustards, turnips, butter beans, black-eyed peas, and green beans. I treasure my grandparents' home-cooked meals and preserves: picked pears, peaches, green tomatoes, carrots, green beans, apples, figs, sauerkraut, blackberry jam, and chow-chow. And I maintain the core values that came from harvesting, sharing, preparing, and cooking meals with community.[64]

Here, he associates this type of eating with spending time with family and building a community based on a set of core values. He grounds his proposed approach to food within the central characteristics associated with soul food—commensality and Southernness—thereby reinforcing the traditional nature of his approach to food.

Another mode of traditionalization that Terry applies involves referencing another form of expressive culture within the black community, specifically music. For example, each recipe in these books is accompanied by a "signature soundtrack," an individual song or album (the majority of which are performed by black artists) that the reader is meant to listen to while cooking and eating each recipe. Additionally, the introduction of *Vegan Soul Kitchen* begins with a quote: "*I know you got soul, if you didn't you wouldn't be in here.*" This is a line from a song written and recorded in 1971 by Bobby Byrd who, working closely with James Brown, was a very influential force in the development of soul and funk music. Within the context of Terry's cookbook, this quote carries several meanings. On the one hand, it calls to mind the concept of soul extracted from food, shifting attention to other ways in which the shared identity of blacks has been articulated in the past, particularly through music. It can also be understood as a statement that addresses the reader directly, constructing the author and reader as part of the same community. Finally, this song was sampled in 1987 by hip-hop artists Eric B. & Rakim in a recording of the same name; although not addressed specifically in the cookbook, the song's connection to hip-hop, a genre of music strongly associated with the black community and characterized by creativity and collaboration, invokes the idea that older cultural forms can be creatively integrated into and revised within new contexts.

Indeed, the theme of remixing is a prominent one in both of Terry's books. The idea is clearly visible in the subtitle of his 2014 book, "Farm-Fresh African, Caribbean & Southern Flavors Remixed," and in *Vegan Soul Kitchen*, he compares himself to a DJ, the quintessential performer of the remix:

> Here, I have imagined new recipes through the prism of the African diaspora—cutting, pasting, reworking, and remixing African, Caribbean, African American, Native American, and European staples, cooking techniques, and distinctive dishes to come up with something all my own. Like a DJ being moved by the energy of the crowd to guide selections, I let the spirits of my ancestors and progeny move me to conjure up these edible treats.[65]

In the introduction to his 2009 book, Terry describes an innovative dish he created that enacted this remix aesthetic, one that served as the inspiration for the book as a whole. For this dish, he took collard greens, a classic soul food dish that he remembered growing in his grandfather's garden when he was a child, and sautéed them with olive oil, minced garlic, and salt, breaking from the traditional way of preparing them by letting them simmer with pieces of fatty meat over low heat for an extended period of time. He then cut them into a chiffonade and added Thompson raisins and freshly squeezed orange juice. This dish, according to Terry, had "Memphis Soul (my past) mixed with Brooklyn Boom-Bap (my present) finished off with a squeeze of Oakland Free-Range Funk (my soon-to-be future)."[66] He frames this dish as representative of the recipes he presents in the book as a whole, reflecting the multidimensional character of what it means to be part of the black community.

The cookbooks examined in this section serve as particularly rich sites for examining issues of traditionalization for, presumably, their authors hope their readers will recreate at least some of their traditional recipes in their own kitchens. Thus, we can view them as more than just sites of reflection on the traditional; they also function as sites of transmission, where knowledge is transferred from one person to another. As Dorothy Noyes reminds us, when we are thinking about the transmission of a traditional practice, we should recognize that what is ultimately being transferred is responsibility. What is "passed down" is not just a thing—e.g., a traditional(ized) recipe— but also metaknowledge about why it is significant and how it should ideally be put into practice.[67] The African American-authored cookbooks discussed here all seek to transform the way black people approach the act of eating by urging readers to rethink food's connections to health and to a shared community across space and time, as well as to change their eating habits accordingly. As these cookbooks reveal, though, what it actually means for individuals to enact their responsibility both to themselves and to the black community through the foods they prepare, serve, and eat continues to be a subject of negotiation.

Notes

I presented an earlier version of this chapter at the 2013 American Folklore Society Annual Meeting as part of a panel entitled "Framing Foodways: Modes and Meanings of Public Contestation." I would like to thank the other panelists—Danille Christensen, Joy Fraser, and Maria Kennedy—as well as the people in the audience for a very productive discussion that significantly helped me think through the issues presented here. I also owe thanks to coeditors Michael Owen Jones and Lucy Long and the anonymous reviewers for their insightful comments and suggestions for revision.

1. Kimberly Nettles, "Saving Soul Food," *Gastronomica* 7, no. 3 (2007): 109.

2. Ibid., 108.

3. Ibid.

4. Culinary historian Michael W. Twitty also addresses the discomforting aspects of Southern foodways in his food blog afroculinaria.com and projects like the Southern Discomfort Tour, though his work focuses more on complicating the ways in which the public image of Southern cuisine renders invisible the labor and contributions of African Americans in the past and the present.

5. Lin T. Humphrey, "Traditional Foods? Traditional Values?" *Western Folklore* 48 (1989): 169–77.

6. Arjun Appadurai, "Introduction: Commodities and the Politics of Value," in *The Social Life of Things: Commodities in Cultural Perspective*, ed. Arjun Appadurai (Cambridge: Cambridge University Press, 1986), 3–63.

7. Danille Elise Christensen, "'Look at Us Now!': Scrapbooking, Regimes of Value, and the Risks of (Auto)Ethnography," *Journal of American Folklore* 124, no. 493 (2011): 179–80.

8. Doris Witt, "From Fiction to Foodways: Working at the Intersections of African American Literary and Culinary Studies," in *African American Foodways: Explorations of History and Culture*, ed. Anne L. Bower (Urbana: University of Illinois Press, 2009), 119.

9. Scholars of African American foodways have recently turned critical attention to the common equation of black food practices with soul food. For example, in her essay looking at "food culture as heritage practice," Psyche Williams-Forson examines the multiple culinary legacies making up black food cultures in the United States and raises important questions about "what practices are overlooked, who is left out of discussions, and to what ends when we reduce a diverse set of people to one group of foods?" See Psyche Williams-Forson, "Take the Chicken Out of the Box: Demystifying the Sameness of African American Culinary Heritage in the U.S.," in *Edible Identities: Food as Cultural Heritage*, eds. Ronda L. Brulotte and Michael A. Di Giovine (Franham: Ashgate, 2014), 93.

10. As textual artifacts, cookbooks can provide great insight into the social and political factors influencing the rhetorical construction of individual and community identities. Scholarship on African American cookbooks specifically has shown how these texts serve as sites of strategic identity construction and negotiation responding to the gendered, racial, and class-based experiences of African Americans. See, for example, Anne L. Bower, "Recipes for History: The National Council of Negro Women's Five Historical Cookbooks," in *African American Foodways: Explorations of History and Culture*, ed. Anne L. Bower (Urbana: University of Illinois Press, 2009), 153–74; Rosalyn Collings Eves, "A Recipe for Remembrance: Memory and Identity in African-American Women's Cookbooks," *Rhetoric Review* 24 (2005): 280–97; Sally Bishop Shigley, "Empathy, Energy, and Eating: Politics and Power in *The Black Family Dinner Quilt Cookbook*," in *Recipes for Reading: Community Cookbooks, Stories, Histories*, ed. Anne L. Bower (Amherst: University of Massachusetts, 1997), 118–31; Doris Witt, *Black Hunger: Soul Food and America* (Minneapolis: University of Minnesota Press, 2004); and Rafia Zafar, "The Signifying Dish: Autobiography and History in Two Black Women's Cookbooks," *Feminist Studies* 25, no. 2 (1999): 449–69.

11. "Heart Disease Facts," Centers for Disease Control and Prevention, 2014, http://www.cdc.gov/heartdisease/facts.htm.

12. L. T. Clark et al., "Coronary Heart Disease in African Americans," *Heart Disease* 3, no. 2 (2001): 97–108.

13. "Diabetes and African Americans," US Department of Health and Human Services Office of Minority Health, 2014, http://minorityhealth.hhs.gov/omh/browse.aspx?lvl=4& lvlID=18.

14. Pan et al., "Differences in Prevalence of Obesity among Black, White, and Hispanic Adults—United States, 2006–2008," *Morbidity and Mortality Weekly Report* 58, no. 27 (2009): 740–44.

15. Richard Handler and Joyce Linnekin, "Tradition, Genuine or Spurious," *Journal of American Folklore* 97, no. 385 (1984): 175–210; and Eric Hobsbawm and Terence O. Ranger, eds. *The Invention of Tradition* (Cambridge: Cambridge University Press, 1983).

16. Dell Hymes, "Folklore's Nature and the Sun's Myth," *Journal of American Folklore* 88, no. 350 (1975): 345–69; and Richard Bauman, "Contextualization, Tradition, and the Dialogue of Genres: Icelandic Legends of the *Kraftaskáld*," in *Rethinking Context*, eds. Alessandro Duranti and Charles Goodwin (Cambridge: Cambridge University Press, 1992), 125–145.

17. Tom Mould, "The Paradox of Traditionalization: Negotiating the Past in Choctaw Prophetic Discourse," *Journal of Folklore Research* 42, no. 3 (2005): 259.

18. Mould, "Paradox of Traditionalization," 257. While acknowledging that "folklorists have typically addressed acts of traditionalization made by the individual performer in the act of performance," Tom Mould also asserts that the "term can refer to any attempt to situate a particular act within a recognized tradition or to elevate a particular cultural practice to a status of the traditional." See Tom Mould, "Traditionalization," in *Folklore: An Encyclopedia of Beliefs, Customs, Tales, Music, and Art*, eds. Charlie T. McCormick and Kim Kennedy White (Santa Barbara, CA: ABC-CLIO, 2011), 1204.

19. Alan Dundes identified the prevalent idea in traditional American thought that "if something is good for you, it must taste bad." See Alan Dundes, "Folk Ideas as Units of Worldview," *Journal of American Folklore* 84, no. 331 (1971): 98. Framed within discourses of taste, the label "healthful" is evaluated negatively. To offer another example, Delores James, in conducting focus groups with African American men and women in northern Florida, found that "several perceived 'eating healthfully' as giving up part of their cultural heritage and trying to conform to the dominant culture." These focus group participants drew on discourses of culture, or tradition, to evaluate "healthful" eating negatively. See Delores James, "Factors Influencing Food Choices, Dietary Intake, and Nutrition-Related Attitudes among African Americans: Application of a Culturally Sensitive Model," *Ethnicity & Health* 9, no. 4 (2004): 357.

20. For studies on the diversity and history of African American foodways that extend beyond the scope of this discussion, see Robert L. Hall, "Food Crops, Medicinal Plants, and the Atlantic Slave Trade," in *African American Foodways: Explorations of History and Culture*, ed. Anne L. Bower (Urbana: University of Illinois Press, 2009), 17–44; Jessica B. Harris, *High on the Hog: A Culinary Journey from Africa to America* (New York: Bloomsbury USA, 2011); Frederick Douglass Opie, *Hog and Hominy: Soul Food from Africa to America* (New York: Columbia University Press, 2008); Andrew Warnes, *Hunger Overcome? Food and Resistance in Twentieth-Century African American Literature* (Athens: University of Georgia Press,

2004); William C. Whit, "Soul Food as Cultural Creation," in *African American Foodways: Explorations of History and Culture*, ed. Anne L. Bower (Urbana: University of Illinois Press, 2009), 45–58; and Anne Yentsch, "Excavating the South's African American Food History," in *African American Foodways: Explorations of History and Culture*, ed. Anne L. Bower (Urbana: University of Illinois Press, 2009), 59–98.

21. Tracy N. Poe, "The Origins of Soul Food in Black Urban Identity: Chicago, 1915–1947," *American Studies International* 37, no. 1 (1999): 4–33.

22. Ibid., 9.

23. Ibid.

24. Ibid.

25. Doris Witt, "Soul Food," in *Encyclopedia of American Studies*, 2010, http://eas-ref.press .jhu.edu/view?aid=176.

26. William A. Van Deburg, *New Day in Babylon: The Black Power Movement and American Culture, 1965–1975* (Chicago: University of Chicago Press, 1992), 194.

27. Adrian Miller, *Soul Food: The Surprising Story of an American Cuisine, One Plate at a Time* (Chapel Hill: University of North Carolina Press, 2013), 1.

28. Opie, *Hog and Hominy*,128.

29. Amiri Baraka [LeRoi Jones], "Soul Food," in *Home: Social Essays*, ed. Amiri Baraka [LeRoi Jones] (New York: Morrow, 1966), 102.

30. Bob Jeffries, *Soul Food Cookbook* (Indianapolis: Bobbs-Merrill, 1969), ix.

31. Ibid., ix.

32. Harris, *High on the Hog*, 2011; Laretta Henderson, "'Ebony Jr! and 'Soul Food': The Construction of Middle-Class African American Identity through the Use of Traditional Southern Foodways," *MELUS* 32, no. 4 (2007): 81–97; Opie, *Hog and Hominy*; Carolyn Rouse and Janet Hoskins, "Purity, Soul Food, and Sunni Islam: Explorations at the Intersection of Consumption and Resistance," *Cultural Anthropology* 19, no. 2 (2004): 226–49; and Doris Witt, *Black Hunger: Soul Food and America* (Minneapolis: University of Minnesota Press, 2004).

33. Opie, *Hog and Hominy*, 173.

34. Elijah Muhammad, *How to Eat to Live: Muhammad Speaks* (Chicago: Muhammad's Mosque of Islam No. 2, 1961–75), 6, quoted in Rose and Hoskins, "Purity, Soul Food," 236.

35. Rouse and Hoskins, "Purity, Soul Food," 240.

36. Muhammad, *How to Eat to Live*, 108.

37. The figure of the grandmother is often referenced in discussions about soul food, both those that frame the traditional cuisine positively and those that frame it negatively. Such references reinforce the idea, most clearly articulated by Marvalene H. Hughes, that "the dominant figure in the cultural translation through food is the Black woman. Her expressions of love, nurturance, creativity, sharing, patience, economic frustration, survival, and the very core of her African heritage are embodied in her meal preparation." See Marvalene H. Hughes, "Soul, Black Women, and Food," in *Food and Culture: A Reader*, eds. Carole Counihan and Penny Van Esterik (New York: Routledge, 1997), 272. Consider, for example, the central role that the character "Big Mama," or Mama Joe, and her cooking played in the 1997 film *Soul Food*. In the words of Psyche A. Williams-Forson, who critiques the

representations of African American women and foodways in the film, Mama Joe's character "is, in essence, the epitome of the strong black woman upon whom the gods had miraculously bestowed culinary gifts." See Psyche A. Williams-Forson, *Building Houses Out of Chicken Legs: Black Women Food, & Power* (Chapel Hill: University of North Carolina Press, 2006), 189. See also Leandris C. Liburd, "Food, Identity, and African-American Women with Type 2 Diabetes: An Anthropological Perspective," *Diabetes Spectrum* 16, no. 3 (2003): 160–65.

38. Opie, *Hog and Hominy*, 168.

39. Nettles, "Saving Soul Food," 112.

40. Opie, *Hog and Hominy*, 155.

41. Harris, *High on the Hog*, 218.

42. Kimberly Nettles and William C. Whit offer lists of these books. See Nettles, "Saving Soul Food," 112–13; and Whit, "Soul Food as Cultural Creation," 56. Not included in these lists, yet still relevant to the current discussion, are *The Family Style Soul Food Diabetes Cookbook* (2006), *Vegan Soul Kitchen* (2009), *By Any Greens Necessary* (2010), and *Afro-Vegan* (2014).

43. Ruby Banks-Payne, *Ruby's Low Fat Soul Food Cookbook* (Chicago: Contemporary Books, 1996), xi.

44. Ibid., xii.

45. Ibid.

46. Ibid.

47. Ibid., v.

48. Patti LaBelle with Laura B. Randolph, *LaBelle Cuisine: Recipes to Sing About* (New York: Broadway Books, 1999), xiii.

49. See also Nettles's insightful comparison of these two cookbooks (2007).

50. Nettles, "Saving Soul Food," 110.

51. Charles L. Briggs and Richard Bauman, "Genre, Intertextuality, and Social Power," *Journal of Linguistic Anthropology* 2, no. 2 (1992): 131–72.

52. Patti LaBelle, *Patti LaBelle's Lite Cuisine: Over 100 Dishes with to-Die-for Taste Made with to-Live-for Recipes* (New York: Gotham Books, 2003), 61.

53. Ibid., xxiii.

54. Ibid., 183.

55. Ibid., 59.

56. Bryant Terry, *Vegan Soul Kitchen* (Cambridge, MA: Da Capo Press, 2009), xxii.

57. Bryant Terry, *Afro-Vegan: Farm-Fresh African, Caribbean, and Southern Flavors Remixed* (Berkeley: Ten Speed Press, 2014), 4.

58. Julie Guthman, "'If They Only Knew': Color Blindness and Universalism in California Alternative Food Institutions," in *Taking Food Public: Redefining Foodways in a Changing World*, eds. Psyche Williams-Forson and Carole Counihan (New York: Routledge, 2012), 211–22; and Julie Guthman, "Bringing Good Food to Others: Investigating the Subjects of Alternative Food Practice," *Cultural Geographies* 15, no. 4 (2008): 431–47.

59. For other recently published works that explicitly speak to this idea, both of which pay homage to the influence of Dick Gregory, see Tracye Lynn McQuirter, *By Any Greens*

Necessary: A Revolutionary Guide for Black Women Who Want to Eat Great, Get Healthy, Lose Weight, and Look Phat (Chicago: Lawrence Hill Books, 2010) and A. Breeze Harper, *Sistah Vegan: Black Female Vegans Speak on Food, Identity, Health, and Society* (New York: Lantern Books, 2010).

60. Terry, *Vegan Soul Kitchen*, xxi.

61. Bryant Terry, "Reclaiming True Grits," *The Root*, February 29, 2008, http://www.the root.com/articles/culture/2008/02/reclaiming_true_grits.html.

62. Terry, *Afro-Vegan*, 59.

63. Ibid., 2.

64. Ibid., 4.

65. Terry, *Vegan Soul Kitchen*, xxii.

66. Ibid., xix.

67. Dorothy Noyes, "Tradition: Three Traditions," *Journal of Folklore Research* 46, no. 3 (2009): 233–68; Rafia Zafar makes a similar point in her analysis of the cookbooks *Spoonbread & Strawberry Wine: Recipes and Reminiscences of a Family* and *Vibration Cooking: or, The Travel Notes of a Geechee Girl*, though she focuses more on issues of gender. She argues that "both [cookbooks] illustrate the ways Black culinary traditions can be imagined or inscribed—by the author, by her readers—as a way of enacting the cultural, expressive, and historical agenda of the African American female. Along with *how-tos*, the Dardens and Smart-Grosvenor give us *whys*." See Rafia Zafar, "The Signifying Dish: Autobiography and History in Two Black Women's Cookbooks," *Feminist Studies* 25, no. 2 (1999): 450–51.

Comfort (and Discomfort) Food: Social Surrogacy and Embodied Memory in Real and Reel Life

LuAnne Roth

It is evident that nothing is simple in memories connected with food.
—Fabio Parasecoli

As suggested by the existence at the 2013 American Folklore Society of two panels on the topic of comfort food, folklorists are acutely aware that, while "under the cloak of the mundane and the quotidian," food is much more than a collection of nutrients.[1] Food assumes social and symbolic functions in people's lives and hides powerful meanings and structures. What we eat has enormous significance as a medium for personal and collective identity creation and maintenance. Five decades ago, psychoanalyst Charlotte Babcock wrote that food is used to relieve anxiety (e.g., eating when upset; clinging to old food habits because they are comforting); to deny one's needs (e.g., dieting or fasting); to gain acceptance and security; or to influence others (e.g., to manipulate and control children), and much research on comfort food still focuses on these emotional uses of food.[2] The term "comfort food" was first recorded in 1977. According to Wikipedia, the fountain of folk knowledge, comfort food is "traditionally eaten food (which often provides a nostalgic or sentimental feeling to the person eating it) or simply provides the consumer an easy-to-digest meal—soft in consistency and rich in calories, nutrients, or both. The nostalgic element held by most comfort food may be specific to either the individual or a specific culture."[3]

This definition leaves much unanswered. Many people intuitively *think* they understand what constitutes comfort food. How complicated can it be?

Yet there are actually many complexities, contingencies, and idiosyncrasies at play when individuals reach for food identified as comforting. Comfort food, therefore, is one of those nebulous terms that leads to much hypothesizing by the folk.[4] If comfort foods "positively pique emotions" and "relieve negative psychological effects,"[5] then I am particularly interested in the role memory plays in these functions and how this becomes relevant to *dis*comfort foods as well. By comparing the results of social science and humanities research, essays from students of my foodways classes and, finally, key scenes from ethnically diverse "food films,"[6] I support the contention that comfort food functions as a form of social surrogacy, and I discuss the technical mechanisms by which filmmakers, despite the limitations of the cinematic medium, manage to call upon organoleptic properties (flavor, smell, mouthfeel) to evoke "the remembering subject."[7] In other words, film works within its confines to visually and auditorally depict memories ordinarily recalled through a range of other senses, such as taste, smell, and mouthfeel.

American studies scholar Warren Belasco encourages reflection on foods laden with autobiographical, emotional, and symbolic meaning by building upon the concept of the madeleine—the tiny, tea-soaked cookie that inspired seven volumes of French novelist Marcel Proust's classic, *Remembrance of Things Past*.[8] Proust's protagonist Swann dips the tiny cookie into his tea and experiences something unexpected and perhaps magical.

No sooner had the warm liquid, and the crumbs with it, touched my palate than a shudder ran through my whole body, and I stopped, intent upon the extraordinary changes that were taking place. An exquisite pleasure had invaded my senses, but individual, detached, with no suggestion of its origin. And at once the vicissitudes of life had become indifferent to me, its disasters innocuous, its brevity illusory—this new sensation having had on me the effect which love has of filling me with a previous essence; or rather this essence was not in me, it was myself. I had ceased to feel mediocre, accidental, mortal. Whence could it have come to me, this all-powerful joy? I was conscious that it was connected with the taste of tea and cake, but that it infinitely transcended those savors, could not, indeed, be of the same nature as theirs. Where did it come from? What did it signify? How could I seize upon and define it? . . .

And suddenly the memory returned. The taste was that of the little crumb of madeleine which on Sunday mornings at Combray, . . . my aunt Leonie used to give me, dipping it first in her own cup of lime-flower tea. And once I had recognized the taste of the . . . madeleine soaked in her decoction of lime-flowers . . . immediately the old grey house . . . rose up like the scenery of a theater to attach itself to the little pavilion, opening on to the garden, which had been built out

behind it for my parents; and with the house the town ... the Square, where I was
sent before luncheon, the streets along which I used to run errands, the country
roads we took when it was fine. And just as the Japanese amuse themselves by
filling a porcelain bowl with water and steeping in it little crumbs of paper which
until then are without character or form, but, the moment they become wet,
stretch themselves and bend, take on color and distinctive shape, that moment
all the flowers in our garden and in M. Swann's park, and the waterlilies on the
Vivonne and the good folk of the village and their little dwellings and the parish
church and the whole of Combray and of its surroundings, taking their proper
shapes and growing solid, sprang into being, towns and gardens alike, from my
cup of tea.[9]

Upon such intense joy, the protagonist seeks the origin of his profound
emotion in the cookie itself, but eventually concludes that the source is hidden elsewhere (perhaps in his very soul).[10]

He realizes something about the process of remembering: that it involves
searching as well as creating—that is, not only retrieving pieces of the past
triggered by a present sensation, such as taste or smell, but actually recreating
the memory in that present moment.[11]

Since the rush of emotion and memory is triggered by the organoleptic
properties of taste and mouthfeel, Proust's madeleine nicely captures food's
power to evoke the deepest of memories and begs the question: How does
food manage to hold such power?[12] Belasco offers an exercise called "Madeleines: We Are What We Ate." Intended to get students to think about their own
equivalent of Proust's madeleine, the exercise asks students to imagine tasting
it and then to begin writing, describing the food as well as the associations,
images, and memories that it conjures: "Is it positive, negative, or somewhere
in between (bittersweet)? Is it a comfort food or a *dis*comfort food? A medium
for conflict or reunion? Is it homemade or commercial? Is it a demographic
'marker' of ethnicity, region, generation, gender, religion, or class? Does eating
this food make you part of a group? Exclude you from other groups?"[13]

For three semesters (2010–2013), I assigned this exercise to undergraduate
students taking a food and culture class I teach at the University of Missouri.
Their ninety responses are as varied as the students themselves, but they seem
to support an association between madeleines and comfort food, as the following examples illustrate (emphasis added).

> *Grandma's* homemade *chicken and noodles.* This was served at all the holidays in
> our family since I was a kid. It is like chicken and dumplings but with homemade
> egg noodles. It *reminds me of all the wonderful times* I have spent with my family.

Everyone wants to take the leftovers home, if there is [*sic*] any! The *holidays* would not be the same without it. The year my grandpa passed away is the only time grandma wasn't going to make it, so the grandkids came and she showed us how so we can always have it. (Female from central Missouri, Spring 2013)

My *grandmother's kabobs*. Persian food is rare in Texas, so I am sure one can imagine how rare it must be in Missouri. Altogether, even if there were 1,000 Persian restaurants in this town of Columbia, no one would make kabobs koobideh like my grandmother Jaleh Lalzalipour. She grills the meat, and shapes the kabobs into planks around the roasting sticks. She has a homemade charcoal grill in the backyard; wooden and old. She rotates the beef kebobs over and over. When she returns into the house with the kabobs, they are nestled together under a circular shape of flat bread on a plate. She enters with the kabobs, but when she walks in it fills the house with the nostalgic aroma. (Female from Texas, Spring 2013)

My *mom's homemade stove-top potatoes with onions*. She's made them my whole life and my whole family begs for them all the time. It reminds me of home and my family and no one can make them like her. My mom makes fried potatoes for us and has since I was little. . . . It's not a complicated dish to make, but we always beg for them at every holiday or dinner she makes when people come over. . . . *They just remind me of home and especially of eating dinner with my sisters and mom* while we joke and talked about our days at school. I think it's indicative of our class and nationality—it's simple, inexpensive and very American in that it's fried potatoes. It definitely makes me feel like part of a group—my family. (Female from Chicago, Spring 2013)

My madeleine is *rice pudding* for the reason that *my mom* would stir the rice and the milk for hours until she got the consistency only she could judge. I have a lot of memories of the kitchen stool pulled up to the stove and my dad, sister, and I taking turns stirring the pudding. (Male from Chicago, Spring 2013)

I would have to say my madeleine is *plátanos fritos* (ripe, sweet plantains fried and salted) for breakfast. By the time I was born, both of my biological grandfathers had passed away and my maternal grandmother had been remarried to Desmond Daniels, a black Panamanian man who I came to know as *Pappy or Grandpa*. When I was a little girl, I was scared of Pappy. A former opera singer, he had a loud, booming voice, and his version of joking was to make scary (but altogether affectionate) faces and voices. However, *I remember the first time we really bonded was over him teaching me to make plátanos* for breakfast. Since then he has become one of my closest friends and mentor. (Female from Kansas City, Missouri, Spring 2013)

Homemade chili. My *grandmother* has always made it for the family when we visit and *especially* holidays (Thanksgiving and Christmas). My mother learned the recipe and now makes it at home for family dinners. It always makes me feel at home and safe; now that my grandma passed away, it's a remembrance of her :). (Female from Iowa, Spring 2012)

My madeleine is *chocolate biscotti.* It brings me images of my childhood and all of my family's shared experiences. It *reminds me of my heritage,* as my grandparents and great-grandparents emigrated here from Italy and grew up in Italian neighborhoods in St. Louis. This is a dish we eat during *holidays,* so images of Christmas trees come to mind as well. (Male from St. Louis, Spring 2012)

Cinnamon apples. Growing up (and now, when I visit), I used to always help my *Grandma Ruby* make cinnamon apples. She would always sneak me some of the Red Hot candies we used to flavor the apples, too! I look forward to it every time we visit Grandma and Grandpa's house. It brings to mind the generation of the Great Depression. We have them at every family meal, so in a way it makes you part of the family group. (Female from Illinois, Spring 2012)

My single most powerful madeleine is *shrimp.* Not only does it evoke my cultural ties but it brings me back to warm days on Bermuda Bluff with my parents, the taste of salt water as I hold the knot in my teeth, the smell of the spices as the pot boils and the feeling of the shells as I spend hours beside my family plucking off shrimp heads and tails. It is a positive homemade comfort food, and I don't get this feeling from shrimp of fast food quality. It binds me to the Low country families, which shrimped and crabbed to supplement their diets. (Male from Beaufort, South Carolina, Spring 2012)

This sampling of my students' testimonials supports the idea that madeleines are associated with ethnic or regional identity, nostalgia, and parental nurturing and, not surprisingly, almost all of them identify their madeleines as comfort food. Also noteworthy, for my students, madeleines are connected with memory, usually positive memories.[14]

Upon entering the body, food inspires memory by linking sensory and cognitive processes through synesthesia—the sensory properties of taste, smell, sound, and appearance.[15] The idea that memory is embedded in food's organoleptic and synesthetic properties is supported in social science research as well as in the humanities. Because memory is embodied, it is worth considering how taste works vis-à-vis memory and the brain.[16] Here I summarize some recent research relevant to the topic of comfort food derived from disciplines outside of the humanities. Cognitive psychologists use computer metaphors to understand the brain's unconscious processes,[17] as both humans and computers constitute thinking engines, although the metaphor has limitations. For one, it is not possible to separate the rational from the emotional elements. Also, brains are like snowflakes in that each is unique. There is tremendous variability of connections in the brains of different individuals because of unique developmental histories and experiences. Even children of the same biological family—being genetically similar and exposed to the same foods—have individualized preferences, tastes, and memories about the same events. In the brain, "synaptic connections change, die, are created every day, and vary in each individual, affecting the way things and events are remembered."[18] In order to taste, "the brain forms its overall perceptions by synthesis of signals, or sensory stimuli, derived from different kinds of receptors on the tongue, in the nose, and at the ends of the nervous tissues in the mouth area."[19] The most important organ for taste is found in the brain's hypothalamus.[20] A "hairnet" of fibers stretching from the brainstem to other parts of the brain "fire each time something startling, unexpected, or important happens," whether a sudden pain or intense pleasure. Upon firing, neuromodulator chemicals are released. These complex dynamics impact memory formation.[21] This memory formation process is nicely explained by the protagonist of television's *Breaking Bad*.[22] Walter White (Bryan Cranston), the high school chemistry teacher who begins making methamphetamines to secure his family's finances after being diagnosed with lung cancer, is invited to break bread with the high-level drug distributor, Gustavo Fring (Giancarlo Esposito), who has prepared a meal of *paila marina*, a Chilean dish prepared "just like my mother used to make it." "It always amazes me," remarks Fring upon tasting the fish stew, "the way the senses work in connection to memory. I mean, this stew is simply an amalgam of ingredients. Taken separately, these ingredients alone don't remind me of anything. I mean, not very much at all. But, in this precise combination, the smell of this meal instantly, it brings you back to my childhood. How is that possible?" Tending toward rational explanations, White responds, "Basically, it all takes place in the hippocampus. Neural connections are formed. The senses make the neurons express signals . . . that go right back to the same part of the brain as before where memory is stored. It's something called relational memory."

Endel Tulving's principle of "encoding specificity" says that "an event is more likely to be remembered if the retrieval conditions and circumstances, including perceptions, thoughts, and emotions, match the subjective qualities at the moment of its encoding in the brain."[23] Because human memory is selective, the computer metaphor proves misleading in understanding food memories. The computer model fails to account for such factors as creativity, imagination, intuition, or aesthetic and sensory appreciation. Unlike accessing computer files, not every human memory is retained or retrieved in the same way. Hence, food memories "are intrinsically multifaceted and variegated."[24] Those engrams or dispositional representations that are created under stress, intense pleasure, or other strong emotional states have a tendency to survive longer."[25]

Psychologists Jordan D. Troisi and Shira Gabriel proposed that comfort food derives its power from cognitive associations with social relationships, so that "the 'comfort' of such food can be understood by examining its effects on loneliness."[26] Loneliness and lack of social connection can be "psychologically and physically perilous," they write, leading to aversive outcomes from hurt feelings, low self-esteem, and depression to physical pain.[27] Since the need to belong is fundamental, humans avoid loneliness by forming relationships with others. When forming relationships with actual people is not possible, the need to avoid loneliness may lead individuals to seek social surrogates,[28] taking the form of television, photographs, letters, smart phones, or comfort food.[29] Troisi and Gabriel gathered college student essays—much like those collected from my students—and coded them for such variables as the type of food; whether it was a favorite food, family, cultural, or holiday tradition, part of her/his past, or otherwise a reminder of home; whether others close to her/him were mentioned; whether the food was salty, sweet, or healthful; and the temperature of the food. After finishing the essays, participants used the UCLA Loneliness Scale[30] to report their feelings of loneliness at the present.[31] Using the quintessential comfort food—chicken soup—the researchers then conducted two experiments to test the hypothesis "that comfort foods are associated with relationships and can reduce lonely feelings."[32] Upon consumption, participants who identified chicken noodle soup as comfort food used more "relationship-related words" compared with those who did not identify the dish as their comfort food.[33] My students' essays showed similar relationship associations, writing not just about kabobs and chicken and noodles, but specifically "my grandmother's kabobs" and "my grandma's homemade chicken and noodles." This finding supports what folklorists have already known: that comfort food *is* cognitively associated with relationships.[34] The second experiment tested whether comfort food actually has the power to reduce feelings of loneliness. The researchers concluded: "Food items become comfort foods because people are repeatedly exposed to them in the presence of relational partners. In other words, because comfort foods are typically initially eaten with primary relationship partners, the perceptual experience of eating these foods is encoded along with the higher-order experience of social comfort.

The first known "food film" is August Lumiere's three-minute silent documentary of his infant daughter being fed lunch (1895), which serves as a
reminder that nourishment is fundamental to human experience and that
our first impressions of the world are formed through the act of eating.

Therefore, the physiological experience of ingesting, or even thinking about
ingesting, comfort food automatically activates the experience of psychological comfort that was initially encoded along with the food."[35]

Deborah Lupton, a cultural studies scholar, conducted an interview-based
study, finding nostalgia to be integral to the meanings ascribed to food. Some
of her interviewees reported that, when feeling sad or sick, they "often experienced the urge to eat the simple, soft, often milky comfort foods of their
childhood such as chocolate, soup, ice cream, French toast and macaroni
cheese," foods that offer pleasure because of their association with emotions
of security and comfort.[36] This also supports the notion of comfort food being
eaten with the deliberate goal of mood alteration.[37] Philosopher Carolyn
Korsmeyer adds that "our pleasant responses to tastes are themselves complex
cognitive responses that involve highly compressed symbolic recognition."[38]
Speaking directly about comfort food, specifically chicken soup (with its
bland, oily quality signifying comfort and care), Korsmeyer observes: "Think
of how what are now called 'comfort foods' blend childhood, nourishment,
and soothing calm into their very tastes."[39] Fittingly, half of the Wikipedia

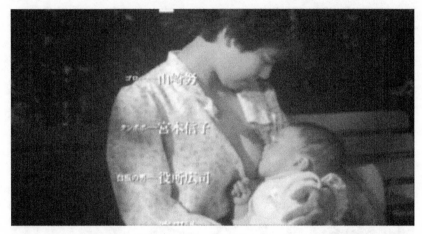

The closing credits of the first modern food film, *Tampopo* (1986), illustrates
the mother's breast as our first sense of comfort and nourishment.

definition quoted at the beginning implies that comfort food is like baby
food—easy to digest, soft, high in calories and nutrients—and this surely is
not coincidental.

By using film as an ethnographic text,[40] cinematic food scenes can shed
light on some of these complex relationships with comfort food. In the first
year of cinema, 1895, August Lumiere created a three-minute silent documentary of his infant daughter being fed lunch. There is no specific mention of comfort food, although it serves as a reminder that nourishment is
fundamental to human experience: "During infancy it constitutes our first
relationship to reality. The mother's breast, or any ersatz food giver, becomes
the first object of the infant's desire and knowledge."[41] In this way, our first
impressions of the world are formed through purely sensual means, as philosopher Jennifer Iannolo writes: "Our surroundings are interpreted by a series
of impressions recorded by our lips, fingers, ears, eyes, and noses. A mother's
breast provides our first sense of comfort and nourishment, when we are not
yet in possession of formal language skills; we cannot articulate what it is we
sense, but we know what brings us pleasures and pain, and we pursue that
which comforts."[42] The first modern food film, *Tampopo* (1986), reinforces
this very notion of the foundational import of food.[43]

The film chronicles the title character Tampopo (Nobuko Miyamoto) and
her pursuit of the perfect ramen noodle restaurant. In addition, director Juzo
Itami's whimsical camera pursues a series of asides—"a pastiche of disjointed
scenes"—that bear thematic relationship to the central narrative.[44] One example takes place during the closing credits, which roll over a long shot of a

mother holding her infant on a park bench while the baby nurses at its mother's breast. The camera slowly pans in to a close-up of the baby contentedly sucking away. Lasting a full three minutes, the scene seems to conclude the central theme of people's preoccupation and obsession with food.[45] Moreover, the extended shot illustrates the type of situation in which the infant's brain forms engrams to remember the experience of being nurtured by its mother.

There are clearly many ways to think about how food and memory work. Anthropologist David Sutton finds that food encompasses structures—both quotidian and ritual—that span days, weeks, or years, which are linked to agricultural, migration, and religious cycles. Drawing evidence from his ethnographic study in Greece, along with four "nostalgia cookbooks" (Cuban, Greek, Italian, and southern US), Sutton finds that these food structures enable memories on a cultural level. "The community members' ability to recall meals years later shows the way in which food facilitates community building"; moreover, the repetition of the meal aids in maintaining "historical consciousness."[46] In this way, the descendants of famine survivors, immigrants, slaves, and war refugees "often cherish the stigmatized foods of their oppressive past as a way to honor their ancestors' courage and endurance."[47] The food at Passover Seders, for example, recalls the ancient story of the Jews' escape from Egypt, as seen in such films as the documentary *Passover: A Celebration*, the fictional comedy *When Do We Eat?* and the existential drama *Crimes and Misdemeanors*.[48] Folklorist Sharon Sherman writes that the home-centered meal is said to create a heightened sense of *communitas* linking Jews from the Exodus, upon which the Seder is based, to the present. As such, a number of key food items on the Seder plate "have acknowledged and deeply engrained meanings"—from lamb shank bone to matzo bread—all of which are recounted in the Haggadah text (prayer book) that structures the meal. For example, Sherman describes the following food symbolism:

A piece of roasted *lamb shank bone* (although any roasted meat bone may be used) represents the Pesach sacrifice. A *roasted egg, called "chagigoh,"* symbolizes a second animal sacrificed in Jerusalem. The first animal had to be entirely eaten before the dawn of the first day. Because the group was large, some only received a small bite, so a second animal (not sacrificed in the Temple) was used for the second night. "*Charoses," a kind of fruit salad* from the early Spring festival, consists of nuts, cinnamon, wine, and apples; it is often said to symbolize the mortar mixed by Jewish slaves for the Pharaoh's buildings in Egypt. It also represents the hope of freedom. *Bitter herbs or "moror,"* usually a piece of horseradish, symbolize the bitterness of the Jews' lives in Egypt. *Greens*, often parsley, lettuce or watercress, dipped in salt water (representing tears) stand for the coming of spring and the hope of redemption. The table setting includes a plate with three pieces of *matzo*, each wrapped separately within a folded cloth. The matzo has three meanings: (1) the bread which the Jews took with them on fleeing Egypt that had not risen (including the dessert matzo or "afikomen"); (2) the bread of poverty; and (3) the bread of the simple life in the desert.[49]

Sherman then reports the difference between the ideal Passover Seder and the reality of how an individual family actually celebrates it, based on ethnographic interviews with members of her own extended family, who are conscious of the circumscribed symbolism of these food items, yet have developed personalized meanings for particular tastes and foods.[50] Sherman concludes that, since each Seder builds on past ones, each participant draws upon her or his memories to create personalized texts, therefore, "food is perhaps more important for the memories it triggers than for its ritual qualities."[51] Consider the way in which Stan's recollection emphasizes the individualized nature of how Seder foods bring the past into the present, as his memories of the taste of matzo and the *charoses* fruit salad are imbricated in nostalgic memories of childhood Seders:

> I think Passover is probably the most symbolic of the holidays . . . we celebrate as Jews. It's the one that . . . I remember as being the happiest when I was a child. We would have . . . Seders at my Grandparent's home or my Grandmother's home and . . . as a child I remember running around and . . . taking . . . bits and pieces of the special foods and it was a holiday that had the smell of cooking, it was a holiday that . . . had a lot of people around, and it wasn't focused on the synagogue, it was focused on the home more than anything else. . . . I remember playing with my cousins, and I remember the taste of various foods. I remember the taste of matzo, and I remember the taste of the *charoses* and as a kid we were allowed to have wine, and that was fun. Very nice and warm and very symbolic kind of holiday.[52]

The film *Soul Food* similarly illustrates the ability of food to recall a history of overcoming oppression for the descendants of African slaves through the Joseph family, a fictional middle-class family living in Chicago.[53] While soul food itself is seen only in the opening and closing of the film, the fact that the narrative revolves around food at different stages of preparation, as well as the memorable close-up shots of the food—including fried chicken, catfish, ham, string beans, greens with ham hocks, corn on the cob, mashed potatoes and gravy, macaroni and cheese, cornbread, and sweet potato pie—render the film a strong contender as a food film. Observers of the film draw attention to the

Soul Food (1997) illustrates the ability of food to
recall a shared history of overcoming oppression.

notion that soul food derives from this history of oppression, contributing to
the meaning individual family members ascribe to food traditions and the
way in which food connects to memory.[54] Even though they were egregiously
oppressed, African Americans retained traditions from their West African
origins while creatively adapting and innovating upon them in the context
of the New World—from oral tradition, religion, music, and dance to material culture and foodways. Food historian Robert L. Hall explains that these
traditional foods, "inextricably linked to slavery," historically

> served to increase the African population and thus support the overseas slave
> trade (as with maize and manioc introduced from the Americas), were used
> cosmetically to make slaves look young and sleek for sale (rubbing with palm
> oil), were fed to slaves as provisions during the infamous Middle Passage (yams,
> peanuts, and rice), were provided to keep slaves healthy during that voyage (cit-
> rus fruit and malagueta peppers), or became plantation products that required
> or used slave labor in the New World (as in the case of rice). The often perversely
> ironic links between the spread of certain foodstuffs and African bondage in
> the Western Hemisphere makes for a good deal of ambivalence about African
> cultural influences among Native Americans, Euro-Americans, and African
> American populations.[55]

In addition, the innovation of the African newcomers profoundly shaped the
culinary tastes of Euro-Americans and Native Americans, a fact most evident
in consumption patterns found in the Southern states.[56] Again, Hall states:

"The continuity, vitality, and creative adaptations of particular culinary traditions in the Americas testify to the richness of African cultures and the resourcefulness of those Africans who were coerced to come yet brought that richness with them and imparted it to host societies."[57]

Pride in this heritage is addressed in the second scene of *Soul Food*, when the partly omniscient narrator, Ahmad (Brandon Hammond), a ten-year-old boy, explains via voiceover that the matriarch, Mama Joe (Irma P. Hall), aka "Big Mama," is the reason the Joseph family has remained close in spite of trials and tribulations: "She was the rock of the Joseph family ... the one that held us all together. One reason we were so tight ... is 'cause we always had Sunday dinners at Big Mama's. That were a tradition started down in Mississippi ... when old folks met at church to talk smack ... and chow down on some good old soul food. Big Mama kept the tradition ... when she and Granddaddy moved to Chicago. Holidays, of course, were bigger. More folks, more eats, more souls ... more soul food." In a scene shortly after, Big Mama alludes to the historical etiology of soul food in a conversation with her youngest child, nicknamed Bird (Nia Long), while admonishing her daughter's overuse of salt: "Ooh. No, baby. That's too much. Just put about four pinches in," to which Bird responds, "How you know how much to put in without using a measuring cup? And why we got to eat ham hocks anyway?" "Ham hocks, pig feet, chitlins," responds Big Mama. "We learn how to make things taste good by trying things out. Soul food cookin' is about cooking from the heart."

After establishing the tight-knit Joseph family, the narrative goes on to describe a series of hardships that threaten to rip the family apart, including sickness, death, pregnancy, birth, adultery, divorce, jail, and career changes. Food functions in the film to negotiate family relationships and, as such, divisiveness is also expressed over food. For example, the contentious relationship between sisters Maxine (Vivica A. Fox) and Teri (Vanessa Williams) is expressed symbolically—"Big Mama said she should have named them Vinegar and Oil"—and the relative status of female family members is expressed according to their cooking skills when Maxine and Teri argue over who cooks the best and when only one person is willing to try Bird's attempt to make fishcakes. Despite these symbolic food conflicts, Big Mama remarks at one point that "green beans, sweet potato pie, and southern fried chicken would settle any dispute." In the end, the Sunday dinner tradition is indeed strong enough to hold the family together through betrayals, conflicts, and petty jealousies. Ahmad's voiceover explains: "Now I understand what soul food was all about. During slavery, black folks didn't have a lot to celebrate. Cooking was how we expressed love for each other. That's what those Sunday dinners meant. More than just eating. It was a time for sharing our joys and sorrows. Something old folks say is missing in today's families." On the whole, soul food functions in the film to create communitas, smoothing ruffled feathers, and promoting love. Everyone in the Joseph family finds stability in the tradition of weekly dinners, as the food brings comfort and solace to those with hurt feelings, serving to remind the family of their shared history. By eating traditional comfort foods together, therefore, food and memory are connected through weekly rituals, as well as through "alimentary exchanges" or the stories people tell about their family's foodways.[58]

In contrast to the comfort food of Sunday dinner creating a sense of communitas, as depicted in *Soul Food*, the food film *Eat Drink Man Woman* presents family members who have great difficulty expressing their feelings for each other.[59] As a result, the intricate preparation of banquet-quality dishes for Sunday dinners by Taiwan's "greatest living chef" becomes a surrogate for unspoken emotions. Indeed, the opening credits roll for four minutes over a series of close-up shots of food preparation by the widower patriarch, Chu (Sihung Lung), who creates complex Chinese recipes.[60] Despite the extraordinary efforts of Chef Chu, the adult daughters cannot appreciate his food. Instead, they seem bored and find fault with it (e.g., "He's losing his sense of taste"). The middle daughter, Jia-Chien (Kuei-Mei Yang), even refers to the collection of culinary masterpieces, which make the film's audience salivate, as the "Sunday dinner torture ritual." As the story progresses, audiences learn that the Sunday ritual brings no gustatory or social enjoyment, that "the participants are merely going through the motions. Despite Chu's fascinating proficiency in exotic and ancient Chinese culinary techniques, his artful meal remains unpalatable for the diners, the empty gestures of a chef who can no longer taste and who creates elaborate meals to hide the fact that he no longer knows how to please and support his daughters, and within the family conversation, the audience can detect thinly veiled hostility."[61] The drama reflects both intergenerational conflict—as the daughters rebel against traditional Chinese customs by pursuing education, Christianity, professional careers, courtship, and marriage—and their lack of appetite for their father's cooking symbolizes their growing alienation from Chinese culture.[62]

Besides providing comfort through a visceral experience of the past, longing for and consuming such foods functions to sustain a sense of personal, cultural, and familial identity.[63] During one revealing alimentary exchange, Jia-Chien prepares dim sum for her ex-boyfriend lover. As the successful airline executive presents one tantalizing dish after another, she describes her yearning to become a master chef and her resentment that her father banished her from the kitchen to prevent this career choice. Upon seeing and smelling the food, she reflects sentimentally on childhood memories that characterize

"It's strange. I don't have any childhood memories unless I cook them into existence," says middle daughter Jia-Chien in *Eat Drink Man Woman* (1994), who is first nostalgic and then sad by the memories prompted by the smell of food.

the difficult relationship with her father: "It's strange. I don't have any childhood memories unless I cook them into existence. You wouldn't believe how fun and warm my father used to be. Back then, after school, before the dinner rush, he'd bake me bracelets made of bread. I used to have a ring full of spices and sugar diamonds made from dough. He enjoyed letting me play in the big kitchen. Jia-Jen was so jealous." Notably, Jia-Chien's personal insight—"All my childhood memories are of cooking. My memory's my nose"—suggests that the smell, taste, or thought of specific foods, if connected to happy or idealized childhood memories, may elicit nostalgia in adult life. "Personal nostalgia may be defined as a kind of homesickness, a sense of loss, a rosy memory of childhood as warm and secure," writes advertising researcher Barbara Stern, "it involves 'a bittersweet longing for home . . . an emotional state in which an individual yearns for an idealized or sanitized version of an earlier time period."[64] Nostalgia does not necessarily depend on a happy childhood; in fact, it often recreates a fictional one, glossing over difference and conflict to construct a more harmonious past,[65] and "this yearning may instigate individuals' attempts to recreate an aspect of this past life by reproducing activities related to the rosy recollections of it," including the consumption of comfort food.[66]

We see another expression of nostalgia and food memories in *Babette's Feast [Bebettes gæstebud]*, which along with *Tampopo*, signaled the coming of age of contemporary food films.[67] Based on a 1950 short story by Isak Dinesen (aka Karen Blixen), the film starts on the Jutland coast of Denmark. Two pious sisters, Martina (Brigette Fedeispiel) and Filippa (Bodil Kjer), devote their lives to a small Lutheran congregation founded by their long-deceased father. Parisian master chef Babette (Stephane Audran) seeks asylum with the sisters in the remote Scandinavian village of Norre Vossberg when her husband and son are executed by General Galliffet in the 1871 Paris uprising. When Babette happens to win the Paris lottery in 1885, she uses all 10,000 francs to provide a "real French meal" to her benefactors. The fact that, above all else, eating is preeminently pleasurable, the apex of sensual activities, produces one of the major conflicts in the film because most of the guests have vowed to reject worldly love, ambition, adulation, and wealth in order to devote themselves to spiritual goals.[68] "Man shall not merely refrain from, but also reject any thought of food and drink," remarks one woman. "Only then can he eat and drink in the proper spirit."

During the seven-course meal (which occupies nineteen minutes of the film), the eleven aging Danes share the gourmet French meal with General Lowenhielm (Gudmar Wivesson), an outsider who provides the critical voice throughout the transcendent dinner in contrast to the austere Danes, who refuse to taste or speak about the food. One major theme of the film is the power of art to uplift or redeem, with the triumph of the "exotic" French dishes over the flock's denial of sensory and sensual appetites. Despite the austere food philosophy that informs the group's approach to the meal, gradually, a sort of miracle occurs. Inspired by the general's praise of the food, the quarrelsome congregation begin to enjoy the Amontillado, turtle soup, champagne, and Blinis Demidoff. Although the food and drink are foreign to the Lutheran flock, it warms their hearts and, like the comfort food of the other films discussed here, it begins to trigger memories. One by one, the dinner guests reminisce about the beloved deceased minister, whose 100th birthday this meal was intended to celebrate. "Do you remember what he taught us?" one woman tenderly recalls. "Little children, love one another." This wisdom is repeated in unison by the group before another memory begins. "Remember the time," begins another woman. "Indeed, it was quite a miracle when our minister had promised to conduct a Christmas sermon at the church across the fjord. For two weeks the weather had been so bad that no captain or fisherman would risk the crossing. The villagers had given up all hope. The minister told them if no boat would take them, he would walk across to them on the waves. And behold, three days before Christmas the storm abated. A cold spell set in and the fjord froze from shore to shore. And this had never happened before in any man's memory."

After tasting the *Cailles en Sarcophage* (quail in a puff pastry shell with *foie gras* and truffle sauce), Babette's signature dish, the worldly general is

After tasting *Cailles en Sarcophage*, Babette's signature dish, General Lowenhielm is reminded of the last time he ate this dish and triumphantly recounts this memory in *Babette's Feast* (1987).

reminded of the last time he ate this dish and triumphantly recounts this memory:

> One day in Paris, after I had won a riding competition, my French fellow officers invited me out to dine at one of the finest restaurants, the Café Anglais. The chef, surprisingly enough, was a woman. We were served *Cailles en Sarcophage*, a dish of her own creation. General Galliffet, who was our host for the evening explained that this woman, this head chef, had the ability to transform a dinner into a kind of love affair. A love affair that made no distinction between bodily appetite and spiritual appetite. General Galliffet said that in the past he had fought a duel for the love of a beautiful woman. But now there was no woman in Paris for whom he would shed his blood—except for this chef. She was considered the greatest culinary genius. What we are now eating is nothing less than *Cailles en Sarcophage*.

It is important to note here that while General Lowenhielm's speech is triggered by eating the exact dish associated with the memory, those recounted by the Lutheran congregation are triggered by food completely foreign to them. While the exotic food cannot be called "comfort food" for the congregation, eating the delicious food nonetheless elicits fond memories and serves as a reminder of the complexity of food and memories.[69]

Tasting the Mayan hot chocolate in *Chocolat* (2000) triggers a powerfully pleasant memory, as the otherwise cantankerous Armande recounts a night of romance and youthful frivolity.

Another example of foreign food that triggers food memories occurs in the film *Chocolat*.[70] Adapted from Jeanne Harris's novel, the story is set in a small, provincial French village and follows the free-spirited protagonist Vianne Rocher (Juliette Binoche) as she opens a chocolaterie. Much to the chagrin of the town's mayor and self-appointed moral compass, Count du Reynaud (Alfred Molina), the shop opens during Lent, a period Catholics set aside for abstemious behavior. The first customer is Vianne's landlady, Armande Voizin (Judi Dench), a cantankerous old woman estranged from her daughter and grandson. Vianne prepares hot chocolate, described as a special Maya recipe sprinkled with chili pepper "to awaken the senses." Given Armande's initial response to the sight of chili pepper (she thinks it is rancid cinnamon), one assumes she has not already had this drink, yet it triggers a powerfully pleasant memory. Upon tasting it, Armande pauses and suddenly warms, remarking, "It tastes like . . . like . . . I don't know," and then chuckles uncharacteristically. When the film returns to this scene a moment later, Armande's disposition has completely transformed as she recounts a story about a night of romance and youthful frivolity: "I was out all night with him. We swam naked in the Thames. At dawn, when I returned to my house and my bed, my mother poked her head in and said, 'Wake up, sleepy head.' She had no idea I'd been gone." Armande and Vianne cackle delightfully at the conclusion of the story. "Are you sure you didn't put booze in here?" Armande asks, surprised at her own sudden mood change.

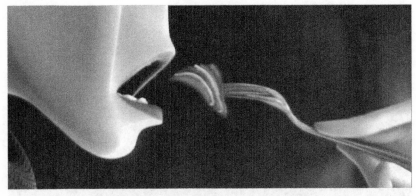

The petulant food critic Anton Ego is poised to take a bite of the titular dish in the animated *Ratatouille* (2007), which will trigger a powerful flashback to childhood.

Tasting the ratatouille triggers a powerful flashback of Ego as a child being comforted by his mother's ratatouille, providing a visceral reminder of the profound connection between food and memory.

Beyond these sorts of alimentary exchanges, in which a character verbally recounts a memory triggered by eating, film can be particularly useful in illuminating the process by which these food memories are sparked. This is seen in *Ratatouille*, an animated food film that follows Remi, an intrepid rat who has the impossible dream of becoming a world-class chef in Paris.[71] Hoping to gain a haughty food critic's approval and therefore restore Gusteau's Restaurant to its former legendary status, in the climactic scene Remi prepares and serves the titular dish—ratatouille (which kitchen staff refer to as "a peasant's dish")—to the petulant food critic aptly named Anton Ego. Adorned with red and yellow sauce, the delicate sculpture of sliced vegetables sits on the plate. Before taking the first bite, a close-up shot shows the critic preparing to take notes for what he anticipates will be a negative review. A medium shot frames the plated ratatouille and Ego's pen on paper—weapons of his trade—as he pauses dramatically and then moves a forkful to his mouth. An extreme close-up of the food entering his mouth, the sound of chewing, and then his stunned expression proceeds a fast zoom from Ego seated in the restaurant to a flashback of him as a young child standing in the doorway of his family's cottage after a bicycle accident. Smiling warmly beside the stove, his mother holds a steaming pot of ratatouille, places a bowl in front of the sniffling boy, and gently grasps his chin to offer encouragement. The boy takes a bite of the food and then the camera zooms from his relieved face to the astounded expression of the adult Ego. Shot from a low-angle, we see Ego's pen fall in slow motion from hand to floor with an amplified bounce as the critic's shock transforms into a warm smile. He proceeds to gobble up the rest of the entrée, gliding his finger on the plate to sop up the last bit of sauce. The emotional experience "knocks him off his hauteur perch," winning the critic's praise, teaching him to appreciate food with modest origins, and providing a visceral reminder of the profound connection between food and memory.[72]

This scene works effectively to show how, as a cinematic device, the flashback provides audiences with visual information the filmmakers are unable to incorporate otherwise. Bridging time, place, and action, the technique progresses the story and reveals information about the character. Perhaps the flashback would more aptly be called "flash present" since the technique functions to reveal what the character is thinking or feeling in the present. As this scene from *Ratatouille* illustrates, flashbacks offer insight into the remembering subject's state of mind and can show how memory is embodied and embedded in organoleptic properties. In this case, the taste of food immediately triggers a positive flashback, showing viewers why ratatouille is comfort food for the critic Ego.

Nostalgic memories, initiated by taste and smell, reveal one of the hallmarks of comfort food, as described in the aforementioned films (*Tampopo, Soul Food, Eat Drink Man Woman, Babette's Feast, Chocolat,* and *Ratatouille*). Many of these cinematic scenes, along with interview data and my students' essays, reinforce the idea that food plays a powerful role in creating a sense of commensality, harmony, nurturance, and positive memories—that "sharing food has almost magical properties in its ability to turn self-seeking individuals into a collaborative group" (Belasco 2008: 18). However, it is important to note that these profound moments, when food triggers memories, need not be positive. "That food functions as a means of opening communication channels and as a weapon to destroy them comes as no surprise," writes Diane Carson.[73] The alimentary exchange recounted in *Eat Drink Man Woman* hints at this dynamic when Jia-Chien is first nostalgic and then saddened by the memories prompted by the smell of food. Rather than functioning as a social surrogate to reduce feelings of loneliness, food has the opposite effect, triggering memories that reinforce a sense of pain and isolation.[74] Another powerful cinematic moment that illustrates this function of *dis*comfort food appears in *301/302*, a South Korean food film in which almost every depiction of food— from procurement and preparation to presentation and consumption—has negative and repulsive associations.[75] The disjointed narrative presents the troubling tale of the title characters—occupants of apartments 301 and 302— who are two isolated neighbors in Seoul's "New Hope" high-rise housing complex. Both struggle with food in their empty and debilitating lives. Fragments of memories—delivered via flashbacks and disembodied voiceover monologues about food—function to immerse viewers in each woman's consciousness and trace the origins of their present problems. Through the omniscient camera, viewers learn that both women had childhoods lacking physical and emotional nourishment and safety, and that both employ food in contrasting ways to respond to this foundational trauma.[76]

Kang Song-hee (Eun-jin Bang), occupant of 301, is recently divorced and hungry for affection. Having become a gourmet cook, 301 is obsessed with food to the point of gluttony. 301 substitutes food for love and sex.[77] A flashback of 301 as a child during the opening credits reveals one source of her disordered relationship to food as the first words of the film are spoken by a child's voiceover: "Our refrigerator is filled with food. But I never eat 'em cold." The young 301 peers into a refrigerator crammed with food. Despite the abundance of food, and her belief that her mother will come home to cook a warm meal, the young girl is actually left to fend for herself. "But because of her work, Mommy didn't come home until late at night," continues the voiceover.[78] The girl sighs and begins to prepare her own meal, chopping a cucumber and what appears to be Spam (a highly processed canned meat product from the US). 301's story reinforces the idea that a lack of social connections can be "psychologically and physically perilous." We see from this brief flashback that 301's use of food to combat loneliness stems from childhood neglect—experiences eventually leading to chronic binging, an obsession with cooking, and a desire to control others through food. Although 301 prepares beautiful dishes that seem to bring her joy, social science research suggests that this sort of emotional eating can have repercussions—that is, "satiating belongingness needs by consuming comfort food may be riskier than using some other social surrogates, as it may lead to overeating or unhealthy eating behavior."[79] 301 is completely preoccupied with food, maintaining a food diary and obsessing over having gained weight. For 301, writes film critic Diane Carson, "the very act of cooking takes on fetishistic importance of its own.... Cooking becomes her voice, killing and preparing a taboo dish her protest."[80]

On the other hand, the occupant of apartment 302, Kim Yoon-hee (Hwang Shin-hye), is an introverted, anorexic writer living a life of austerity and self-deprivation. Unlike her neighbor, 302 finds both food and sex repulsive and indigestible. This is ironic because she is employed as an advice column writer on those very topics. Disjointed flashbacks reveal 302's disturbing background, with the sight and sound of a saw cutting through raw red meat followed by an extreme close-up of the adolescent's lips as the child's voiceover explains: "Our refrigerator is big. It's always filled with fresh meat. My mom's an expert in slicing the meat." Following additional shots of meat being carved with a sharp knife, the voiceover continues: "But I always imagined how nice it would be if our fridge was filled with yellow orange juice or green apples." As counterpoint to 301's philosophy that "eating is everything," 302 elaborates later on her neurosis: "I just can't eat things. My body rejects everything. It's not that I'm dieting. I just can't eat. My body is filled with dirtiness. So how am I supposed to have a man in me or put food in my stomach? I just want to disappear."

Later scenes establish the fact that 302's hatred of her body and self-starvation comes in response to the trauma of being sexually abused at the hands of her stepfather, who runs the family butcher shop. Soon after moving into the apartment complex, 301 cooks sausage mignon and delivers it to her neighbor. "No, thank you. Especially not sausage," says 302, to which 301 bluntly replies, "You must not like sex. Were you raped? Not me. I crave it as much as cooking. I enjoyed having sex with my ex-husband even without love." As 301 begins eating the sausages herself, 302 becomes nauseas, eventually running to the toilet gagging as 301 looks directly at the camera and remarks, "Sex isn't disgusting; love is." Both the sausage incident and 302's explanation about her inability to eat suggest that 302 associates anything taken into the body as a sort of phallic violation.[81] Ironically, 302's "self-destructive tyranny" functions as a form of self-assertion and a site of independence.[82]

Upon discovering her neighbor's dislike of food, 301 becomes determined to make 302 eat. This leads to a twisted relationship between the two women and an exploration into the traumatic memories influencing each woman's relationship with food. While 301's motivation initially seems to derive from a belief that 302 needs encouragement and support to develop an appetite, 301 becomes increasingly vengeful upon discovering that 302 has been surreptitiously throwing away the gifts of food. Since this refusal to eat challenges

Almost every depiction of food has negative and repulsive associations in *301/302* (1995). Here, 301 brutally force-feeds 302,
which triggers a flashback of traumatic childhood memories.

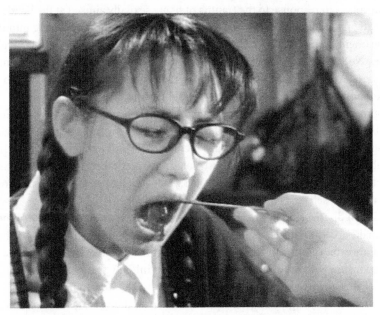

The act of being force-fed as an adult triggers 302's memories of being both
forced to eat and sexually abused at the hands of her lecherous stepfather.

301's compulsion to control others through food, 301 becomes enraged. She yanks the food from the trash, arranges it on plates, begins eating it herself, and also tries to force-feed 302. As 302 watches 301 eat, the camera zooms to a close-up of red sauce dripping from her lips, and "once again the color red—red meat, red sauce, blood on knives, red illumination—triggers 302's agonizing memories and negative food associations,"[83] leading to another red-infused flashback of her own childhood, the butcher shop, her predatory stepfather, and her mother who, too distracted counting money, turned a blind eye and failed to protect her daughter.[84]

Furious at her neighbor's refusal to eat, 301 force-feeds 302. As 302 gags on the food being pushed into her mouth, the camera cuts to other painful memories triggered by the food; we see a teenaged 302 being pressured to eat with her money-grubbing mother and depraved stepfather and later a flashback of her stepfather sexually molesting her. "There is no humor to make the subject matter palatable," observes film scholar Steve Zimmerman. "Instead, dish after dish, each one beautifully prepared and photographed, is shoved down your throat to the point of revulsion."[85] Not for the faint of heart (or for the weak of stomach), 301/302 is the sort of food film that ruins rather than stimulates appetites and reminds its audience that "one of the most basic of all human needs—nutritional sustenance—becomes *the* catalyst for self-destructive behavior" and that "our own more or less satisfactory association with food implicates our deepest psychological and emotional nature."[86]

Unlike the climactic scene from *Ratatouille*, in which the title dish triggers the flashback, in *301/302*, the particular food itself is not as significant (the phallic symbolism of sausage notwithstanding) as the fact that 301 and 302 use any food to either gain power or to resist it. As the research of Tulving (quoted earlier) suggests, memories created under duress or strong emotional states tend to survive longer. Hence, violating 302 through a sort of oral rape triggers one of the many disturbing flashbacks that illustrate why all edibles are discomfort food for the beleaguered 302.[87] Whereas 301 employs food to comfort herself and reduce feelings of loneliness, for 302 the term "comfort food" is itself an oxymoron. Instead of the experience of ingesting or even thinking about food activating the experience of comfort, as Troisi and Gabriel's study suggests, for 302 any food causes the discomfort that was initially encoded during her adolescence.

Altogether, this comparison exercise—of reflections on madeleines and comfort food, studies by researchers in the humanities and social sciences, and key scenes from a number of international food films—sheds light on the process by which food evokes a wide range of memories, both positive and negative. By using film (reel life) as ethnography of food memories in context, we can interpret the role of food in real life. Film benefits from its ability to visually depict bodily memory, the process of remembering, and "people's subjective perceptions of foods past."[88] The ability to juxtapose images—of food and then flashbacks of memories—renders film uniquely adept at representing organoleptic properties and the emotional weight of food, eating, social surrogacy, and food's profound ability to encapsulate and evoke powerful memories.

Filmography

"Abiquiu." Produced by Vince Gilligan, 2010. *Breaking Bad*, Season 3, Episode 3. Santa Monica, CA: High Bridge Productions, 2010.

Bebettes gæstebud [Babette's Feast]. Directed by Gabriel Axel, 1987. Los Angeles: MGM Studios, 2001. DVD.

Chocolat. Directed by Lasse Hallström, 2000. Santa Monica, CA: Miramax Home Entertainment, 2001. DVD.

Crimes and Misdemeanors. Directed by Woody Allen, 1989. Los Angeles: 20th Century Fox, 2001. DVD.

Eat Drink Man Woman. Directed by Ang Lee, 1994. Los Angeles: MGM World Films, 2002. DVD.

Last Supper. Directed by Mats Bigert and Lars Bergström, 2005. Stockholm, Sweden: Bigert & Bergström, 2005. DVD.

Passover: A Celebration. Directed by Sharon R. Sherman, 1983. Eugene, OR: Sharon R. Sherman.

Ratatouille. Directed by Brad Bird, 2007. Emeryville, CA: Disney-Pixar, 2007. DVD.

Smoke Signals. Directed by Chris Eyre, 1997. La Crosse, WI: Echo Bridge Home Entertainment, 2011. DVD.

Soul Food. Directed by George Tillman, Jr., 1997. Los Angeles: 20th Century Fox, 2001. DVD.

Soulfood Junkies. Directed by Byron Hurt, 2012. Plainfield, NJ: God Bless the Child Productions, 2012. DVD.

Tampopo. Directed by Juzo Itami, 1985. Tokyo, Japan: Itami Productions, 2005. DVD.

301/302. Directed by Chul-soo Park, 1995. South Korea: Park Chul-Soo Films, 2003. DVD.

When Do We Eat? Directed by Salvador Litvak, 2005. New York: Virgil Films, 2006. DVD.

Notes

1. David E. Sutton, *Remembrance of Repasts: An Anthropology of Food and Memory* (New York: Berg, 2001), 3.

2. Charlotte Babcock, "Food and Its Emotional Significance," *Journal of the American Dietetic Association* 24 (1948): 390–93.

3. "Comfort Food," Wikipedia, accessed October 1, 2013, http://en.wikipedia.org/wiki/Comfort_food.

4. Experimental psychologist Brian Wansink and his colleagues conducted a study of over 400 North American college students to determine the most common comfort foods and quantify these preferences according to gender and age. The researchers placed these foods into four categories—convenience foods, indulgence foods, nostalgic foods, and physical comfort foods. In the end, they found that the selection of particular foods may have the deliberate goal of mood alteration. While the identification of particular items as comfort food may prove idiosyncratic, Wansink writes elsewhere, patterns can be detected. In one study of American preferences, "males preferred warm, hearty, meal-related comfort foods (such as steak, casseroles, and soup), while females instead preferred comfort foods that were more snack related (such as chocolate and ice cream). In addition, younger people preferred more snack-related comfort foods compared to those over 55 years of age." The study also revealed connections between the actual consumption of comfort foods and guilty feelings. Brian Wansink and Cynthia Sangerman, "Engineering Comfort Foods" (2000): 66–67; and Brian Wansink, Matthew M. Cheney, and Nina Chan, "Exploring Comfort Food Preferences across Age and Gender," *Physiology and Behavior* 79 (2003): 739–47.

5. "Comfort Food."

6. From comedy to high drama, films historically employed food in three main ways—as a prop, as a transition device, and as symbol or metaphor. These uses of food dominated until the 1980s, when several directors discovered the visual, aesthetic, and box-office appeal of food, making movies in which food played a leading role or received notable attention. The success of *Tampopo* and *Babette's Feast* spawned a new genre. Because food films lack the heritage of more established genres (e.g., Westerns and musicals), some critics argue that they should be called a movement or style within other genres, but not a separate genre. To qualify as a food film, the film must contain the following to varying degrees: 1) Food must be an essential part of the plot; 2) Food must be seen on screen, in close-up, throughout the film; 3) The preparation and cooking of food must be featured; 4) The serving of food (the eating occasion, if not eating itself) must be shown; and 5) Food must be influential in the life of at least one character. Steve Zimmerman and Ken Weiss, *Food in the Movies* (Jefferson, NC: McFarland & Company, 2005).

7. Sutton, *Remembrance of Repasts*, 9.

8. Marcel Proust, *Du Côté de chez Swann*, in *Remembrance of Things Past*, trans. C. K. Scott Moncreiff (New York: Henry Holt and Company, 1922).

9. Proust, *Du Côté de chez Swann*, 58–62.

10. "It is the same for our past. We would exert ourselves to no result if we tried to evoke it, all the efforts of our intelligence are of no use. The past is hidden outside its realm and its range, in some material objects (in the sensation this object would give us) of which we do not suspect. . . . It is deep uncertainty every time the spirit feels to be defeated by itself; when the searching spirit is at the same time the obscure land that has to be searched, where its luggage will have no use. Searching? Not only: creating. The spirit faces something that does not exist yet and that only the spirit itself can make real and then make it enter its light." Proust, *Du Côté de chez Swann*, 59.

11. Fabio Parasecoli, "Hungry Engrams: Food and Non-Representational Memory," in *Food and Philosophy: Eat, Think and Be Merry*, eds. Fritz Allhoff and Dave Monroe (Malden, MA: Blackwell Publishing, 2007), 108.

12. This profound power of madeleines may help account for the popularity of food memoirs.

13. Warren Belasco, *Food: The Key Concepts* (New York: The Berg, 2008), 26.

14. Only one student recounted a negative madeleine: "*Peas.* I hate peas. The texture, the smell, the color—it all disgusts me. Growing up, my parents forced me to eat them, despite my distaste. They thought I hated peas because I'd never tried them before. Seeing that I was eight, it's a valid argument. But one day, after months of pretending to like them, I just gave in and refused to eat peas anymore. I guess it excludes me [from the group], but I know a lot of people who don't like peas, so I don't feel excluded" (Female from Chicago, Illinois, Spring 2012).

15. Sutton, *Remembrance of Repasts*, 15.

16. In 1904, a German scientist named Richard Semon developed a theory for how memory works, arguing that "memory can be preserved through generations by heredity" through something he called an "engram," "the long-lasting change in the nervous system that encodes information into memory and that lies dormant until something brings it back to consciousness." Parasecoli, "Hungry Engrams," 109.

17. Ibid., 105.

18. Ibid., 106.

19. Ibid.

20. Ibid., 112.

21. Ibid.

22. "Abiquiu," produced by Vince Gilligan (2010; *Breaking Bad*, season 3, episode 3; Santa Monica, CA: High Bridge Productions, 2010).

23. Quoted in Parasecoli, "Hungry Engrams," 110.

24. Parasecoli, "Hungry Engrams," 113.

25. Ibid.

26. Jordan D. Troisi and Shira Gabriel, "Chicken Soup Really Is Good for the Soul: 'Comfort Food' Fulfills the Need to Belong," *Psychological Science* 22 (2011): 747–53.

27. Ibid., 747.

28. J. L. Derrick, S. Gabriel, and K. Hugenberg, "Social Surrogacy: How Favored Television Programs Provide the Experience of Belonging," *Journal of Experimental Social Psychology* 45 (2009): 352–62.

29. Ibid., 748.

30. D. Russell, L. A. Peplau, and C. E. Cutrona, "The Revised UCLA Loneliness Scale: Concurrent and Discriminant Validity Evidence," *Journal of Personality and Social Psychology* 39 (1980): 472–80.

31. Troisi and Gabriel, "Chicken Soup Really Is Good for the Soul," 750.

32. Ibid., 748.

33. Ibid., 749.

34. Ibid.

35. Ibid., 748.

36. Deborah Lupton, *Food, the Body and the Self* (Thousand Oaks, CA: Sage Publications, 1996), 50.

37. Wansink and Sangerman, "Engineering Comfort Foods," 66–67.

38. Carolyn Korsmeyer, "Delightful, Delicious, Disgusting," in *Food and Philosophy: Eat, Think and Be Merry*, eds. Fritz Allhoff and Dave Monroe (Malden, MA: Blackwell Publishing, 2007), 147.

39. Ibid., 148.

40. Emiko Ohnuki-Tierney, "The Ambivalent Self of the Contemporary Japanese," *Cultural Anthropology* 5 (1990): 196–215.

41. Parasecoli, "Hungry Engrams," 109.

42. Jennifer L. Iannolo, "Food and Sensuality: A Perfect Pairing," in *Food and Philosophy: Eat, Think and Be Merry*, 242.

43. *Tampopo*, directed by Juzo Itami (1985; Tokyo, Japan: Itami Productions, 2005), DVD.

44. James R. Keller, *Food, Film and Culture: A Genre Study* (Jefferson, NC: McFarland & Company, 2006), 7.

45. See the following for more on *Tampopo*: Michael Ashkenazi, "Food, Play, Business, and the Image of Japan in Itami Juzo's *Tampopo*," in *Reel Food: Essays on Food and Film*, ed. Anne L. Bower (New York: Routledge, 2004), 27–40; Charles Shiro Inouye, "In the Show House of Modernity: Exhaustive Listing in Itami Juzo's *Tampopo*," in *Word and Image in Japanese Cinema*, eds. Dennis Washburn and Carole Cavanaugh (Cambridge, UK: Cambridge University Press, 2001), 126–46; Keller, *Food, Film and Culture*; and Ohnuki-Tierney, "The Ambivalent Self of the Contemporary Japanese," in Steve Zimmerman, *Food in the Movies*, 2nd edition (Jefferson, NC: McFarland & Company), 2009.

46. Sutton, *Remembrance of Repasts*, 26.

47. Belasco, *Food: The Key Concepts*, 30.

48. *Passover: A Celebration*, directed by Sharon R. Sherman (1983; Eugene, OR, Sharon R. Sherman); *Crimes and Misdemeanors*, directed by Woody Allen (1989; Los Angeles: 20th Century Fox, 2001), DVD; *When Do We Eat?* directed by Salvador Litvak (2005; New York: Virgil Films, 2006), DVD.

49. Sharon R. Sherman, "The Passover Seder: Ritual Dynamics, Foodways, and Family Folklore," in *Food in the USA: A Reader*, ed. Carole M. Counihan (New York: Routledge, 2002 [1988]), 200, emphasis added.

50. For example, when Sherman questions Stan about the bitter herbs, he responds: "Those things are intellectually symbolic, I think, rather than emotionally symbolic. The matzo's very emotional. The bitter herbs and the egg and the neck of the chicken . . . they're interesting symbols, but you don't *feel* them as much as you do the matzo" (2002 [1988]: 201).

51. Sherman, "The Passover Seder," 202.

52. Quoted in Sherman, "The Passover Seder," 202.

53. *Soul Food*, directed by George Tillman, Jr. (1997; Los Angeles: 20th Century Fox, 2001), DVD.

54. See Bower (2007) for a history of soul food and Williams-Forson (2006) for a critique of the film *Soul Food*, which she accuses of gender and "culinary malpractice

homogenizing ... the eating practices of African Americans." Psyche Williams-Forson, "Still Dying for Some Soul Food?" in *Building Houses Out of Chicken Legs: Black Women, Food and Power* (Chapel Hill: University of North Carolina Press, 2006), 186.

55. Robert L. Hall, "Food Crops, Medicinal Plants, and the Atlantic Slave Trade," in *African American Foodways: Explorations of History and Culture*, ed. Anne L. Bower (Urbana: University of Illinois Press, 2007), 35.

56. Ibid., 35–36.

57. Ibid., 17–18.

58. For more on the topic of soul food and the film *Soul Food*, see Tina Harris, "Deconstructing the Myth of the Dysfunctional Black Family," in *Food for Thought: Essays on Eating and Culture*, ed. Lawrence C. Rubin (Jefferson, NC: McFarland & Company, 2008); Marvalene H. Hughes, "Soul, Black Women, and Food," in *Food in the USA: A Reader*, ed. Carole M. Counihan (New York: Routledge, 2002); Keller, *Food, Film and Culture*; Tracey N. Poe, "The Origins of Soul Food in Black Urban Identity: Chicago, 1915–1947," in *Food in the USA: A Reader*, ed. Carole M. Counihan (New York: Routledge, 2002); Psyche Williams-Forson, "Still Dying for Some Soul Food?" in *Building Houses Out of Chicken Legs: Black Women, Food and Power* (Chapel Hill: University of North Carolina Press, 2006); and *Soulfood Junkies*, directed by Byron Hurt (2012; Plainfield, NJ: God Bless the Child Productions, 2012), DVD.

59. *Eat Drink Man Woman*, directed by Ang Lee (1994; Los Angeles: MGM World Films, 2002), DVD.

60. Zimmerman, *Food in the Movies*, 377.

61. Keller, *Food, Film and Culture*, 169.

62. Tarja Laine, "Family Matters in *Eat Drink Man Woman*: Food Envy, Family Longing, or Intercultural Knowledge through the Senses?" in *Shooting the Family: Transnational Media and Intercultural Values*, ed. Patricia Pisters and Wim Staat (Amsterdam: Amsterdam University Press, 2005); and Ming-Yeh T. Rawnsley, "Cultural Representation of Taste in Ang Lee's *Eat, Drink, Man, Woman*," in *Food for Thought: Essays on Eating and Culture*, ed. Lawrence C. Rubin (Jefferson, NC: McFarland & Company, 2008).

63. Julie L. Locher, William Yoels, Donna Maurer, and Jillian van Ells, "Comfort Foods: An Exploratory Journey into the Social and Emotional Significance of Food," *Food and Foodways: Explorations in the History and Culture of Human Nourishment* 13 (2005): 278.

64. Barbara Stern, "Historical and Personal Nostalgia in Advertising Text: The *fin de siècle* Effect," *Journal of Advertising* 11 (1992): 11. See also the documentary film *Last Supper*, in which death row inmates select a last meal to eat prior to the execution. *Last Supper*, directed by Mats Bigert and Lars Bergström (2005; Stockholm, Sweden: Bigert & Bergstrom, 2005), DVD. See also Michael Owen Jones, "Dining on Death Row: Last Meals and the Crutch of Ritual," forthcoming in *Journal of American Folklore* 127 (503): 3–26.

65. Rutherford, *Men's Silences*, 126.

66. Stern, "Historical and Personal Nostalgia in Advertising Text," 16. See also Lupton, *Food, the Body and the Self*, 49–50.

67. *Bebettes gæstebud [Babette's Feast]*, directed by Gabriel Axel (1987; Los Angeles: MGM Studios, 2001), DVD.

68. Sutton, *Remembrance of Repasts*, x.

69. See Ron Hansen, "Babette's Feast," in *Writers at the Movies: 26 Contemporary Authors Celebrate 26 Memorable Movies*, ed. Jim Shepard (New York: Perennial, 2000); Keller, *Food, Film and Culture*; Margaret McFadden, "Gendering the Feast: Women, Spirituality, and Grace in Three Food Films," in *Reel Food: Essays on Food and Film*, ed. Anne L. Bower (New York: Routledge, 2004); and Zimmerman, *Food in the Movies*.

70. *Chocolat*, directed by Lasse Hallström (2000; Santa Monica, CA: Miramax Home Entertainment, 2001), DVD.

71. *Ratatouille*, directed by Brad Bird (2007; Emeryville, CA: Disney-Pixar, 2007), DVD.

72. Zimmerman, *Food in the Movies*, 411.

73. Diane Carson, "Transgressing Boundaries: From Sexual Abuse to Eating Disorders in *301/302*," in *Seoul Searching: Culture and Identity in Contemporary Korean Cinema*, ed. Frances Gateward (Albany: State University of New York Press, 2007), 274–75.

74. Troisi and Gabriel, "Chicken Soup Really Is Good for the Soul."

75. *301/302*, directed by Chul-soo Park (1995; South Korea: Park Chul-Soo Films, 2003), DVD.

76. Carson, "Transgressing Boundaries," 275–77. Carson offers a metaphorical interpretation of the film as well, saying that it explores the boundaries of resistance to both personal and national subjugation, as Koreans had historically struggled for independence from both colonizers and occupiers.

77. Cynthia Baron, Diane Carson, and Mark Bernard, *Appetites and Anxieties: Food, Film, and the Politics of Representation* (Detroit: Wayne State University Press, 2014); Carson, "Transgressing Boundaries"; Joan Kee, "Claiming Sites of Independence: Articulating Hysteria in Pak Ch'ol-su's *301/302*," *Positions* 9 (2001): 449–66; and Zimmerman, *Food in the Movies*, 204.

78. This translation is on my copy of the DVD. For a slightly different translation of these lines, see Baron et al., *Appetites and Anxieties*; and Carson, "Transgressing Boundaries."

79. Troisi and Gabriel, "Chicken Soup Really Is Good for the Soul," 751.

80. Carson, "Transgressing Boundaries," 269.

81. Ibid., 272.

82. Ibid., 277.

83. Baron et al., *Appetites and Anxieties*, 121–22.

84. Carson interprets the mother's obsessive money counting as a metaphor for the idea that "capitalism trumps care." Carson, "Transgressing Boundaries," 274.

85. Zimmerman, *Food in the Movies*, 204.

86. Carson, "Transgressing Boundaries," 267.

87. For more on food being used to assert sexual power, and as a form of oral rape, see the discussion of *American History X* in LuAnne Roth, "Beyond *Communitas*: Cinematic Food Events and the Negotiation of Power, Belonging, and Exclusion," in *Folklore/Cinema: Popular Film as Vernacular Culture*, ed. Sharon R. Sherman and Mikel J. Koven (Logan: Utah State University Press, 2007 [2005]).

88. Sutton, *Remembrance of Repasts*, 7.

Haunted Tongues and Hollow Comforts: Examples of Culinary Conscience in Indonesian Fiction

Annie Tucker

Writing Indonesian Comfort Food

Comfort food as a popular culinary genre originated in the United States, and much of comfort food research to date has been conducted in North America, but can the concept be productively transferred to other food cultures throughout the world?

Over recent years, as food has assumed a new precedence in global popular discourse, Indonesia has enthusiastically refashioned itself as a destination for culinary tourism,[1] and is even lauding its first bad-boy "celebrity chef."[2] Depictions of regional and national Indonesian dishes are also emerging in Indonesian literature, and some of these seem intriguing analogues to comfort foods as they have come to be understood in the United States. Through the following analysis of culinary fiction by Puthut EA, a young writer from Yogyakarta, Central Java, I will address wider themes in burgeoning comfort food research relevant to scholarship on fictional depictions of comfort food in different cultural places. I discuss why the dishes in question can be considered to be Indonesian comfort food, and what implications the discourse around such comfort food might have on Indonesian aesthetic or expressive culinary practices, food culture, or other aspects of daily life.[3] In this I aim to contribute to the currently quite minimal Indonesian foodways research and the comparative global inquiry into comfort food, particularly with regard to the way it may be deployed to evoke uncomfortable ideas and encourage difficult conversations.

Puthut EA's short stories have frequently appeared in major national periodicals and he has published numerous anthologies.[4] Puthut's writing addresses family, romance, politics, and the general ethos of post-Suharto millennial Indonesian—and, in particular, Javanese—life. He is also well-known for being a "culinary" writer, and his stories have been praised for depicting "special dishes that we encounter all the time but are rarely discussed."[5] In his stories, these everyday foods are clearly rendered, described with careful attention—so redolent with meaning that they become vibrant characters in their own right, catalysts of reflection and action.

While the "comfort food" concept has yet to be widely applied in Indonesian food culture, some of the dishes Puthut chooses to focus on in his stories fall within this category. He writes about typical foods found in variation throughout the archipelago, dishes that are at once simple, hearty, casual, and easy to prepare; nostalgic and sentimental, associated with childhood and tradition; and imbued with a sense of home and humble origins. These parameters are associated with comfort food in the United States and prove to be comforting for his Indonesian characters as well, at least at first. Ultimately, however, within Puthut EA's fiction these cherished dishes strikingly unsettle the stomach as he evokes their familiar positive meanings and associations only to complicate them. An analysis of the symbolism and narrative impact of three different foods—a spicy dish known as *sambal*, Indonesian style fried rice or *nasi goreng*, and cooked papaya leaves—in three different short stories will both demonstrate the relevance of the comfort food concept within the works and investigate how the author imbues these foods with a kind of "culinary conscience," forcing characters to confront truths that are hard to swallow while asking readers what happens when daily staples of identity become spoiled by doubt, tainted with anxiety, or haunted by painful memories.

This analysis suggests a compelling line of inquiry in the study of comfort food. Why is it that many beloved comfort foods, so easy to prepare, so delicious to eat, and so reminiscent of home, end up eliciting a psychological discomfort in those who consume them? And why and how does this discomfort manifest itself outside particularly American concepts of health, morality, and food? The associations of comfort foods with unpleasant feelings and an uneasy conscience is particularly notable in the Indonesian examples to be discussed because, unlike familiar North American comfort foods (such as Spam, macaroni and cheese, and ice cream) that may elicit some discomfort in diners and health professionals due to dubious ingredients or health effects, the Indonesian comfort foods discussed in Puthut's short stories are not associated with negative feelings because of their *nutritional* content. They are not deep-fried, processed, filled with mystery ingredients, devoid of nutritional value, or high in salt, sugar, fat, or calories the way iconic Western comfort foods tend to be.[6] In fact, Indonesia has no shortage of such comfort foods with unsettling ingredients and back stories:[7] There are the *bakso* meatballs that, according to urban legend, are made with Borax or formaldehyde to prevent the meat from rotting,[8] instant noodles soaked in chemicals rumored to cause autism,[9] free-flowing sweet tea associated with diabetes,[10] and beloved deep-fried snacks that people know are fattening and contribute to high cholesterol.[11] These delicious comfort foods are somewhat ambivalent due to ingredients that might ultimately be quite unhealthful. In contrast, an Indonesian who enjoys the sambal, fried rice, and leafy greens depicted in Puthut EA's stories would be enjoying a comparatively nutritious and balanced meal. And yet, despite the ways these dishes deviate from the standard understandings of tasty but potentially un-nutritious comfort food, in these stories these healthful foods do ultimately become associated with uncomfortable meanings and memories that link acts of personal consumption to issues of significant social and cultural concern. This theme of ambivalent connotation is traced across the selected stories, chosen for the range of settings where the comfort food is consumed—from family table to town square to informal restaurant far from home—and for the range of issues they address, from overbearing parental authority to brutal political violence to ruthless exploitation.

Intimate Domination in "Family *Sambal*"

> I cannot deny how that irreplaceable food has become so much more, full of hints and cues and subtle signals for our entire family. It's like the weavings of a mental web that is mysterious and full of secrets.
> —"Family Sambal"[12]

Sambal is a ubiquitous Indonesian condiment, found in infinite variation throughout the archipelago according to regional food traditions and personal touch. Sambal can be raw or cooked, range from perfectly mild to infernally hot, and taste simple and clean or funky and complex. The base of most sambal consists of garlic, shallots, salt, oil and chili pepper, and often (but not always) tomato. Additional ingredients are versatile; the menu at the popular casual dining franchise Spesial Sambal in Yogyakarta, Central Java (where "spesial" is the Indonesian spelling of the English word "special"), offers a whopping twenty choices of sambal, with ingredients that range from tempeh, the fermented soybean cake, to eggplant to green mango to shrimp paste to eel to gizzard. To prepare sambal, raw or cooked ingredients are ground and mashed together with a mortar and flat-bottomed pestle known as a *cobek* until they achieve the consistency of a creamy paste or a wetter, chunkier chutney.[13] Sambal is most often used as a flavor enhancer, added on top of food or on the side of the plate; however, it is not uncommon for Indonesians to eat just a plate of white rice with sambal.[14] Sambal is among the most common "loan" words in the languages of the countries to which Indonesian people migrate, indicating its significance to Indonesians, who bring it with them wherever they go.[15]

In his story "Family *Sambal*," Puthut EA depicts sambal as comfort food, although he describes its comforting qualities rather than specifically using the phrase, at once reflecting the condiment's central (if often "supporting") role in Indonesian cuisine and associating it with family identity and the warm and stable atmosphere of home. Throughout the narrator's childhood, it is served every day, beloved and even given affectionate nicknames by each member of the family: "fierce *sambal*," because it is so spicy, "happy *sambal*" because it makes the family so happy to eat all together, "lazy *sambal*" because it makes the diners dawdle so they won't have to bring the meal to a close. When the narrator moves away to go to college, sambal remains intimately associated with his family and hence becomes imbued with nostalgia, synonymous with the experience of being at home. He says, "When I followed my older sister to college, we often tried to make the dish together, but . . . it was never exactly like it was when we ate it at home with our parents. . . . After we had moved away from home, whenever we gathered with our family, we ate the *sambal* hungrily as a kind of renewal, as if to reinforce something that we all thought was important."[16]

When it becomes time for the character and his older sister to choose a mate and settle down, however, the meanings of sambal are destabilized as the dish is used as a sign of exclusion rather than a vehicle of reassuring family connection. The narrator realizes that "if a guest spends the night at our house . . . the dish will be hidden, disappear from our dining room table. It's as if we are sending each other the message, 'Now there is someone else.'"[17] The sambal is brought out to the family table only if his parents are willing to consider the interloper as a potential member of the family's inner circle. Each sibling has brought romantic partners home in hopes of their parents' approval for a marriage, but the sambal has never appeared, to the point that the narrator renames it "test *sambal*" and his older sister begins calling it the "*sambal* of death." She finally finds a man to pass the test; they marry and have a child. The story concludes as the narrator sits down to a family meal with his current girlfriend. After great anticipation and amidst great anxiety, the sambal appears on the table, and his mother invites the guest to partake of the dish. However, after she helps herself, she says, "I often make this *sambal* for my grandmother . . . but I like it best with a little *kecap*,"[18] and pours extra soy sauce all over it—ruining the familiar taste, both literally and figuratively violating the sacrosanct mixture of the family sambal. While the author leaves readers hanging, we can guess that the unlucky girl will never be invited back, and the narrator will find himself without a mate.

The quick switch and moment of realization in "Family *Sambal*" is humorous but palpably uncomfortable, serving to change the main character's relationship to his family and the reader's evaluation of them: rather than being warm and caring, his parents suddenly seem domineering, controlling, and close-minded. Sambal, instead of being a vehicle of comfort, reassurance, and tangible expression of love for the narrator now becomes a domestic weapon of manipulation, coercion, and exclusion. In this family melodrama, the subversion of comfort food serves as a potentially playful and potentially more serious jibe at the Javanese platitude of *rukun*, which is commonly glossed as "harmony." Rukun is much touted as a core family value that resonates out into broader Javanese culture and even national politics.[19] However, rukun is not achieved without a cost; in her classic ethnography on the Javanese family, Hildred Geertz says that the appearance of rukun may be more important than its actual substance, and to achieve a veneer of collective peace and accord, individual family members must often swallow their desires and silently stew.[20]

Like other anthropologists of the region, Geertz explicitly relates the value of rukun to foodways practices, specifically the early practice of hand- or spoon-feeding children long past an age where they are capable of feeding themselves; on the one hand, this can seem like overindulgence, feeding children so they do not have to become independent, anticipating their needs so they never have to be hungry. But it is also a subtle form of discipline: the implied message being that the child eats what and when the parent chooses for them.[21] Puthut EA's short story echoes and illustrates these Javanese family dynamics through his story about sambal. On the one hand, this comfort food seems emblematic of family warmth and stability, but ultimately such warmth is underpinned by steely authority, and such stability is earned at the cost of personal choice and fulfillment. While on the surface the family ritual is preserved and the comfort food status of the sambal is publicly maintained within the domestic domain, privately for the narrator and his sister, it has taken on a more complicated meaning, at times filling them with dread or resentment.

This re-signification of food and the ensuing revelation of the largely unspoken cultural truths it references may seem tongue-in-cheek in "Family *Sambal*," but quickly become sinister in the next story, "Koh Su."

Political Violence and Partial Amnesia: The Missing Ingredient in "Koh Su"

I don't know exactly whether it is because of Koh Su or not, but nasi goreng is clearly the signature dish of this city. . . . The first cooking lesson to be taught, the first thing any child learns how to do, is ngosu, also known as making fried rice.
—"Koh Su"[22]

Fried rice, or nasi goreng, is another dish that could be considered a comfort food. It is enjoyed by Indonesians across the archipelago and, like sambal, it is one of the few Indonesian foods to achieve broad international recognition.[23] While fried rice is popular throughout Asia, Indonesians identify strongly with their sweeter and spicier version, and it has been called one of Indonesia's few national dishes.[24] Nasi goreng is a humble, flexible, and forgiving dish. It is made from a base of cold, plain rice, which is often left from previous meals, with supplemental ingredients that usually depend on whatever scraps of meat or bits of vegetables are available in the kitchen; the rice is mixed with beef, egg, shrimp, scallions, or simply fried on its own with the addition of chili powder, white pepper, coriander, tamarind, or other spice blends, and *kecap*, which is a thick soy-based sauce. Depending on the region, nasi goreng can be served with sides of *sate* or skewered meat, *acar*, a bowl of pickles, and *krupuk*, crispy prawn crackers. Nasi goreng is almost always available at larger restaurants, but is most often consumed by locals at breakfast or as a late-night snack sold at casual food stalls or via the *kaki lima*, the roving sellers who traverse neighborhoods pushing mobile cook-stations, stopping to fry up a portion for diners while they wait eagerly outside their houses or sit on an unfurled mat on the sidewalk. Nasi goreng, like sambal, can be considered a comfort food: as indicated by Puthut EA in his story, it is simple, hearty, easy to prepare, and associated with casual or home cooking as well as with childhood—unlike sambal, it is even high in carbohydrates, as are so many familiar North American comfort foods.[25]

Puthut's short story "Koh Su" captures the role of fried rice in Indonesian daily rhythms and culinary life—people lining up in the evenings to enjoy the meal at a food stall, going home to a friend's house to cook up a quick batch after school, and constantly comparing recipes and techniques. In his story, however, nasi goreng has a particular draw due to the local preoccupation with a mythologized sidewalk cook who disappeared without sharing his secret recipe. The cook, Koh Su, is surrounded by rumors. People are not sure of his origins, although many think he might have been Chinese; they are not sure what went into his secret brown sauce; and they are not sure how or why he disappeared. Some conjecture that he "meditated until he vanished, risen directly up to heaven," befitting his almost mystical status, although others suggest that he was killed during "the bloody events" and "buried along with dozens of communists in an old well behind the public school."[26] Amidst all the mystery, what people are sure of is that Koh Su's fried rice recipe was the most divinely delicious anyone has ever tasted or will likely ever taste again. As one villager describes it, the distance between Koh Su's dish and heaven was only as wide as a cigarette. Koh Su and fried rice are so tied together in people's minds that the two become synonymous. The narrator explains: "The name Koh Su turned into a verb for the activity of making fried rice. If someone said, 'This morning I ngohsu,' that meant that earlier that morning he had made nasi goreng. Or if someone said, 'Come on, let's ngohsu . . .' that meant she was inviting you to make some fried rice."[27]

The rumors of Koh Su's disappearance are wrapped up in one of the largest—and least discussed—mass killings in world history. Beginning in late September 1965, and continuing into the early months of 1966, Indonesia was wracked by vicious attacks against communists, who were believed to have murdered six high-ranking military officials as part of a purported coup.[28] Indonesians of Chinese descent were targeted in these killings, in part because China was a leading communist country and in part due to long-standing prejudice against ethnic Chinese across Indonesia, which has been expressed in numerous incidents of violence both before and since 1965.[29] Suharto took power of the nation during this episode, enforcing a monolithic silence about these events for the entire course of his forty-year rule—any remaining purported communists and their supporters and families were scapegoated, blacklisted, monitored, and "disappeared," blamed for the very violence in which they were victims.[30] After a half-century of almost total silence, Indonesian scholars, artists, documentarians, and writers are beginning to slowly reckon with not only a horrific episode in the nation's past, but the chilling silence that followed; they are beginning to openly grapple with their previous failure to address this violence in any way, which to some suggests widespread national complicity in these murders.[31]

This buried past is reanimated within the narrative of "Koh Su" when, after a string of chefs try their hand at selling nasi goreng and fail, a new fried-rice cook comes to town. He looks like the vanished man, he cooks like the vanished man, and he uses a secret sauce like the vanished man. The narrator samples the food, and the fried rice is indeed perfect, just like Koh Su's fabled meal. However, when he goes to his local coffee stall to talk it over with his friends, they all believe something is still missing in the taste of the rice. As the story ends, it is revealed that not only did Koh Su probably disappear in the violence, but the entire village where he used to get his rice was also wiped out. The fried rice will never taste the same again not just because Koh Su is gone, as is his secret recipe, but because the source and network of foodways wisdom, from field to table, has been destroyed.

Comfort food can often be a favorite food linked to a particular person, place, or time in such a way that evokes pleasant or positive social connotations;[32] however, in this short story, despite being linked to both an individual association with the narrator's childhood and home, the most pleasant aspects of that connotation are perpetually deferred. One the one hand, the dish represents a nostalgic yearning for the past, a reminder of a more perfect life before the mass violence. On the other hand, the comfort of this original dish makes its new simulacrum discomforting. It turns out that the most integral food of the town—the dish from which the city gets its identity—revolves around a hollow core, a missing man, and a massacred community. In Puthut EA's short story, fried rice is like a macabre madeleine, and rather than pleasurable memories that come rushing back to the narrator, along with an exquisite taste that captures or even exceeds tastes from childhood, Indonesia's hidden history of state violence, local complicity in mass murder, and collective amnesia about these atrocities are evoked—a history that, much like the character of Koh Su in the story, has only been addressed through rumor, conjecture, suspicion, and oblique references that have grown into a kind of urban legend. Puthut EA serves up a deeply unsettling juxtaposition of transcendence—a traditional food product whose taste brings the diner close to heaven—and disillusioning terror.

This story ends in a moment of publicly acknowledged horror and conflicted discomfort; the last story, however, suggests that the taste of comfort food and the act of eating it can be a revelation and can also instigate meaningful moral action that might reconnect Indonesians with their roots, their core values, and their better selves.

The Delicious Bitterness of "Papaya Flowers"

> When the vegetable was in my mouth, I wanted to swallow it immediately, but as soon as
> I had swallowed it, I wanted to taste its strange flavor again. After breakfast, I was lost in
> thought. I opened my laptop . . . I knew that it was bizarre, but I was going to do it: I typed
> my resignation letter with the taste of papaya flowers and leaves on my tongue. . . .
> —"Papaya Flowers"[33]

Many standard Indonesian meals have two main components: white rice and *lauk*, or side dishes. One common genre of lauk is stewed or sautéed leaves. These leaves can come from a variety of trees or other plants, although some of the most commonly found leaves are cassava, mustard, and papaya. With Indonesia's fertile soil, in rural and less developed residential neighborhoods, these plants might even be grown in one's own garden or foraged from the side of the road. At first consideration, it may seem that stewed leaves are a theoretical opposite to comfort food, being leafy greens low in fat and high in nutritional value, and (unlike the usual preparation of collard greens in the United States) more likely to be cooked in water, thin broth, or coconut milk, or sautéed in vegetable oil, than in animal fat. But such a dish shares other qualities with comfort food—the most salient to this discussion being its humble or common origins, associated with plain or village folk from the peasant class. In essence it is not just associated with home, but with Indonesia's historic, indigenous, and literal "roots."

Comfort food has been conceptualized as "grandma's cooking" by scholars as well as the American general public, and many Indonesians have mothers and grandmothers who still cook them papaya leaves.[34] Indeed, in a country that has experienced such rapid development and Westernization in the past four decades, this plain family cooking symbolizes more than just the comfort of home: it symbolizes authentic, indigenous Indonesian values of humble origins, modest desires, asceticism, and sustainable living. Humble comfort food has also been valued in the West for its function as a repository of history, for being food that represents defiant survival during harsh times, and for the achievement of creating something tasty out of slim resources.[35] In this case, papaya leaves and other readily accessible leafy greens indicate the pride of Indonesia's incredibly fertile land, where according to a popular song lyric, the oceans are made of milk, the fish swim right up to you, and even the stones sprout into edible plants.[36] At the same time, they reference the reliance of the Indonesian people, who have been able to get by on little during times of politically induced hardship, including World War II and the war for independence.

In "Papaya Flowers," this stew is eaten by a businesswoman from Jakarta who is on a trip to a remote island of the archipelago, to audit a subsidiary of the large fishing conglomerate whose headquarters are based back in the capital. She is unsatisfied with and disconnected from her work; it is exhausting, and something about it seems to be troubling her conscience, although she does not tell the reader exactly what. In her downtime, she eats at a small local canteen and she strikes up a conversation with a man who is also alone, in town on a fishing trip. He explains how he befriended some local fishermen as they escorted him on their boats and even saved his life in a fearsome episode where he capsized and went overboard.

There is a charge between the two characters—at first, it seems the frisson might be erotic, as after their parting, the narrator remarks, "I could still feel the warmth of his grasp in the palm of my hand." However, it turns out the man ultimately arouses a different feeling in her. When they meet again, he invites her to share a meal of papaya flowers and leaves. In a pointed exchange over the food he states: "I like this vegetable. Its preparation and seasonings are simple—papaya flowers and young papaya leaves are sautéed with slices of garlic, tomato, salt, and a little bit of oil. But it has a powerful taste." The businesswoman counters, "I don't like papaya flowers and leaves. They are too bitter." But her new acquaintance insists: "That's exactly where its thrill is."[37]

The man quickly segues into a discussion with the woman about the fishing conglomerate she works for, explaining how the corporation is making life very difficult for the local fishermen by holding a monopoly over much-needed ice, cheating them at the scales and underpaying them for their catch, all for the sake of their own profit. She grows angry and defensive, excuses herself, and returns to Jakarta without ever seeing the man again. Ultimately, however, the taste of papaya leaves haunts her and she finds herself taking action, preparing the food for herself and sending in the resignation letter that concludes the story.

In this story, food is imbued with class significance and wrapped up in a history of rapid economic development and social change Indonesia has coped with since the 1980s, when the country experienced infrastructural growth and development and opened up to global trade. A sector of the Indonesian population experienced astronomic financial success working with extraction industries and other large corporations. The people of this sector have often been critically depicted in Indonesian film and literature as "neo-colonialists," going in to rural areas and strong-arming people into signing over their land to industries that pollute the land and disrupt the local economy.[38] From this perspective, prosperous, "modernized," and Westernized

Indonesians are also those who may have lost sight of their moral compass, those who are abusing their nation while claiming to help "develop" it.

This tension and ambivalence is signaled by the character of the city-dwelling, white-collar Jakarta businesswoman in "Papaya Flowers" and her initial negative, perhaps even disdainful, reaction to eating simple village comfort food. The fact that she does not enjoy or appreciate stewed papaya leaves and flowers immediately signals something about her orientation towards village cuisine, and given her role in local exploitation, signals her disconnection from average village people. Indeed, someone of her position is most likely to eat "Western" food or other global cuisine such as sushi; a similar character in a short story by Puthut EA's contemporary, the author Linda Christanty, mentions eating "spaghetti and salmon steak."[39] In this environment and orientation towards status eating, certain Indonesian foods are relegated to a beloved but denigrated category of *ndeso* or "village" food,[40] a derogatory term used in Indonesian middle-class urban circles to distinguish themselves from the rural population.[41]

Simple peasant food, then, evokes a familiar split and an ambivalence in Indonesian identity; indicating poverty and backwardness in a fast-growing and forward-looking country on its way to ever-greater affluence and economic relevance in Southeast Asia and the world on the one hand, and a cherished past of agrarian values on the other, where there is nothing fancy to be found, but nothing unhealthful either, in honest, locally sourced nourishment. All this is referenced in a "simple but powerful" leaf, which, with such conflicting connotations, can at once taste "delicious" and yet "bitter." Going further, within the narrative of the story, "delicious bitterness" can be taken as a gustatory analogue for the joy to be found in simple life, where one gives up creature comforts and ambitions of economic advancement or cosmopolitan competition in exchange for taking only what you need, living in peace and harmony with the environment; in other words, the joys of living more like a local fisherman than a corporate executive. The taste of the dish symbolizes the pleasure to be found in leaving an affluent but exploitative lifestyle—complete with the watered-down taste of globalized food—behind.

"Papaya Flowers" provides an interesting counterpoint to the two previous examples. While, in all three short stories, the comfort food consumed carries moral weight, instead of only leading to a chilling revelation about Indonesia's horrific shameful past or skewering its hypocritical family values, in this story the taste of common comfort food has the ability to *do* something, catalyzing an introspection that leads to a change of heart: the rejection of exploitation and an implied realignment with village values understood to be at the very core of Indonesia's true identity. And this taste seems to have an accelerating effect, as the more comfort food is eaten, the more it is desired, and the more powerful becomes its pull toward the life it represents. If, over the course of the first two stories, comfort food is stripped of its restorative and nostalgic power by its current iteration, in the last story, it is finally able to comfort, encourage, and reorient a character who has lost her way.

Comfort Food and Culinary Conscience

It is widely discussed that depictions of food in fiction often signal ethnic and class identity, express family dynamics, trace and commemorate cultural history, and comment on intergenerational stability and change.[42] This has also been true for writers and filmmakers depicting the contemporary Asian and Asian diasporic experience.[43] Puthut EA's work both adheres to and diverges from this familiar culinary symbolic; more specifically, he establishes the familiar meanings and associations of comfort foods—such as family, regional, and ethnic identity, belonging and bonding—only to subvert them to address incidences of coercion, brutality, and erasure that call Indonesian familial, cultural, and political values and practices into question.

Rather than using comfort foods as a soothing shorthand, Puthut disorients his characters and readers through processes of eating and cooking, insisting on a more complicated elaboration between public history and personal meaning, between consumption and memory. If, in daily practice, comfort food is typically used to *manage* difficult and troubling emotions by recalling past experiences of intimacy and communion,[44] its use in this literature is to precisely the opposite effect; it *triggers* difficult and troubling emotions in both characters and readers by recalling or animating experiences of discord, betrayal, resentment, guilt, and loss. In the pacing of the narrative, as the comfort food is re-conceptualized, the action suddenly grinds to a halt; a reader can almost see spoons suspended midair and has an experience akin to losing one's appetite and pushing away a plate. Puthut's performative writing does not merely describe but also enacts the ambivalent reconsideration of comfort food, and by extension, its most cherished associations.

Puthut EA achieves this effect through his narrative structure and by deploying ambivalent or polyvalent sensory associations. Food is a "potent" site for the construction of embodied memory and associated meaning particularly because of its sensual power,[45] but in fiction and nonfictional writing about food, the culturally constructed meanings of these sensory impressions differ "in the perspectives of the authors who construct and construe the object of food in often very different ways."[46] Therefore the taste of sambal, a perfect blend of "a few green chili peppers, with a small piece of garlic and enough salt, sprinkled with a few drops of still-warm oil leftover in the frying pan," is "enticing as an accompaniment to any other dish"[47] and yet can reprimand the tongue and punish the stomach, "burning"[48] when consumed in excess; just like a mother and father's love can comfort and ground a grown child throughout the vagaries of life but can also chafe when too overbearing. Nasi goreng can evoke rapture with its diligent preparation and exquisite presentation where the rice "is truly a beauty to behold. Every single grain is the same exact color, evenly mixed with spices and evenly cooked" and "its aroma is also perfect."[49] Yet this uniformity in appearance and taste uncannily resonates with concerns about origin and a country's history in which practically an entire group of people was eliminated in the name of a more homogenous national development. Is such uniformity the sign of shared meanings and identities or does it represent the erasure of differences? Is the process of "crushing shrimp heads"[50] to create a base flavor for the fried rice simply a process required to create enticing flavor or is it an encoded memory of violent murder?

It is integral to the craft and dynamic impact of these stories that the foods depicted are the (perhaps rare) specimens of healthful comfort food, associated with old-fashioned home cooking rather than the comparatively newer, processed, convenience comfort foods mentioned at the opening of this chapter that to a certain extent represent what could be called a recent "epochal transformation"[51] of Indonesian culture. Such long-standing comfort foods, because they are a continuation of centuries-old enduring foodways practices, hark back to an idealized Indonesian past and identity, one that is imagined as preexisting many of the complicated issues addressed in these short stories. If the comfort foods depicted were not so integral to Indonesian identity—if they were not so evocative of this idealized past—then the re-association would not be so unsettling. It is the purity of their idealized associations that allows them to move from the role of providing culinary comfort to culinary conscience.

In this dynamic deployment of conscience, the tastes, textures, and contexts of eating and serving comfort food act to remind both eater and readers of aspects of their history and identity they may have unconsciously forgotten or prefer not to think about and to encourage reflection or maybe even action. This fits, in a perhaps unexpected way, with one social use of comfort foods in everyday life. It has been proposed that comfort food enables memory on a cultural level; the enduring and repetitive preparation of certain meals or dishes aids in maintaining a historical consciousness for the people who prepare and consume them.[52] However, this historical consciousness is usually a consciousness of the positive and shared aspects of a group: the aforementioned survival, knowledge, aesthetics, and intergenerational continuity, which may become especially important when a group has been marginalized or subjugated. In Puthut EA's literary vision, however, comfort food appears especially to point out to Indonesian characters and readers what has been *left out* of their historic consciousness—what they have chosen *not* to acknowledge in their narrative of themselves, suggesting that we eat to (perhaps unconsciously) forget as much as we eat to consciously remember.[53] By imbuing certain comfort foods with a "culinary conscience," this consciousness must be reconstituted; negative or elided elements must be brought to light in order for the meaning of true comfort to be reassessed. After eating the foods and understanding their full context, neither the characters nor readers can find placation or satiation; they are instead left to reckon with the complexities of Indonesian family politics, political history, and national practice.

This aspect of culinary conscience implicates the reader and not just the character in the story. Puthut EA is known for ending his stories in a moment of suspense, so that the readers themselves must decide what will happen next and how the story will end.[54] He seems to be challenging the reader. Can cherished and familiar dishes still provide solace or sustenance, or do they now only leave a bitter taste in the mouth? Can comfort food be truly comforting when eaten with a haunted tongue? Once you have tasted the truth, must you change your behavior? While he leaves it up to readers to make their own decisions, the impact of his stories is more than an unsettling disillusionment; the questions he raises with his fiction are an implicit call for the realignment of Indonesian cultural and national identity, and mindful acts of sustainability and consumption, true nurture and sustenance, and commemoration.

This has just been one example of how the comfort food concept might be productively applied to better understand the meanings of food and its representation in a cultural place outside of North America. Puthut EA's short stories suggest that while the concept may never be explicitly mentioned, certain local foods may fit well into the genre, and by playing with its associations, authors can deploy these foods and their associations to powerful narrative effect. It may be that in a global perspective, certain aspects of comfort food may remain salient while others become less so; associations with simple home cooking, for example, may ultimately be more important cross-culturally than carbohydrate or fat content or taste profile. For those seeking to investigate these global similarities or differences, fiction will certainly prove ripe for analysis, since in literature such associations and meanings are so purposefully and performatively explored and manipulated.

Notes

1. Nurfika Osman, "Iconic Dishes Set the Scene for RI Culinary Tourism," *Jakarta Globe,* accessed September 1, 2015, http://www.thejakartapost.com/news/2012/12/15/iconic-dishes-set-scene-ri-culinary-tourism.html.

2. Logan Connor, "Interview: Rahung Nasution," *Southeast Asia Globe,* accessed September 1, 2015, http://sea-globe.com/rahung-nasution-indonesia-southeast-asia-globe/.

3. Indeed, one might question the use of the term "Indonesian," as opposed to regional terminology such as "Javanese," "Balinese," etc., regarding the foods Indonesians eat; however, this nuance is not the focus of my discussion here, and as I argue, the comfort foods discussed are found throughout much of the archipelago. For further discussion, see Michiko Kubo, "The Development of an Indonesian National Cuisine: A Study of a New Movement of Instant Foods and Local Cuisine," in *Globalization, Food, and Social Identities in the Asia Pacific Region,* ed. James Farrer (Tokyo: Sophia University Instituted of Comparative Cultures, 2010).

4. A representative sample of these are Puthut EA, *Dua Tangisan Pada Satu Malam* (Jakarta: Penerbit Buku Kompas, 2003); *Sebuah Kitab Yang Tak Suci* (Yogyakarta: Sumbu, 2001); and *Seekor Bebek Mati Di Pinggir Kali* (Yogyakarta: Insist Press, 2009). The short stories discussed here are anthologized in his two newest compilations, *Sebuah Usaha Menulis Surat Cinta* (Yogyakarta: EA Books, 2014) and *Drama Itu Berkisah Terlalu Jauh* (Yogyakarta: EA Books, 2014).

5. Arman Dhani Bustomi, "Padamulanya Adalah Luka," in *Seubah Usaha Menulis Surat Cinta,* by Puthut EA (Yogyakarta: EA Books, 2014), x. Throughout this chapter, all translations from quotes taken from the Indonesian are mine.

6. Michael Owen Jones, "'Stressed' Spelled Backwards."

7. Sojin Kim and Mark Livengood, "Ramen Noodles & Spam: Popular Foods, Significant Tastes," *Digest: An Interdisciplinary Study of Food and Foodways* 15 (1995): 2–11. Also Sara E. Newton "The Jell-O Syndrome: Investigating Popular Culture/Foodways," *Western Folklore* 51 (1992): 249–67.

8. For a comparative example of this rumor in literary narrative, see Kurniawan, *Cantik.*

9. Annie Tucker, *Interpreting and Treating Autism in Javanese Indonesia,* PhD dissertation, University of California, Los Angeles, 2013.

10. Steve Ferzacca, *Healing the Modern in a Central Javanese City* (Durham, NC: Carolina Academic, 2001).

11. Ibid.

12. Puthut EA, "Sambal Keluarga," in *Sebuah Usaha,* 138.

13. A full menu of Spesial Sambal offerings can be found at http://hargamenu.com/daftar-menu-waroeng-spesial-sambal-ss/, accessed February 16, 2015.

14. Tineke Hellwig and Eric Tagliacozzo, *The Indonesia Reader: History, Culture, Politics* (Durham: Duke University Press, 2009), 1–12.

15. Ron Witton, "Indonesian and Malay Loan Words in Australian English," *Review of Indonesian and Malaysian Affairs* 41 (2007): 149–77. Also C. D. Grijns, "Indonesian

Terminology and Globalism," *Archipel* 58 (1999): 47–71. While perhaps as yet largely unfamiliar in the United States, with a small Indonesian population compared to the Netherlands and Australia, a Balinese-style sambal, Sambal Matah, has recently been made available in the nationally popular Trader Joe's chain.

16. Puthut EA, "Sambal Keluarga," in *Sebuah Usaha*, 159.

17. Ibid., 158.

18. Ibid., 165.

19. Hildred Geertz, *The Javanese Family: A Study of Kinship and Socialization* (New York: Free Press of Glencoe, 1961).

20. Ibid.

21. Ibid.; Margaret Mead and Gregory Bateson, *Growth and Culture* (New York: Putnam, 1951).

22. Puthut EA, "Koh Su," in *Drama Itu*, 44.

23. Anneke Otterloo, "Chinese and Indonesian Restaurants and the Taste for Exotic Food in the Netherlands: A Global-Local Trend," in *Asian Food: The Global and the Local*, eds. Katarzyna Cwiertka and Boudewijn Walraven (New York: Routledge, 2002), 153–66. See also Kubo, "Indonesian National Cuisine."

24. Barbara Crosette, "Fare of the Country: Spicy Staple of Indonesia," *New York Times*, July 6, 1986, accessed July 31, 2015, http://www.nytimes.com/1986/07/06/travel/fare-of-the-country-spicy-staple-of-indonesia.html?sec=travel.

25. Locher et al., "Comfort Foods" (2005).

26. Puthut EA, "Koh Su," in *Drama Itu*, 46.

27. Ibid., 44.

28. Benedict Anderson, "How Did the Generals Die," *Indonesia* 43 (1987): 109–34. Also Robert Cribb, ed. *The Indonesian Killings of 1965–1966: Studies from Java and Bali* (Clayton, Australia: Centre of Southeast Asian Studies, Monash University, 1990); and John Roosa, *Pretext for Mass Murder* (2006).

29. Purdey, *Anti-Chinese Violence* (2006).

30. Robert Lemelson, *40 Years of Silence* (Boston: Documentary Educational Resources, 2009). Also Robert Lemelson, Ninik Supartini and Emily Ng, "*Anak PKI*: A Longitudinal Case Study of the Effects of Ostracism, Political Violence, and Bullying on an Adolescent Javanese Boy," in *Formative Experiences: The Interaction of Caregiving, Culture, and Developmental Psychobiology*, eds. Carol M. Worthman et al. (Cambridge: Cambridge University Press, 2010), 378–89.

31. Mary Zurbuchen, *Beginning to Remember: The Past in the Indonesian Present* (Seattle: University of Washington Press, 2005).

32. Roth, this volume; Locher et al., "Comfort Foods" (2005).

33. Puthut EA, "Bunga Papaya," 65–66.

34. For example, you can find a recipe for papaya leaves on the Indonesian recipe blog "Mother's Cooking" with the tag line, "it will make you want to go straight home." http://resepibumemasak.blogspot.com/2013/04/resep-tumis-bunga-dan-daun-pepaya-bunda.html, accessed February 16, 2015.

35. Sheila Bock, "I Know You Got Soul: Traditionalizing a Contested Cuisine," in *Comfort Food: Meanings and Memories*, eds. Michael Owen Jones and Lucy Long (Jackson: University Press of Mississippi, forthcoming).

36. From the song "Kolam Susu," or "Oceans of Milk," written and made popular in the 1970s by the Band Koes Plus. Complete lyrics in Indonesian available via http://lirik.kapan-lagi.com/artis/koes_plus/kolam_susu. Retrieved February 16, 2015.

37. Puthut EA, "Bunga Papaya," 62. Ibid., p 62.

38. For representative examples of this portrayal, see Utami, *Saman* (2005), Kurniawan, *Cantik Itu Luka* (2004), and Madasari, *Entrok* (2010).

39. Linda Christanty, "Kesedihan," *Koran Tempo*, February 21, 2010, accessed February 16, 2015, https://lakonhidup.wordpress.com/2010/02/21/kesedihan/.

40. An illustrative example culled from popular culture can be found in a short video made by Last Day Production, a group specializing in humorous shorts parodying upper-class Jakarta lifestyles. In a short entitled *Rich Kids*, an affluent young man is entertaining a guest when his servant brings him out a plate of fried catfish and rice. Embarrassed, he quickly orders her to take the food away, reassuring his guest that he has no idea why she prepared him such a meal, since he never eats like that. As soon as the guest has gone, however, he calls the servant back in, ready for his food. She reports that she has thrown the food away as he instructed, and he appears crestfallen. The final shot is of the youth eating the same meal in a casual roadside stall, relishing every bite. Short available on YouTube, accessed February 16, 2015, https://www.youtube.com/watch?v=YVZzlMSEiS8.

41. Martin Slama, "The Agency of the Heart: Internet Chatting as Youth Culture in Indonesia," *Social Anthropology* 18 (2010): 316–30.

42. Emily Gowers, *The Loaded Table: Representations of Food in Roman Literature* (Oxford: Clarendon Press, 1993). Also Robert Warnes, *Hunger Overcome? Food and Resistance in Twentieth-Century African American Literature* (Athens: University of Georgia Press, 2004).

43. For representative examples in contemporary literature and film, see Amy Tan, *The Joy Luck Club* (New York: Penguin, 2006). Also Kirsten Chen, *Soy Sauce for Beginners* (New York: Houghton Mifflin, 2013). For scholarly considerations of similar representations, see Wenying Xu, *Eating Identities Reading Food in Asian American Literature* (Honolulu: University of Hawai'i Press, 2008). Also Jennifer Ann Ho, *Consumption and Identity in Asian American Coming-of-Age Novels* (New York: Routledge, 2005).

44. Locher et al., "Comfort Foods." See also Michael Owen Jones, "'Stressed' Spelled Backwards is 'Desserts,'" in *Comfort Food: Meanings and Memories*, eds. Michael Owen Jones and Lucy Long (Jackson: University Press of Mississippi, forthcoming).

45. David E. Sutton, *Remembrance of Repasts: An Anthropology of Food and Memory* (London: Berg, 2001); and Jon Holtzman, "Food and Memory," *Annual Review of Anthropology* 35 (2006), 362.

46. Holtzman, "Food and Memory."

47. Puthut EA, "Sambal Keluarga," 155.

48. Ibid., 160.

49. Puthut EA, "Koh Su," 53.

50. Ibid., 50.
51. Holtzman, "Food and Memory."
52. Sutton, *Remembrance of Repasts.*
53. Holtzman, "Food and Memory."
54. Bustomi, *Sebuah Usaha,* 2014, vii.

BIBLIOGRAPHY

Appadurai, Arjun. "Introduction: Commodities and the Politics of Value." In *The Social Life of Things: Commodities in Cultural Perspective*, ed. Arjun Appadurai, 3–63. Cambridge: Cambridge University Press, 1986.

Arce, Marilyn, Vasiliki Michopoulos, Kathryn N. Shepard, Quynh-Chau Ha, and Mark E. Wilson. "Diet Choice, Cortisol Reactivity, and Emotional Feeding in Socially Housed Rhesus Monkeys." *Physiology & Behavior* 101 (2010): 446–55.

Babcock, Charlotte. "Food and Its Emotional Significance." *Journal of the American Dietetic Association* 24 (1948): 390–93.

Balthrope, Robin. "Food as Representative of Ethnicity and Culture in George Tillman Jr.'s *Soul Food*, Maria Ripoll's *Tortilla Soup*, and Tim Reid's *Once Upon a Time When We Were Colored*." In *Reel Food: Essays on Food and Film*, ed. Anne L. Bower, 101–113. New York: Routledge, 2004.

Baraka, Amiri [LeRoi Jones]. "Soul Food." In *Home: Social Essays*, ed. Amiri Baraka [LeRoi Jones], 101–104. New York: Morrow, 1966.

Baron, Cynthia, Diane Carson, and Mark Bernard. "Foodways Structured to Convey Disorder and Dysfunction." In *Appetites and Anxieties: Food, Film, and the Politics of Representation*, 107–27. Detroit: Wayne State University Press, 2014.

Barthel, D. "Modernism and Marketing: The Chocolate Box Revisited." *Theory of Culture and Society* 6 (1989): 429–38.

Bauman, Richard. "Contextualization, Tradition, and the Dialogue of Genres: Icelandic Legends of the *Kraftaskáld*." In *Rethinking Context*, eds. Alessandro Duranti and Charles Goodwin, 125–45. Cambridge: Cambridge University Press, 1992.

Belasco, Warren. *Food: The Key Concepts*. New York: The Berg, 2008.

Benford, Rebecca, and Brendan Gough. "Defining and Defending 'Unhealthy' Practices: A Discourse Analysis of Chocolate 'Addicts'" Accounts." *Journal of Health Psychology* 11 (2006): 427–40.

Benton, D., and R. T. Donohoe. "The Effects of Nutrients on Mood." *Public Health Nutrition* 2 (1999): 403–409.

Boggiano, Mary M., Bulent Turan, Christine R. Maldonado, Kimberly D. Oswald, and Ellen S. Shuman. "Secretive Food Concocting in Binge Eating: Test of a Famine Hypotheses." *International Journal of Eating Disorders* 46 (2012): 212–25.

Bower, Anne L. "Recipes for History: The National Council of Negro Women's Five Histori-cal Cookbooks." *African American Foodways: Explorations of History and Culture*, ed. Anne L. Bower, 153–74. Urbana: University of Illinois Press, 2009.

———. "Watching Food." In *Reel Food: Essays on Food and Film*, ed. Anne L. Bower, 1–13. New York: Routledge, 2004.

Boym, Svetlana. *The Future of Nostalgia*. New York: Basic Books, 2001.

Brady, Erika, ed. *Healing Logics: Culture and Medicine in Modern Health Belief Systems*. Logan: Utah State University Press, 2001.

Briggs, Charles L., and Richard Bauman. "Genre, Intertextuality, and Social Power." *Journal of Linguistic Anthropology* 2, no. 2 (1992): 131–72.

Brothers, Joyce. "Psychological Problems Play a Part in Obesity." *Des Moines Regis-ter*, November 6, 1966. Accessed February 2, 2015. http://www.newspapers.com/newspage/1131300/.

Burns-Booth, Karen S. "Nursery Puddings, Slow Sunday and Old Fashioned Baked Rice Pudding, Lavender and Lovage." September 4, 2011. Accessed February 21, 2015. http://www.lavenderandlovage.com/2011/09/nursery-puddings-slow-sunday-and-html.

cafepress.com/mf/17205589/chocolate-voices-ash-grey_tshirt. Accessed June 13, 2013.

Chambers, Erve. *Native Tours: The Anthropology of Travel and Tourism*. Prospect Heights, IL: Waveland Press, 2000.

Christensen, Danille Elise. "'Look at Us Now!': Scrapbooking, Regimes of Value, and the Risks of (Auto)Ethnography." *Journal of American Folklore* 124, no. 493 (2011): 175–210.

Cizza, Giovanni, and Kristina I. Rother. "Was Feuerbach Right: Are We What We Eat?" *Jour-nal of Clinical Investigation* 121 (2011): 2969–71.

Coakley, Linda. "Polish Encounters with the Irish Foodscape: An Examination of the Losses and Gains of Migrant Foodways." *Food and Foodways: Explorations in the History and Culture of Human Nourishment*, 20, no. 3–4 (2012): 307–325. DOI: 10.1080/07409710.2012.715968.

Counihan, Carole M. *The Anthropology of Food and Body: Gender, Meaning, and Power*. New York: Routledge, 1999.

Dallman, Mary F., Susan F. Akana, Susanne E. la Fleur, Francisca Gomez, Hani Houshyar, M. E. Bell, Seema Bhatnagar, Kevin D. Laugero, and Sotara Manalo. "Chronic Stress and Obesity: A New View of 'Comfort Food.'" *Publications of the National Academy of Sci-ences* 100 (2003): 11696–701.

Dallman, Mary F., Norman C. Pecoraro, and Susanne E. la Fleur. "Chronic Stress and Com-fort Foods: Self-Medication and Abdominal Obesity." *Brain, Behavior, and Immunity* 19 (2005): 275–80.

Davidson, Alan. *Oxford Companion to Food*. 2nd edition. Oxford: Oxford University Press, 2006.

Dawkins, Nicole. "The Hunger for Home: Nostalgic Affect, Embodied Memory and the Sensual Politics of Transnational Foodways." *Undergraduate Journal of Anthropology* 1 (2009): 33–42.

Dillinger, Teresa L., Patricia Barriga, Sylvia Escarcega, Martha Jimenez, Diana Salazar Lowe, and Louis E. Grivetti. "Food of the Gods: Cure for Humanity? A Cultural History of the Medicinal and Ritual Use of Chocolate." *Journal of Nutrition* 130 (2000): 2057S–72S.

Dubé, Laurette, Jordan L. LeBel, and Ji Lu. "Affect Asymmetry and Comfort Food Consumption." *Physiology & Behavior* 86 (2005): 559–67.

Dundes, Alan. "Folk Ideas as Units of Worldview." *Journal of American Folklore* 84, no. 331 (1971): 93–103.

Duneier, Mitchell. *Slim's Table: Race, Respectability, and Masculinity.* Chicago: University of Chicago Press, 1992.

Ellis, Carolyn, and Arthur P. Bochner. "Autoethnography, Personal Narrative, Reflexivity: Researcher as Subject." In *Handbook of Qualitative Research*, eds. Norman K. Denizen and Yvonna S. Lincoln, 733–68. 2nd edition. Thousand Oaks, CA: Sage, 2000.

Esterick, Penny Van. "From Hunger Foods to Heritage Foods: Challenges to Food Localization in Laos." In *Fast Food/Slow Food: The Cultural Economy of the Global Food System*, ed. Richard Wilk, 83–96. Altamira Press, 2006.

Evers, Catharine, F. Marijn Stok, and Denise T. D. deRidder. "Feeding Your Feelings: Emotion Regulation Strategies and Emotional Eating." *Personality and Social Psychology Bulletin* 36 (2010): 792–804.

Eves, Rosalyn Collings. "A Recipe for Remembrance: Memory and Identity in African-American Women's Cookbooks." *Rhetoric Review* 24, no. 3 (2005): 280–97.

Ferzacca, Steve. *Healing the Modern in a Central Javanese City.* Durham, NC: Carolina Academic, 2001.

Fischler, Claude. "Food, Self, and Identity." *Social Science Information* 27, no. 2 (1988): 275–92.

Garmey, Jane. *Great British Cooking: A Well-Kept Secret.* New York: Harper Collins, 1992.

Georges, Robert A., and Michael Owen Jones. *Folkloristics: An Introduction.* Bloomington: Indiana University Press, 1995.

Gibson, Edward Leigh. "Emotional Influences on Food Choice: Sensory, Physiological and Psychological Pathways." *Physiology & Behavior* 89 (2006): 53–61.

Gould, Jillian. "Toronto Blueberry Buns: History, Community, Memory." *Material History Review* 57 (Spring 2003): 30–39.

Grieshop, James I. "The *Envios* of San Pablo Huixtepec, Oaxaca: Food, Homes, and Transnationalism." *Human Organization* 65 (2006): 400–406.

Grigson, Jane. *English Food.* London: Penguin Books, 1998 [1974].

Gowers, Emily. *The Loaded Table: Representations of Food in Roman Literature.* Oxford: Clarendon Press, 1993.

Guthman, Julie. "Bringing Good Food to Others: Investigating the Subjects of Alternative Food Practice." *Cultural Geographies* 15, no. 4 (2008): 431–47.

———. "'If They Only Knew': Color Blindness and Universalism in California Alternative Food Institutions." *Taking Food Public: Redefining Foodways in a Changing World*, eds. Psyche Williams-Forson and Carole Counihan, 211–22. New York: Routledge, 2012.

Hall, C. Michael, Liz Sharples, Richard Mitchell, Niki Macionias, and Brock Cambourne, eds. *Food Tourism around the World: Development, Management and Marketing* (Boston: Elsevier Butterworth Heinemann, 2003.

Hall, Carl T. "'Comfort Food' Research Finds Medicinal Effect / High-Fat Fare Helps Rats in Dealing with High Stress Levels." *San Francisco Gate.* Accessed February 19, 2013. http://www.sfgate.com/health/article/Comfort-food-research-finds-medicinal-effect-2573565.php. 2003.

Handler, Richard, and Joyce Linnekin. "Tradition, Genuine or Spurious." *Journal of American Folklore* 97, no. 385 (1984): 175–10.

Hansen, Ron. "Babette's Feast." In *Writers at the Movies: 26 Contemporary Authors Celebrate 26 Memorable Movies*, ed. Jim Shepard, 102–114. New York: Perennial, 2000.

Harper, A. Breeze. *Sistah Vegan: Black Female Vegans Speak on Food, Identity, Health, and Society.* New York: Lantern Books, 2010.

Harris, Jessica B. *High on the Hog: A Culinary Journey from Africa to America.* New York: Bloomsbury USA, 2011.

Harris, Tina. "Deconstructing the Myth of the Dysfunctional Black Family." In *Food for Thought: Essays on Eating and Culture*, ed. Lawrence C. Rubin, 211–24. Jefferson, NC: McFarland & Company, 2008.

Harrison, Julia. "Spam." In *Fat: The Anthropology of an Obsession*, eds. Don Kulick and Anne Meneley, 185–98. New York: Jeremy P. Tarcher/Penguin, 2005.

Henderson, Laretta. "Ebony Jr! and 'Soul Food': The Construction of Middle-Class African American Identity through the Use of Traditional Southern Foodways." *MELUS* 32, no. 4 (2007): 81–97.

Hjalager, Anne-Mette, and Greg Richards, eds. *Tourism and Gastronomy.* London: Routledge, 2002.

Ho, Jennifer Ann. *Consumption and Identity in Asian American Coming-of-Age Novels.* New York: Routledge, 2005.

Hobsbawm, Eric, and Terence O. Ranger, eds. *The Invention of Tradition.* Cambridge: Cambridge University Press, 1983.

Holtzman, Jon D. "Food and Memory." *Annual Review of Anthropology* 35 (2006): 361–78.

Hubbell, Amy. "(In)Edible Algeria: Transmitting Pied-Noir Nostalgia through Food." In *Edible Alterities: Perspective from La Francophonic*, special issue, eds. Angela Giovanangeli and Julie Robert. *Portal: Journal of Multidisciplinary International Studies* 10, no. 2: 1–18.

Hughes, Marvalene H. "Soul, Black Women, and Food." In *Food and Culture: A Reader*, eds. Carole Counihan and Penny Van Esterik, 272–80. New York: Routledge, 1997.

Humphrey, Lin T. "Traditional Foods? Traditional Values." *Western Folklore* 48 (1989): 169–77.

Hymes, Dell. "Folklore's Nature and the Sun's Myth." *Journal of American Folklore* 88, no. 350 (1975): 345–69.

Iannolo, Jennifer L. "Food and Sensuality: A Perfect Pairing." In *Food and Philosophy: Eat, Think and Be Merry*, eds. Fritz Allhoff and Dave Monroe, 239–49. Malden, MA: Blackwell Publishing, 2007.

Inouye, Charles Shiro. "In the Show House of Modernity: Exhaustive Listing in Itami Juzo's *Tampopo*." In *Word and Image in Japanese Cinema*, eds. Dennis Washburn and Carole Cavanaugh, 126–46. Cambridge: Cambridge University Press, 2001.

James, Delores. "Factors Influencing Food Choices, Dietary Intake, and Nutrition-Related Attitudes among African Americans: Application of a Culturally Sensitive Model." *Ethnicity & Health* 9, no. 4 (2004): 349–67.

Japhe, Brad. "Japanese Comfort Food at Del Rey Kitchen from Satoru Yokomori and Michael Yee." *LA Weekly*, November 10, 2014. http://m.laweekly.com/squidink/2014/11/10/japanese-comfort-food-at-del-rey-kitchen-from-satoru-yokomori-and-michael-yee.

Jones, Michael Owen. "Afterward: Discovering the Symbolism of Food Customs and Events." In *"We Gather Together": Food and Festival in American Life*, eds. Theodore C. Humphrey and Lin T. Humphrey, 235–45. Ann Arbor, MI: UMI Press, 1988.

———. "Dining on Death Row: Last Meals and the Crutch of Ritual." *Journal of American Folklore* 127 (2014): 3–26.

———. *Exploring Folk Art: Twenty Years of Thought on Craft, Work, and Aesthetics*. Ann Arbor, MI: UMI Research Press, 1987.

———. "Food Choice, Symbolism, and Identity: Bread-and-Butter Issues for Folkloristics and Nutrition Studies (American Folklore Society Presidential Address, October 2005)." *Journal of American Folklore* 120 (2007): 129–77.

———. "Latina/o Local Knowledge about Diabetes: Emotional Triggers, Plant Treatments, and Food Symbolism." In *Diagnosing Folklore: Perspectives on Health, Trauma, and Disability*, eds. Trevor J. Blank and Andrea Kitta, 97–103. Jackson: University Press of Mississippi, 2015.

Kalčik, Susan. 1984. "Ethnic Foodways in America: Symbol and Performance of Identity." In *Ethnic and Regional Foodways in the United States: The Performance of Group Identity*, eds. Linda Kelly Brown and Kay Mussell, 37–65. Knoxville: University of Tennessee Press, 1984.

Kandiah, Jayanthi, Melissa Yake, James Jones, and Michaela Meyer. "Stress Influences Appetite and Comfort Food Preferences in College Women." *Nutrition Research* 26 (2006): 118 23.

Keller, James R. *Food, Film and Culture: A Genre Study*. Jefferson, NC: McFarland & Company, 2006.

Kim, Sojin, and R. Mark Livengood. "Ramen Noodles & Spam: Popular Foods, Significant Tastes." *Digest. An Interdisciplinary Study of Food and Foodways* 15 (1995): 2–11.

Kirshenblatt-Gimblett, Barbara. "Kitchen Judaism." In *Getting Comfortable in New York, 1880–1950*, eds. Susan Braunstein and Jenna Weissman Joselit, 94. New York: The Jewish Museum, 1990.

———. "Objects of Memory: Material Culture as Life Review." In *Folk Groups and Folklore Genres: A Reader*, ed. Elliot Oring, 329. Logan: Utah State University Press, 1989.

Korsmeyer, Carolyn. "Delightful, Delicious, Disgusting." In *Food and Philosophy: Eat, Think and Be Merry*, eds. Fritz Allhoff and Dave Monroe, 145–61. Malden, MA: Blackwell Publishing, 2007.

Kubo, Michiko. "The Development of an Indonesian National Cuisine: A Study of a New Movement of Instant Foods and Local Cuisine." In *Globalization, Food, and Social Identities in the Asia Pacific Region*, ed. James Farrer. Tokyo: Sophia University Instituted of Comparative Cultures, 2010.

Laine, Tarja. "Family Matters in *Eat Drink Man Woman*: Food Envy, Family Longing, or Intercultural Knowledge through the Senses?" In *Shooting the Family: Transnational*

Media and Intercultural Values, eds. Patricia Pisters and Wim Staat, 103–114. Amsterdam: Amsterdam University Press, 2005.

Leach, Helen. "The Pavlova Wars: How a Creationist Model of Recipe Origins Led to an International Dispute." *Gastronomica: The Journal of Food and Culture* 2 (2010): 24–30. Accessed January 25, 2015. http://www.jstor.org/stable/10.1525/gfc.2010.10.2.24.

Levitan, Robert D., and Caroline Davis. "Emotions and Eating Behaviour: Implications for the Current Obesity Epidemic." *University of Toronto Quarterly* 79 (2010.): 783–99.

Lewis, George H. "From Minnesota Fat to Seoul Food: Spam in America and the Pacific Rim." *Journal of Popular Culture* 34, no. 2 (2000): 83–105.

Liburd, Leandris C. "Food, Identity, and African-American Women with Type 2 Diabetes: An Anthropological Perspective." *Diabetes Spectrum* 16, no. 3 (2003): 160–65.

Lindemann, Bernd, Yoko Ogiwara, and Yuzo Ninomiya. "The Discovery of Umami." *Chemical Senses* 27 (2002): 843–44.

Lloyd, Timothy Charles. "The Cincinnati Chili Complex." *Western Folklore* 40, no. 1 (1981): 28–40.

Locher, Julie L. "Comfort Food." In *Encyclopedia of Food and Culture*, ed. S. Katz. New York: Charles Scribner's Sons, 2002.

Locher, Julie L., William C. Yoels, Donna Maurer, and Jillian Van Ells. "Comfort Foods: An Exploratory Journey into the Social and Emotional Significance of Food." *Food & Foodways* 13 (2005): 273–97.

Lockwood, Yvonne R., and William G. Lockwood. "Pasties in Michigan's Upper Peninsula: Foodways, Interethnic Relations, and Regionalism. In *Creative Ethnicity: Symbols and Strategies of Contemporary Ethnic Life*, eds. Stephen Stern and John Allan Cicala, 3–20. Logan: Utah State University Press, 1991.

Long, Lucy M. "Culinary Tourism." In *The Oxford Handbook of Food History*, ed. Jeffrey M. Pilcher, 389–408. Oxford: Oxford University Press, 2012.

———. "Culinary Tourism: A Folkloristic Perspective on Eating and Otherness." In *Culinary Tourism*, ed. Lucy Long, 20–50. Lexington: University Press of Kentucky, 2004.

———. "Greenbean Casserole and Midwestern Identity: A Regional Foodways Aesthetic and Ethos." *Midwestern Folklore* 33, no. 1 (2007): 29–44.

Long, Lucy M. ed. *The Food and Folklore Reader.* New York: Bloomsbury, 2015.

Lukovitz, Karlene. "Does Meaning of 'Comfort Foods' Vary by Age?" July 31, 2009. Accessed February 22, 2013. http://www.mediapost.com/publications/article/110781/does-meaning-of-comfort-foods-vary-by-age.html#axzz2Leodj8ws.

Lupton, Deborah. *Food, the Body and the Self.* Thousand Oaks, CA: Sage Publications, 1996.

Manekar, Purnima. "India Shopping: Indian Grocery Stores and Transnational Configurations of Belonging. *Ethnos* 67, no. 1: 75–80.

Mannur, Anita "Culinary Nostalgia, Authenticity, Nationalism and Diaspora." In *Culinary Fictions: Food in South Asian Diasporic Culture*, 27–78. Philadelphia: Temple University Press, 2010.

McFadden, Margaret. "Gendering the Feast: Women, Spirituality, and Grace in Three Food Films." In *Reel Food: Essays on Food and Film*, ed. Anne L. Bower, 117–28. New York: Routledge, 2004.

McGee, Harold. *On Food and Cooking: The Science and Lore of the Kitchen*. New York: Charles Scribner's Sons, 1984.

Michener, Willa, and Paul Rozin. "Pharmacological Versus Sensory Factors in the Satiation of Chocolate Craving." *Physiology & Behavior* 56 (1994): 419–22.

Miller, Adrian. *Soul Food: The Surprising Story of an American Cuisine, One Plate at a Time*. Chapel Hill: University of North Carolina Press, 2013.

Milligan, Rhonda-Jane, Glenn Waller, and Bernice Andrews. "Eating Disturbances in Female Prisoners: The Role of Anger." *Eating Behaviors* 3 (2002): 123–32.

Mintz, Sidney. "Eating American." In *Food in the USA: A Reader*, ed. Carole M. Counihan, 23–34. New York: Routledge, 2002.

Mould, Tom. "The Paradox of Traditionalization: Negotiating the Past in Choctaw Prophetic Discourse." *Journal of Folklore Research* 42, no. 3 (2005): 255–94.

———. "Traditionalization." *Folklore: An Encyclopedia of Beliefs, Customs, Tales, Music, and Art*, eds. Charlie T. McCormick and Kim Kennedy White. 1 vol. Santa Barbara, CA: ABC-CLIO, 2011.

Nabhan, Gary. 2008. "Place-based Foods at Risk in New England." Place Based Foods, February 7, 2014. http://garynabhan.com/i/place-based-foods.

"A Nation Turns to Comfort Food." *ABC News*, November 7, 2006. Accessed February 20, 2013. http://abcnews.go.com/US/story?id=92217&page=1.

Nettles, Kimberly. "'Saving' Soul Food." *Gastronomica* 7, no. 3 (2007): 106–13.

Neustadt, Kathy. 1988. "'Born among the Shells': The Quakers of Allen's Neck and Their Clambake." In *"We Gather Together": Food and Festival in American Life*, eds. Theodore C. Humphrey and Lin T. Humphrey, 89–110. Ann Arbor, MI: UMI Press, 1998.

Newton, Sarah E. "The Jell-O Syndrome: Investigating Popular Culture/Foodways." *Western Folklore* 51 (1992): 249–67.

Norwalk, Mary. *English Puddings: Sweet & Savory*. London: The Book People, 2010.

Noyes, Dorothy. "Tradition: Three Traditions." *Journal of Folklore Research* 46, no. 3 (2009): 233–68.

Ohnuki-Tierney, Emiko. "The Ambivalent Self of the Contemporary Japanese." *Cultural Anthropology* 5 (1990): 196–15.

Ong, L. S., H. I. Jzerman, and A. K. Leung. "Is Comfort Food Really Good for the Soul?: A Replication of Troisi and Gabriel's (2011) Study 2." *Frontiers in Psychology* 6 (2015): 314.

Opie, Frederick Douglass. *Hog and Hominy: Soul Food from Africa to America*. New York: Columbia University Press, 2008.

Oring, Elliott. "Legend, Truth, and News." *Southern Folklore* 47 (1990): 163–77.

Osman, Jamie L., and Jeffery Sobal. "Chocolate Cravings in American and Spanish Individuals: Biological and Cultural Influences." *Appetite* 47 (2006): 290–301.

Otterloo, Anneke H. Van. "Chinese and Indonesian Restaurants and the Taste for Exotic Food in the Netherlands: A Global-Local Trend." In *Asian Food: The Global and the Local*, eds. Katarzyna Cwiertka and Boudewijn Walraven, 153–66. New York: Routledge, 2002.

Oxford English Dictionary. "Comfort Food." Accessed February 19, 2013. oed.com/view/Entry/36890?redirectedFrom=comfort+food#eid8985487.

Papazian, Gretchen. "Anorexia Envisioned: Mike Leigh's *Life is Sweet*, Chul-soo Park's *301/302*, and Todd Hayne's *Superstar*." In *Reel Food: Essays on Food and Film*, ed. Anne L. Bower, 147–66. New York: Routledge, 2004.

Parasecoli, Fabio. *Bite Me: Food in Popular Culture*. Oxford: Berg, 2008.

———. "Hungry Engrams: Food and Non-Representational Memory." In *Food and Philosophy: Eat, Think and Be Merry*, ed. Fritz Allhoff and Dave Monroe, 102–114. Malden, MA: Blackwell Publishing, 2007.

Parker, Scott, Niveen Kamel, and Debra Zellner. "Food Craving Patterns in Egypt: Comparisons with North America and Spain." *Appetite* 40 (2003): 193–95.

Parker, Gordon, Isabella Parker, and Heather Brotchie. "Mood State Effects of Chocolate." *Journal of Affective Disorders* 92 (2006): 149–59.

Pocius, Gerald L. *A Place to Belong: Community Order and Everyday Space in Calvert, Newfoundland*. Montreal: McGill-Queen's University Press, 2000.

Poe, Tracy N. "The Origins of Soul Food in Black Urban Identity: Chicago, 1915–1947." *American Studies International* 37 (1999): 4–33.

Prescott, John. *Taste Matters. Why We Eat the Food We Do*. London: Reaktion Books, 2012.

Proust, Marcel. "*Du Côté de chez Swann*" [Swann's Way]. In *Remembrance of Things Past*. Trans. C. K. Scott Moncreiff. New York: Henry Holt and Company, 1922.

Quinzio, Jeri. *Pudding: A Global History*. London: Reaktion Books, 2012.

Raman, Parvathi. "'Me in Place, and the Place in Me': A Migrant's Tale of Food, Home and Belonging." *Food, Culture, and Society* 14, no. 2 (2011): 165–80.

Rawnsley, Ming-Yeh T. "Cultural Representation of Taste in Ang Lee's *Eat, Drink, Man, Woman*." In *Food for Thought: Essays on Eating and Culture*, ed. Lawrence C. Rubin, 225–36. Jefferson, NC: McFarland & Company, 2008.

Richman, Phyllis. "She May Not Have Coined the Term, But She's an Expert Nonetheless." *Washington Post*, December 16, 2013. Accessed February 2, 2015. http://www.washington post.com/lifestyle/food/comfort-food-she-may-not-have-coined-the-term-but-shes-an -expert-nonetheless/2013/12/16/eb32c150–61c5–11e3–8beb–3f9a9942850f_story.html.

———. *Washington Post*, December 25, 1977.

Robertson, Jenny. *Nursery Puddings: Comforting Desserts from Childhood*. Kindle edition. February 11, 2012

Rogers, Peter J., and Hendrick J. Smit. "Food Craving and Food 'Addiction': A Critical Review of the Evidence from a Biopsychosocial Perspective." *Pharmacology, Biochemistry & Behavior* 66 (2000): 3–14.

Romm Cari. "Why Comfort Food Comforts." *The Atlantic*, April 3, 2015. Accessed May 15, 2015. http://www.theatlantic.com/health/archive/2015/04/ why-comfort-food-comforts/389613/.

Rosenfield, Israel. *The Invention of Memory: A New View of the Brain*. New York: Basic Books, 1988.

Roth, LuAnne. "Beyond *Communitas*: Cinematic Food Events and the Negotiation of Power, Belonging, and Exclusion." In *Folklore/Cinema: Popular Film as Vernacular Culture*, eds. Sharon R. Sherman and Mikel J. Koven, 197–220. Logan: Utah State University Press, 2007 [2005].

Rouse, Carolyn, and Janet Hoskins. "Purity, Soul Food, and Sunni Islam: Explorations at the Intersection of Consumption and Resistance." *Cultural Anthropology* 19, no. 2 (2004): 226–49.

Rozin, Elizabeth. *Ethnic Cuisine: The Flavor Principle Cookbook.* Brattleboro, VT: Stephen Greene, 1983.

———. "The Role of Flavor in the Meal and the Culture." In *Dimensions of the Meal: The Science, Culture, Business, and Art of Eating*, ed. Herbert L. Meiselman, 134–42. Gaithersburg, MD: Aspen, 2000.

Rozin, P., E. Levine, and C. Stoess. "Chocolate Craving and Liking." *Appetite* 17 (1991): 199–212.

Russell, D., L. A. Peplau, L. A., and C. E. Cutrona. "The Revised UCLA Loneliness Scale: Concurrent and Discriminant Validity Evidence." *Journal of Personality and Social Psychology* 39 (1980): 472–80.

Rutherford, J. *Men's Silences: Predicaments in Masculinity.* London: Routledge, 1992.

Saltzman, Rachelle H. "Identity and Food." In *Food Issues: An Encyclopedia*, ed. Ken Albala. Thousand Oaks, CA: Sage Publications, 2015.

———. *A Lark for the Sake of Their Country: The 1926 General Strike Volunteers in Folklore and Memory.* Manchester: Manchester University Press, 2012.

———. "Rites of Intensification: Eating and Ethnicity in the Catskills." In *Culinary Tourism*, ed. Lucy Long, 97–113. Lexington: University Press of Kentucky, 2004.

———. "Terroir." In *Food Issues: An Encyclopedia*, ed. Ken Albala. Thousand Oaks, CA: Sage Publications, 2015.

Sherman, Sharon. "The Passover Seder: Ritual Dynamics, Foodways, and Family Folklore." In *Food in the USA: A Reader*, ed. Carole M. Counihan, 193–204. New York: Routledge, 2002 [1988].

Shigley, Sally Bishop. "Empathy, Energy, and Eating: Politics and Power in *The Black Family Dinner Quilt Cookbook*." In *Recipes for Reading: Community Cookbooks, Stories, Histories*, ed. Anne L. Bower, 118–31. Amherst: University of Massachusetts, 1997.

Sims, Rebecca. "Food, Place, and Authenticity: Local Food and the Sustainable Tourist Experience." *Journal of Sustainable Tourism* 17, no. 3 (2009): 321–36.

Singer, Eliot. "Conversion through Foodways Enculturation: The Meaning of Eating in an American Hindu Sect." In *Ethnic and Regional Foodways in the United States: The Performance of Group Identity*, eds. Linda Kelly Brown and Kay Mussell, 195–216. Knoxville: University of Tennessee Press, 1984.

Slotkin, Daniel E. "What's Your Comfort Food?" *New York Times*, May 25, 2012. Accessed August 11, 2013. http://learning.blogs.nytimes.com/2012/05/25/whats-your-comfort -food/?_r=1&apage=2#comments.

Smith, Catrin. "Punishment and Pleasure: Women, Food and the Imprisoned Body." *Sociological Review* 50 (2002): 197–214.

Smith, Valene L. *Hosts and Guests.* Philadelphia: University of Pennsylvania Press, 1989.

Stein, Joel. "You Eat What You Are." *Time*, October 18, 2007.

Stein, Karen. "Comfort Foods: Bringing Back Old Favorites." *Journal of the American Dietetic Association* 108, no. 3 (March 2008): 412, 414.

Stern, B. "Historical and Personal Nostalgia in Advertising Text: The *fin de siècle* Effect." *Journal of Advertising* 11 (1992): 11–22.

Stewart, Susan. *On Longing: Narratives of the Miniature, the Gigantic, the Souvenir, the Collection*. Durham: Duke University Press, 1993.

Stowers, Susan L. "Gastronomic Nostalgia: Salvadoran Immigrants Craving for Their Ideal Meal." *Ecology of Food and Nutrition* 51, no. 5: 374–93.

Style, Sue. "Toad in the Hole is Uniquely British Comfort Food." *Zester Daily*, January 27, 2015.

Sutton, David E. *Remembrance of Repasts: An Anthropology of Food and Memory*. New York: Berg, 2001.

Swislocki, Mark. *Culinary Nostalgia: Regional Food Culture and Urban Experience in Shanghai*. Palo Alto: Stanford University Press, 2008.

Thorn, Bret. "Seeking Comfort, Diners Indulge in Feel-Good Fare." *Nation's Restaurant News* 35 (2001): 32.

Tierney, John. "Comfort Food, for Monkeys." *New York Times*, May 20, 2008.

Tisdale, Sallie. *The Best Thing I Ever Tasted. The Secret of Food*. New York: Riverhead Books, 2000.

Tomiyama, A. Janet, Mary F. Dallman, and Elissa S. Epel. "Comfort Food Is Comforting to Those Most Stressed: Evidence of the Chronic Stress Response Network in High Stress Women." *Psychoneuroendocrinology* 36 (2011): 1513–19.

Torres, Nora Gomez. "Cubans Finding Comfort, Nostalgia in Russian Products." *Miami Herald*, November 14, 2014. Accessed February 10, 2014. www.miamiherald.com/news/ . . ./article3936801.html.

Troisi, Jordan D., and Shira Gabriel. "Chicken Soup Really Is Good for the Soul: 'Comfort Food' Fulfills the Need to Belong." *Psychological Science* 22 (2011): 747–53.

Troisi, Jordan D., S. Gabriel, J. L. Derrick, and A. Geisler. "Threatened Belonging and Preference for Comfort Food among the Securely Attached." *Appetite*, July 1, 2015: 58–64. DOI: 10.1016/j.appet.2015.02.029.

Tuan. *Yi-Fu. Space and Place: The Perspective of Experience*. Minneapolis: University of Minnesota Press, 2005 [1977].

Turner, Patricia A. "Church's Fried Chicken and The Klan: A Rhetorical Analysis of Rumor in the Black Community." *Western Folklore* 46 (1987): 294–306.

Twitty, Michael. "Soul Food Cooked By Others Hands." *American Prospect*, October 31, 2013. http://prospect.org/article/soul-foods-contested-history.

Tye, Diane. *Baking As Biography: A Life Story in Recipes*. Montreal: McGill-Queen's University Press, 2010

Valentine, Gill, and Beth Longstaff. "Doing Porridge: Food and Social Relations in a Male Prison." *Journal of Material Culture* 3 (1998): 131–52.

Van Oudenhove, Lucas, Shane McKie, Daniel Lassman, Bilal Uddin, Peter Paine, Steven Coen, Lloyd Gregory, Jan Tack, and Qasim Aziz. "Fatty Acid–Induced Gut-Brain Signaling Attenuates Neural and Behavioral Effects of Sad Emotion in Humans." *Journal of Clinical Investigation* 121 (2011): 3094–99.

Viteri, Maria Amelia. "Nostalgia Food and Belonging: Ecuadorans in New York City." In *Ethnicity, Citizenship, and Belonging: Practice, Theory, and Spatial Dimensions*, eds. Sarah

Albiez, Nelly Castro, Lara Jüssen, and Eva Youkhana, 221–36. Vervuert: Iberoamericana, 2011. Accessed February 19, 2014. http://www.academia.edu/nostalgia

Wagner, Heather Scherschel, Britt Ahlstrom, Joseph P. Redden, Zata Vickers, and Traci Mann. "The Myth of Comfort Food." *Health Psychology* 33, no. 12 (December 2014): 1552–57. Accessed May 15, 2015. http://dx.doi.org/10.1037/hea0000068.

Wan, Julie. "Fat Might Be the Sixth Basic Taste." *Washington Post*, June 4, 2012. Accessed February 17, 2013. http://articles.washingtonpost.com/2012–06–04/national/35462005 _1_fat-taste-nada-abumrad-meatiness.

Wansink, Brian, and Cynthia Sangerman. "Engineering Comfort Foods." *American Demographic*, July 2000: 66–67.

Wansink, Brian, Matthew M. Cheney, and Nina Chan. "Exploring Comfort Food Preferences across Age and Gender." *Physiology and Behavior* 79 (2003.): 739–47.

Ward, Paul. *Britishness since 1870.* London: Routledge, 2004.

Warnes, Andrew. *Hunger Overcome? Food and Resistance in Twentieth-Century African American Literature.* Athens: University of Georgia Press, 2004.

Watson, James L., and Melissa L. Caldwell. Introduction to *The Cultural Politics of Food and Eating*, 1–10. Malden, MA: Blackwell Publishers, 2005.

Weingarten, H. P., and D. Elston. "Food Cravings in a College Population." *Appetite* 17 (1991): 167–75.

———. "The Phenomenology of Food Cravings." *Appetite* 15 (1990): 231–46.

Wenk, Gary. "Why Does Fat Taste So Good? The Importance of Fat-Tasting Proteins on the Tongue." *Psychology Today*, January 2012.

Whit, William C. "Soul Food as Cultural Creation." In *African American Foodways: Explorations of History and Culture*, ed. Anne L. Bower, 45–58. Urbana: University of Illinois Press, 2009.

Wilk, Richard. *Home Cooking in the Global Village: Caribbean Food from Buccaneers to Ecotourists.* Oxford: Berg, 2006.

Wilk, Richard, ed. *Fast Food/Slow Food: The Cultural Economy of the Global Food System.* Altamira Press, 2006.

Williams-Forson, Psyche. *Building Houses Out of Chicken Legs: Black Women Food, & Power.* Chapel Hill: University of North Carolina Press, 2006.

———. "Take the Chicken Out of the Box: Demystifying the Sameness of African American Culinary Heritage in the U.S." In *Edible Identities: Food as Cultural Heritage*, eds. Ronda L. Brulotte and Michael A. Di Giovine, 93–107. Franham: Ashgate, 2014.

Wilson, M. E., J. Fisher, A. Fischer, V. Lee, R. B. Harris, and T. J. Bartness. "Quantifying Food Intake in Socially Housed Monkeys: Social Status Effects on Caloric Consumption." *Physiology & Behavior* 94 (2008): 586–94.

Witt, Doris. *Black Hunger: Soul Food and America.* Minneapolis: University of Minnesota Press, 2004.

———. "From Fiction to Foodways: Working at the Intersections of African American Literary and Culinary Studies." In *African American Foodways: Explorations of History and Culture*, ed. Anne L. Bower, 101–25. Urbana: University of Illinois Press, 2009.

———. "Soul Food." *Encyclopedia of American Studies.* 2010.

Wood, Paulette, and Barbra D. Vogen. "Feeding the Anorectic Client: Comfort Foods and Happy Hour." *Geriatric Nursing* 19 (1998): 192–94.

Wood, Stacy. "The Comfort Food Fallacy: Avoiding Old Favorites in Times of Change." *Journal of Consumer Research* 36 (2010): 950–63.

Wright, Patrick. *On Living in an Old Country: The National Past in Contemporary Britain.* London: Verso, 1985.

Xu, Wenying. *Eating Identities: Reading Food in Asian American Literature.* Honolulu: University of Hawai'i Press, 2008.

Yentsch, Anne. "Excavating the South's African American Food History." In *African American Foodways: Explorations of History and Culture,* ed. Anne L. Bower, 59–98. Urbana: University of Illinois Press, 2009.

Yoder, Don. "Folk Cooker." In *Folklore and Folklife,* ed. Richard M. Dorson. Chicago: University of Chicago Press, 1972.

Yoder, Lonnie. "The Funeral Meal: A Significant Funerary Ritual." *Journal of Religion and Health* 25 (1986): 149–60.

Young, Simon N. "How to Increase Serotonin in the Human Brain without Drugs." *Journal of Psychiatry and Neuroscience* 32 (2007): 394–99.

Yuker, H. E. "Perceived Attributes of Chocolate." In *Chocolate: Food of the Gods,* ed. Alex Szogyi, 35–43. Westport, CT: Greenwood Press, 1997.

Zafar, Rafia. "The Proof of the Pudding: Of Haggis, Hasty Pudding, and Transatlantic Influence." *Early American Literature* 2 (1996): 133–49.

———. "The Signifying Dish: Autobiography and History in Two Black Women's Cookbooks." *Feminist Studies* 25, no. 2 (1999): 449–69.

Zellner, D., A. Garriga-Trillo, E. Rohm, S. Centeno, and S. Parker. "Food Liking and Craving: A Cross-Cultural Approach." *Appetite* 33 (1999): 61–70.

Zellner, Debra A., Ana Garriga-Trillo, Soraya Centeno, and Elizabeth Wadsworth. "Chocolate Craving and the Menstrual Cycle." *Appetite* 42 (2004): 119–21.

Zimmerman, Steve. *Food in the Movies.* 2nd edition. Jefferson, NC: McFarland & Company, 2009.

Zurbuchen, Mary Sabina. *Beginning to Remember: The Past in the Indonesian Present.* Seattle: University of Washington Press, 2005.

CONTRIBUTORS

Barbara Banks, a longtime resident of the South Side of Chicago, retired from Cook County Hospital in 2008 after forty years of working in medical administration. She earned an Associates Degree from Harold Washington College in Business Administration, and later received a BA. In addition to writing, especially about food traditions, Barbara is a world traveler and studies French, yoga, Zumba, and other dance exercises in her spare time.

Sheila Bock is Assistant Professor of Interdisciplinary studies at University of Nevada, Las Vegas. While her research spans a range of topics, the majority of her work employs narrative and performance models of analysis to examine how people make sense of their own and others' experiences with illness, particularly in contexts of stigma. Other research interests include foodways, performance as a mode of negotiating differential identities, and the intersections between folklore and popular culture. Her articles and book chapters appear in the *Journal of Folklore Research*; *Western Journal of Black Studies*; *Health, Culture, and Society*; the *Journal of Medical Humanities*; the *Journal of Folklore and Education*; *Western Folklore*; *Patient Experience*; and *Diagnosing Folklore*.

Susan Eleuterio is a folklorist, educator, and consultant to nonprofits. She holds an MA in American Folk Culture from the Cooperstown Graduate Program (SUNY/Oneonta) and a BA in English/Education from the University of Delaware. She is the author of *Irish American Material Culture: A Directory of Collections, Sites and Festivals in the United States and Canada*, as well as essays in *The Encyclopedia of Chicago History, The Encyclopedia of American Folklore, The Encyclopedia of Women's Folklore and Folklife*, and *Ethnic American Food Today: A Cultural Encyclopedia*. She has conducted fieldwork and developed public programs including exhibits, performances, folk arts education workshops and residencies in schools, and professional development programs for teachers, students, adults, and artists for schools, museums, arts education agencies, and arts organizations across the United States. She is an adjunct faculty member of Goucher College's Masters in Cultural Sustainability program.

Jillian Gould is Assistant Professor, Department of Folklore, Memorial University of Newfoundland, where she introduces students to folklore, fieldwork, and ethnography. Jillian has enjoyed writing about food since graduate school and is the author of several food-related articles, including "Candy Stores and Egg Creams" in *Jews of Brooklyn* (2002), "Toronto Blueberry Buns: History, Community, Memory" in *Material History Review* (2003), and, more recently, "A Nice Piece of Cake and a Kibitz: Re-inventing Sabbath Hospitality in an Institutional Home" in *Home Cultures* (2013). The Sabbath Hospitality article grew out of her PhD dissertation, which explores how the elderly residents of a Jewish retirement home in Toronto create and recreate "home" through their memories, rituals, and material culture—including foodways. She has been a workshop presenter on Foodways and Community Traditions for the Tombolo Multicultural Festival (St. John's, Newfoundland) and has facilitated a staged oral history about fish and chips at Newfoundland's provincial museum. Her current research explores the early life and WPA fieldwork of folklorist Herbert Halpert (1911–2000).

Phillis Humphries is a longtime resident of Chicago who also lived briefly in New York. After attending school in Chicago, she served as a medical advocate and is a former facilitator for the group Healing Racism. She is a founding member of St. Thomas the Apostle's Anti-Racism group, located in the Hyde Park community in Chicago. Phillis is a published writer and wrote for the Neighborhood Writing Alliance from 2006 to 2012. Her hobbies include speed walking and small weight lifting. She has been an avid fan of Valois' restaurant for years.

Michael Owen Jones (MA and PhD in Folklore) taught courses at UCLA on food customs and symbolism, folk art, organizational symbolism, folk medicine, and other topics for forty years until his retirement in 2008. He has authored more than 160 publications. His essays on foodways explore such matters food handlers' slang; food choice affected by sensory deprivation; food and disgust; food choice, symbolism, and identity; last meals on death row; eating behind bars; and Percy Shelley (the first "celebrity vegan"). Among his eleven books are *Foodways and Eating Habits* (coedited), *Putting Folklore to Use* (edited), *People Studying People* (with R. A. Georges), *Craftsman of the*

Cumberlands, Exploring Folk Art, Studying Organizational Symbolism, and *Folkloristics* (with R. A. Georges).

Alicia Kristen, a Little Rhody native, studied anthropology and literature at Rhode Island College. Her first major ethnography, "Tutors' Tales: Narratives & Initiation in Rhode Island College's Writing Center," won the James Houston Award in Anthropology and the John Omohondro Prize at the Northeastern Anthropological Association conference. After presenting research at diverse conferences and herding goats for a few years, Alicia's interest in communities of practice drew her to place-based education. She mentored undergraduate students in designing K-5 curricula titled Critters & Currents (2014) and Restoring Connections (2015), and publishing articles about them in *Clearing* magazine. At the University of Oregon, while teaching and pursuing concurrent MAs in Environmental Studies and Public Folklore, she developed a digital game that uses coyote mentoring practices to reconnect young adults with nature and place. Alicia now works as instructor and director of Fox Den for Whole Earth Nature School in Eugene, Oregon.

William G. Lockwood is Professor Emeritus of Anthropology at the University of Michigan, Ann Arbor. His research has been conducted in Yugoslavia, among the Croatian minority of Austria, Roma of Bosnia, Italy and the United States, and ethnic, immigrant, and regional communities of the United States. His primary research interests are ethnicity and interethnic relations, peasant market systems, and food and foodways.

Yvonne R. Lockwood is Curator Emeritus of Folklife and Senior Academic Specialist Emeritus at the Michigan State University Museum. Her formal training is in folklore, history and Slavic Languages and Literatures. Her decades of historical and cultural research in the former Yugoslavia, Burgenland, Austria, and the United States, especially the Great Lakes region, have resulted in publications, exhibitions, festivals, and workshops. Her primary research interests include foodways, textile traditions, and folklore of ethnic and regional communities.

Lucy Long, folklorist and food studies scholar, founded and directs the nonprofit Center for Food and Culture, which develops educational materials and programs around the many ways in which food connects us all. She is an adjunct assistant professor at Bowling Green State University, where she has taught since 1987 in Popular Culture, American Culture Studies, International Studies, and Tourism. She is the author and editor of numerous publications on food, including *Culinary Tourism* (2004), *Regional American Food Culture* (2009), *Ethnic American Food Today: A Cultural Encyclopedia* (2015), *The Food and Folklore Reader* (2015), and *Ethnic American Cooking: Recipes for Living in a New World* (2016). She is past editor of *Digest*, past convener of the Foodways section of the American Folklore Society, and currently on the executive board of the Association for the Study of Food and Society.

LuAnne Roth is an Assistant Teaching Professor in the English Department at the University of Missouri. Her research and teaching focus on folklore, film/media, and food studies. She is particularly interested in how food is used to negotiate the nexus of belief, class, ethnicity, gender, and race. Her foodways research appears as articles in the journals *Food, Culture and Society*, *Digest*, and *Western Folklore* and as chapters in the volumes *Unsettling Assumptions: Tradition, Gender, Drag* (2014) and *Folklore/Cinema: Popular Film as Vernacular Culture* (2007). Roth is currently working on a book manuscript—"Talking Turkey," which examines media representations of the American Thanksgiving meal—and she maintains a digital archive of scenes related to food/culture. Her interest in comfort food grows out of this archive along with observations of students in her Food, Culture, and Film course, during which the topic of comfort food is a clear favorite.

Rachelle H. Saltzman joined the Oregon Folklife Network as Executive Director in 2012 after nearly eighteen years as the Iowa Arts Council's Folklife Coordinator. Saltzman writes about food and culture for popular and academic audiences, organizes food festivals, and works in culinary tourism. She teaches Foodways and Folklore (University of Oregon), serves on the Local Food Connections conference planning team, and writes a regular column for Oregon's *Take Root* magazine. Saltzman also serves on Travel Oregon's Agritourism Leadership Working Group. Her book, *A Lark for the Sake of Their Country: The 1926 General Strike Volunteers in Folklore and Memory* (Manchester University Press, 2012), explores folklore, memory, and the politics of identity.

Charlene Smith, a resident of Chicago and a longtime educator, now retired, taught elementary and special education in the Chicago Public Schools for forty years. She received her associate's degree from Wilson Junior College, and later completed a BA from Illinois State University and an MA from the University of Illinois. She often wrote and published essays about her southern background in the *Journal of Ordinary Thought*. The Neighborhood Writing Alliance published the *Journal of Ordinary Thought*, held weekly workshops in writing, and encouraged the belief that "everyone is a philosopher" for over seventeen years. Charlene loves to travel and to discover the richness and history of people, places, and things. She enjoys musical concerts, walking, shopping, cooking, mediation practice, and learning about the secrets of life and living.

Annie Tucker is a researcher, writer and translator focused on contemporary Indonesian arts, literature, and culture. She received her PhD in Culture and Performance with a concentration in Folklore Studies from UCLA in 2013, where she is currently a lecturer for the Disability Studies minor. She lives in Los Angeles and works as a research assistant and writer for Elemental Productions, an ethnographic film company exploring culture and personal experience in Indonesia. She also translates Indonesian fiction. Her work has been recognized by PEN/America, the Association for Asian Studies Council on Southeast Asian Studies, and the American Literary Translator's Association, and her translation of the novel *Beauty Is a Wound*, by critically acclaimed author Eka Kurniawan, has just been published by New Directions.

Diane Tye is Professor and former Head of the Department of Folklore, Memorial University. She is author of *Baking as Biography: A Life Story in Recipes* and coeditor, with Pauline Greenhill, of *Undisciplined Women: Tradition and Culture in Canada* and *Unsettling Assumptions: Tradition, Gender, Drag*. Her articles have appeared in a wide range of journals, including *Ethnologies, Western Folklore, Women's Studies International Forum, Fabula, Food and Society*, and *CuiZine*. She is a past president of the Folklore Studies Association of Canada, a member of the Executive Board of the American Folklore Society, and coeditor with Michael Lange of *Digest*, the online journal of the American Folklore Society's Foodways section.

INDEX

CPSIA information can be obtained
at www.ICGtesting.com
Printed in the USA
BVOW11s0608200317
478849BV00001B/2/P